Wanted TO BUY

7TH EDITION

A listing of serious buyers paying CASH for everything collectible!

COLLECTOR BOOKS
A Division of Schroeder Publishing Co., Inc.

The current values in this book should be used only as a guide. They are not intended to set prices, which vary from one section of the country to another. Auction prices as well as dealer prices vary greatly and are affected by condition and demand. Neither the editors nor the publisher assumes responsibility for any losses which might be incurred as a result of consulting this guide.

Searching For A Publisher?

We are always looking for knowledgeable people considered experts within their fields. If you feel that there is a real need for a book on your collectible subject and have a large comprehensive collection, contact Collector Books.

Cover Design: Beth Summers

Collector Books
P.O. Box 3009
Paducah, KY 42002-3009

Introduction

This book was compiled to help put serious buyers in contact with non-collecting sellers all over the country. Most of us have accumulated things that are not particularly valuable to us but could very well be of interest to one of the buyers in this book. Not only does this book list the prices that collectors are willing to pay on thousands of items, it also lists hundreds of interested buyers along with the type of material each is buying. *Wanted to Buy* is very easy to use. The listings are alphabetically arranged by subject, with the interested buyer's name and address preceding each group of listings. In the back of the book, we have included a special section which lists the names and addresses of over 250 buyers along with the categories that they are interested in. When you correspond with these buyers, be sure to enclose a self-addressed, stamped envelope if you want a reply. If you wish to sell your material, quote the price that you want or send a list. Ask if there are any items on the list that they might be interested in and the price that they would be willing to pay. If you want the list back, be sure to send a SASE large enough for it to be returned.

Packing and Shipping Instructions

Special care must be exercised in shipping fragile items in the mail and UPS double boxing is a must when shipping glass and china pieces. It is extremely important that each item be wrapped in several layers of newspaper. First, put a four-inch layer of wadded newspaper in the bottom of the box. Secondly, start placing the well-wrapped items on top of the crushed newspaper, making certain that each piece of glass or china is separated from the others. Make sure that there are at least four inches of cushioning newspaper or foam between each item. When the box is nearly full, place more cushioning material on top of the contents and then seal the box.

Finally, place this box and contents in a large box cushioned again with at least four inches of newspaper on all four sides, top and bottom. This double boxing is very important. Our Postal Service and United Parcel Service are efficient; however, we must pack well just in case there is undue bumping in handling.

When shipping coins and precious metals, be sure to register your shipment and request a return slip so that you will know that the buyer received the goods, as well as the date that they were delivered. All materials should be insured for full value. Remember, always use strong boxes, lots of packing, and good shipping tape.

Advertising

We buy **advertising items of almost any kind**: Planters Peanut, Freedomland, Campbell Kids, Coke, Elsie the Cow, Esso, Howard Johnsons, Pepsi, Reddy Kilowatt, Speedy Alka-Seltzer, Stork Club, Coney Island-related items, advertising clocks, plates/dishes with advertising logos, all country store collectibles, tins, displays, World's Fair items, gasoline and car memorabilia, etc. Also wanted are **airline memorabilia, plates and dishes with logos** from any of the previously mentioned categories or anything similar. We are always looking for rare and hard-to-find items. If you are not sure if the item is new or old, please contact us. We reimburse actual UPS and insurance charges.

Marty Blank
P.O. Box 405
Fresh Meadows, NY 11365
516-485-8071
MartyAdver@aol.com

	We Pay
Advertising Pot Scrappers w/colorful graphics	**50.00+**
Advertising Vinyl or Composition Ad Characters	**50.00+**
Coke Memorabilia	**Call**
Elsie the Cow Cookie Cutter, 2-pc set	**20.00**
Freedomland View-Master, 3-reels w/pamphlet	**25.00+**
Mr Peanut Bank (not tan/red/light blue or regular green), **We pay high...Our specialty**	**Call**
Needle Books w/advertising	**5.00+/Call**
Pepsi-Cola Memorabilia	**Call**
Advertising signs, porcelain	**Call**
Prohylactic Tins	**15.00**
Speedy Alka-Seltzer Ad Figure (counter), good condition	**250.00**
Spice Tins, old only	**20.00+**
Tins, advertising	**Call**
Tins, typewriter	**10.00+**
World's Fair Items	**10.00+**

Beretta handgun paper advertising items for the years 1915 through the early 1960s are wanted. Items include boxes, manuals, promotional items, magazine articles, suit ties, cuff links, tie tacks, lapel pins, and any memorabilia in general.

Also wanted are **old advertising items from Waterloo, Iowa, manufacturing companies; Iowa chauffeur badges for the years 1923, 1925, 1927, and 1928; and a Gem doughnut machine (need not be working, but must be complete).** Gem doughnut machine advertising pieces are also wanted.

Orrin E. Miller
1920 Franklin St.
Waterloo, IA 50703-5022

Presently, I collect cardboard **advertising fans**. These may be cardboard with a picture on the back and wood handle, or they may be a three-piece cardboard style with a picture on one side. Other wants include **old cigar boxes, fast-food toys, and Strawberry Shortcake dolls**.

Vicki T. Roberts
11521 E Rodney Griffin St.
Centralia, MO 65240-9303

	We Pay
Advertising Fans	**1.00-6.00**
American Flags	**50¢-5.00**
Cigar Boxes, colorful pictures inside lid	**1.00-6.00**
Fast-food Items	**25¢-2.00**
Strawberry Shortcake Dolls	**25¢-3.00**

I am a collector of **General Electric refrigerator promotional items** from the 1920s through the 1930s pertaining to the monitor top refrigerator. I collect only pre-1960s items and do not want salt and pepper shakers or paper advertisements. I am interested in clocks, coin banks, water bottles, and G.E. chiller glass trays. I'm also interested in Frigidaire, Sewel, Westinghouse, and Norge promotional items. Please send description along with your asking price.

Larry Wessling
2805 Kingsridge Dr.
Blue Springs, MO 64015

We buy **any jigsaw puzzles that were used as advertising or given away**. They must have the product or service advertised printed on the face of the puzzle, or the pieces may be cut into their shape. Complete puzzles only are wanted. If they have the original box or envelope, we would pay a higher price. Age and condition are very important and determine the final price.

Also wanted are **figural advertising paperweights** that are miniatures of what they advertise. They must have a manufacturer name or product as part of the design. Condition, age, and uniqueness will determine a higher price.

Donald Friedman
660 W Grand Ave.
Chicago, IL 60610
312-226-4741
DFRIED4141@AOL.COM

Advertising Jigsaw Puzzles	**We Pay**
Automobiles, Trucks & Busses	**25.00+**
Candies & Gum	**20.00+**
Coke (**no Springbok**)	**100.00**
Farm Equipment	**20.00+**
Food Products	**20.00+**
Gasoline & Oil Products	**25.00+**
Radio Shows	**20.00+**
Soft Drinks	**20.00+**
World's Fair	**25.00+**

Advertising Paperweights	**We Pay**
Automobiles (fenders, springs, bumpers)	**35.00**
Bathroom Fixtures (tubs, toilets, sinks)	**25.00**
Bricks or Similar Clay Items	**10.00**
Motors	**20.00**
Railroad Wheels	**20.00**
Sewer Tiles & Sewer Pipes	**15.00**
Telephones	**40.00**

I have been collecting **M&M's promotional items** since 1972. I buy, sell, and trade! I have no specific wants and am looking for other collectors.

Fred Kraut
120 Covington Dr.
Warwick, RI 02886
401-738-2277
Uki845@aol.com

I am interested in purchasing **Morton Salt memorabilia**. Any Morton Salt advertising collectibles, especially items featuring the girl with the umbrella are wanted — but any and all will be considered, regardless of condition. Please call or write.

Cheri Signorelli
3900 Arizona St.
Kenner, LA 70065
504-468-1331 (home)
504-279-4375 (work)

I am a private collector of **early phonograph and radio advertising.** I'm mainly looking for early tin, porcelain, and cardboard signs depicting phonographs or radios. Condition is very important, **no repos or magazine ads please**. Below is just a small list of what I am currently seeking.

Kirk Lahey
170 Collins Gr. Unit 22
Dartmouth, NS
Canada B2W4E6
902-434-7877 or 902-468-9642
fax 902-468-9643
phono@ns.sympatico.ca

We Pay

Advertising Doll, RCA Radiotron, jointed wood, 15½", EX condition only ..**800.00+**
Banner, RCA Victor Tubes 1939, cloth (see pg 122 *America for Sale* by Congdon-Martin) ....**700.00+**
Banner, Victor, Victrola w/opera stars around border (see pg 452, item 983 *Collectors Guide to His Masters Voice* by Ruth Edge) ....**1,000.00+**
Banner, Victor, flapper girl sitting before Victrola (see pg 452, item 984 *Collectors Guide to His Masters Voice* by Ruth Edge) ....**1,200.00+**
Clock, Victor Sessions (see pg 24 *Advertising Clocks* by Michael Bruner) ..**1,000.00+**

Counter Display Sign, Victor, electric (see pg 158, item 567 *Collectors Guide to His Masters Voice* by Ruth Edge)........**1,000.00+**
Lamp, Victor, revolving, 1929 (see pg 102, item 160 *Collectors Guide to His Masters Voice* by Ruth Edge)........**500.00+**
Lighter, RCA, silvered metal, microphone shape, 1940s (see pg 128 *Hake's Guide to Advertising Collectibles*........**100.00+**
Mirror, Victor, celluloid, 1914 (see pg 104, item 163 *Collectors Guide to His Masters Voice* by Ruth Edge)........**250.00+**
Needle Display Case, Victor, tin & glass (see pg 158, item 567 *Collectors Guide to His Masters Voice* by Ruth Edge)........**1,000.00**
Shot Glass, RCA, aluminum, 1940s, 2" (see pg 128 *Hake's Guide to Advertising Collectibles*)........**50.00**
Sign, Pathe........**600.00+**
Sign, World Phonograph, tin, young girl in front of phonograph........**1000.00+**
Sign, Mandel Phonograph, tin........**600.00+**
Sign, advertising trolley car, cardboard........**150.00+**
Sign, Sonora Radios, light-up (see pg 60 *Radios — The Golden Age* by Phillip Collins)........**350.00+**
Sign, Sylvania Radio Tubes w/Donald Duck, cardboard (see pg 90 *Hake's Guide to Advertising Collectibles*)........**250.00**
Sign, Victor, shadow box, light-up (see pg 430, item 925 *Collectors Guide to His Masters Voice* by Ruth Edge)........**800.00+**
Thermometer, Columbia Records, tin, 5x1 ft........**800.00+**

We collect, buy, and trade **glass jars and trays many companies supplied their vendors**. These had a company logo or name included in their design. (The list below does not include those jars with the names only on their bottom.) Some of these early jars would also have decal-type labels in addition to the embossed name, while the more recent jars eventually had only painted-on names or painted labels. *We are generally only interested in embossed items, not painted or paper labeled only jars.* Below are some of the names that are known to exist, but there are many regional companies that supplied jars with their names to local stores that may not be listed.

Generally, jars with embossed names will be priced between $50.00 and $200.00, with rarity and condition the determining factors. Chips and missing lids will devalue items. Original decal/paper labels on embossed jars will add value. I also buy old spare lids for these jars (marked or unmarked).

Also buying **any glass store advertising display cases, jars, trays, old penny candy jars, or any top for these items**. Note: Many of the Planters jars have been reproduced. (Original Planters jars were only made in clear glass, no colored at all, and all original jars are marked 'Made in USA' embossed in the bottom.)

Craig Ehlenberger
Abalone Cove Antiques
7 Fruit Tree Rd.
Portugese Bend, CA 90275
310-377-4609 or fax 310-544-6792
CEhlenberger@worldnet.att.net

Jars Wanted

After Dinner Famous Peanuts Jar, difficult
American Nut Co., rare
Barsam Bros Jar, difficult
Beich's, difficult
Borden's, relatively common
Dad's Oatmeal Cookies, lg, relatively common jar
Dillings Candy, rare
Double-Kay Nuts, sm, metal top, rare
Elephant Peanuts, rare
Items, stackable, relatively common
Kis-Me Gum, relatively common
Lance, 2 embossed designs, rare
National Biscuit, difficult
Nut House Peanut, various styles, metal tops, relatively common to rare
Pittsburgh Pretzel, rare
Pitcain Water Spar, difficult
Planters Peanuts, corner peanut, rare
Planters Peanuts, fishbowl, relatively common
Planters Peanuts, football, rare
Planters Peanuts, pennant, relatively common
Planters Peanuts, running Mr Peanut, difficult
Planters Peanuts Jar, sq, relatively common
Reeds, lg, rare
Royal Marshmallows, rare
Sawyer Biscuits, rare
Squirrel Peanuts, relatively common
Sunshine Biscuits/Loose Willis, difficult
Taylor Biscuits, rare
Uneeda/Nabisco, stackable, relatively common
US Nuts, metal tops, rare
Van Houten Hot Chocolate, metal tops, difficult
Water Spar Varnish, rare
Wilholte's Peanut Butter Sandwiches, metal tops, difficult

I am interested in buying all **unusual Planters Peanuts and Mr. Peanut memorabilia**, especially containers that held Planters products and point-of sale display items. I am also interested in any material from the many Planters

Peanuts stores that existed throughout the country, such as signs, neon clocks, etc. I will always reimburse your postage or UPS and insurance costs. A SASE will guarantee a reply to any written inquiry. Please write or call if unsure of any item or if not listed below. Unwanted items include magazine ads, plastic cups, metal dishes, pocketknives, plastic banks, and items made after 1970.

Sherwin Borsuk
80 Parker Ave.
Meriden, CT 06450
203-237-8042

	We Pay
Boxes, cardboard, held Planters products, 1920s or 1930s	150.00+
Boxes, cardboard, held Planters products, 1940s	100.00+
Boxes, cardboard, held Planters products, 1950s or 1960s	50.00+
Store Display, cardboard or paper, featuring Mr Peanut	100.00+
Coloring Books, unused, before 1950	10.00+
Glass Jars, clear glass, not reproduction w/lids	45.00+
Glass Jars, clear glass w/paper label(s)	85.00+
Letter Opener, from Planters Chocolate & Nut Co	500.00
Statue, metal, legs crossed	400.00+
Statue, rubber Mr Peanut	500.00+
Store Display, metal	400.00+
Metal Can or Jar, held Planters Oil	25.00+
Costume, Mr Peanut	250.00+
Peanut Block Display, metal	600.00+
Night Light, plastic Mr Peanut	100.00+
Figure, papier-mache Mr Peanut, hollow, held peanuts	150.00+
Figure, papier-mache Mr Peanut on base, electric, blinks	1,500.00+
Figure, papier-mache Mr Peanut on base, electric, taps cane	2,000.00+
Martini Glass, plastic, various colors	25.00+
Postcard, showing Planters stores or factories	5.00+
Hand Puppet, rubber Mr Peanut	500.00+
Tin, held Planters Peanuts, pocket size	500.00+
Tin, held Planters Nuts, under 1-lb size	15.00+
Tin, held Planters Nuts, 5-lb size	50.00+
Tin, held Planters Nuts, 10-lb size	35.00+
Tin, held Planters Nuts, over 10-lb size	200.00+
Trolley Card Ad, cardboard	75.00+
Shipping Crates, Planters, wood	150.00+

Years ago most companies had very decorative envelopes and letterheads with great graphics on them. This was thought to be a very good way to advertise their products. I am interested in buying **old advertising envelopes and letterheads from firearms, ammo, trap, and powder companies** (Winchester, Remington, Savage, Stevens, Cortland Trap, L.C. Smith, Ithaca, Parker, Hazard, DuPont, Peters, Newhouse, Taylor, etc.)

Bob Bowering
P.O. Box 420
E Wilton, ME 04234
207-778-6724

I buy authentic **advertising signs of all kinds:** paper, tin, or porcelain. I will buy one of a kind or in quantities of several hundred. Also of interest are **pocket mirrors, advertising pin-back buttons, Presidential campaign items, political pins, and political posters.**

David Beck
P.O. Box 435
Mediapolis, IA 52637
319-394-3943

	We Pay
Calendars, ea	**10.00-1,000.00**
Calendar, gun powder	**100.00-1,000.00**
Sign, seed corn, tin	**10.00-50.00**
Sign, Coca-Cola	**50.00-2,000.00**
Sign, gas or oil	**50.00-500.00**

Wanted: **older advertising signs and tins**. Items must be in very good condition and include service station items, tobacco items, spices, coffee products, food items, drink products, gun powders, etc. Any early signs will be considered.

Frank Vernaua Jr.
P.O. Box 522
Swampscott, MA 01907
781-396-0479

Advertising

Antique advertising trade cards are wanted — especially those that date to the turn-of-the-century. Please write.

Manfred Rothstein
1308 Medical Dr.
Fayetteville, NC 28304-4442

Arm & Hammer premium cards are wanted in sets or singles. I'm especially looking for fish and animal cards. Name your price! Other wants include **Ocean liner and all Queen Mary memorabilia, ruby-flashed souvenir items, calendar plates with pictures, and aluminum bar soap cases used for traveling.**

Lisa
Box 7173
Eureka, CA 95502
707-443-9125

	We Pay
Arm & Hammer Premium Cards	**Call or Write**
Calendar Plates	**Call or Write**
Ocean Liner Memorabilia	**up to $100.00**
Ruby-Flashed Souvenir Items	**up to $100.00**
Soap Cases, embossed or stamped aluminum	**Call or Write**

Wanted: **advertising whistles**. These whistles are about 2" long and are made of aluminum. They have an embossed band around the bottom. Send a photocopy (if possible) and your asking price.

Bernie Biske
47529 Cheryl Ct.
Shelby Twp., MI 48315-4707
810-731-3295

Animal Dishes

Old milk glass covered animal dishes such as Flaccus, Atterbury, McKee, Vallerysthal, Challinor & Taylor, and slag glass are wanted. (**Other slag glass items** are wanted as well.) **Powder jars with animal or human figures** are also sought.

Sharon Thoerner
15549 Ryon Ave.
Bellflower, CA 90706
562-866-1555
sharnantiques@juno.com

Art

We are interested in purchasing quality **American and European paintings from the late 19th century to the mid-20th century**. Please send photos with descriptions, dates, condition, etc. All letters are answered within a few days. We are especially interested in garden scenes, mothers and children, beach scenes with people, western works, and still life paintings featuring money. We have listed below prices we are willing to pay for major examples of the following artists. We are interested in smaller examples as well as works by artists not listed. We will also purchase entire collections or estates of artists. Please feel free to call.

Cincinnati Art Galleries
635 Main St.
Cincinnati, OH 45202
513-381-2128 or fax 513-381-7527

Major Works by Artist	We Pay
Adams, J.O.	10,000.00-25,000.00
Albert, E.	5,000.00-10,000.00
Amick, W.	5,000.00-10,000.00
Bacher, O.	25,000.00-50,000.00
Baker, G.	10,000.00-25,000.00
Bannister, E.	25,000.00-50,000.00

Beal, G.	10,000.00-25,000.00
Beal, R.	10,000.00-25,000.00
Beard, J.	5,000.00-10,000.00
Beard, W.	5,000.00-10,000.00
Beaux, C.	10,000.00-25,000.00
Beckwith, J.	25,000.00-50,000.00
Betts, L.	10,000.00-25,000.00
Birney, W.	5,000.00-10,000.00
Bischoff, F.	25,000.00-50,000.00
Black, L.	10,000.00-25,000.00
Blenner, C.	5,000.00-10,000.00
Bloch, A.	10,000.00-25,000.00
Bluemner, O.	25,000.00-50,000.00
Boggs, F.	5,000.00-10,000.00
Borein, E.	10,000.00-25,000.00
Botke, J.	10,000.00-25,000.00
Bradford, W.	25,000.00-50,000.00
Bricher, A.	25,000.00-50,000.00
Bridgman, R.	5,000.00-10,000.00
Brookes, S.	10,000.00-25,000.00
Brown, J.G.	10,000.00-25,000.00
Brown, W.	5,000.00-10,000.00
Brush, G.	25,000.00-50,000.00
Bundy, J.	5,000.00-10,000.00
Butler, T.	25,000.00-50,000.00
Butterworth, J.	25,000.00-50,000.00
Cadmus, P.	25,000.00-50,000.00
Cassidy, I.	10,000.00-25,000.00
Chalfant, J.	25,000.00-50,000.00
Christy, H.	5,000.00-10,000.00
Coleman, C.	25,000.00-50,000.00
Couse, E.	25,000.00-50,000.00
Cucuel, E.	10,000.00-25,000.00
Curran, C.	25,000.00-50,000.00
Davey, R.	10,000.00-25,000.00
David, S.S.	10,000.00-25,000.00
Davies, A.	10,000.00-25,000.00
Deas, C.	25,000.00-50,000.00
Delano, G.	5,000.00-10,000.00
Deming, E.	5,000.00-10,000.00
Dewing, M.	5,000.00-10,000.00
Dixon, M.	25,000.00-50,000.00
Dodge, W.	5,000.00-10,000.00
Dolph, J.	5,000.00-10,000.00
Dougherty, P.	5,000.00-10,000.00
Dougherty, T.	25,000.00-50,000.00
Dow, A.	10,000.00-25,000.00
Dubois, G.	25,000.00-50,000.00

Dubreuil, V.	10,000.00-25,000.00
Dufner, E.	5,000.00-10,000.00
Duncanson, R.	10,000.00-25,000.00
Dunn, H.	10,000.00-25,000.00
Dunning, R.	10,000.00-25,000.00
Dunton, W.	10,000.00-25,000.00
Durand, A.	25,000.00-50,000.00
Durrie, H.	25,000.00-50,000.00
Duveneck, F.	25,000.00-50,000.00
Edmonds, F.	10,000.00-25,000.00
Ellis, F.	5,000.00-10,000.00
Enneking, J.	5,000.00-10,000.00
Fairman, J.	5,000.00-10,000.00
Forsyth, W.	5,000.00-10,000.00
Francis, J.	10,000.00-25,000.00
Frost, A.	5,000.00-10,000.00
Gamble, J.	10,000.00-25,000.00
Garber, D.	25,000.00-50,000.00
Gaspard, L.	25,000.00-50,000.00
Gaugengigl, I.	5,000.00-10,000.00
Gaul, W.	5,000.00-10,000.00
Gay, W.	5,000.00-10,000.00
Gignoux, R.	10,000.00-25,000.00
Gilchrist, W.	5,000.00-10,000.00
Gile, S.	5,000.00-10,000.00
Gollings, R.	10,000.00-25,000.00
Graves, A.	10,000.00-25,000.00
Gruelle, J.	5,000.00-10,000.00
Gruppe, E.	5,000.00-10,000.00
Guy, S.	25,000.00-50,000.00
Hahn, W.	25,000.00-50,000.00
Hale, E.	10,000.00-25,000.00
Hale, P.	25,000.00-50,000.00
Hall, G.	5,000.00-10,000.00
Hamilton, H.	5,000.00-10,000.00
Hart, J.	5,000.00-10,000.00
Hart, W.	10,000.00-25,000.00
Harvey, G.	10,000.00-25,000.00
Haseltine, W.	10,000.00-25,000.00
Hawthorne, C.	25,000.00-50,000.00
Hennings, E.	25,000.00-50,000.00
Henri, R.	25,000.00-50,000.00
Henry, E.	25,000.00-50,000.00
Henshaw, G.	5,000.00-10,000.00
Herter, A.	10,000.00-25,000.00
Herzog, H.	10,000.00-25,000.00
Hibbard, A.	5,000.00-10,000.00
Higgins, V.	10,000.00-25,000.00

Hill, T.	25,000.00-50,000.00
Hills, L.	5,000.00-10,000.00
Hirst, C.	5,000.00-10,000.00
Hitchcock, G.	25,000.00-50,000.00
Hoffbauer, C.	5,000.00-10,000.00
Hopkins, J.	5,000.00-10,000.00
Horton, W.	5,000.00-10,000.00
Hovenden, T.	10,000.00-25,000.00
Hudson, G.	10,000.00-25,000.00
Hunt, W.	10,000.00-25,000.00
Hurd, P.	10,000.00-25,000.00
Hurley, E.	5,000.00-10,000.00
Innes, G.	25,000.00-50,000.00
Johnson, D.	25,000.00-50,000.00
Johnson, E.	25,000.00-50,000.00
Johnson, F.	25,000.00-50,000.00
Jones, H.	5,000.00-10,000.00
Kaelin, C.	5,000.00-10,000.00
Kaye, O.	10,000.00-25,000.00
Keith, W.	10,000.00-25,000.00
Kensett, J.	25,000.00-50,000.00
Key, J.	5,000.00-10,000.00
Krieghoff, C.	10,000.00-25,000.00
Kosa, E.	5,000.00-10,000.00
Kroll, L. Jr.	5,000.00-10,000.00
Kuehne, M.	5,000.00-10,000.00
Kuhn, W.	25,000.00-50,000.00
Kuniyoshi, Y.	25,000.00-50,000.00
Lambdin, G.	10,000.00-25,000.00
Lane, F.	25,000.00-50,000.00
Laurence, S.	10,000.00-25,000.00
Lie, J.	5,000.00-10,000.00
Lorenz, R.	10,000.00-25,000.00
Marsh, R.	25,000.00-50,000.00
Maurer, A.	25,000.00-50,000.00
McCloskey, W.	25,000.00-50,000.00
McEntee, J.	10,000.00-25,000.00
Meakin, L.	5,000.00-10,000.00
Melchers, G.	25,000.00-50,000.00
Melrose, A.	10,000.00-25,000.00
Mignot, L.	10,000.00-25,000.00
Miller, A.	25,000.00-50,000.00
Moeller, L.	5,000.00-10,000.00
Mora, F.	5,000.00-10,000.00
Moran, E.	5,000.00-10,000.00
Mosler, H.	10,000.00-25,000.00
Mowbray, H.	10,000.00-25,000.00
Mulhaupt, F.	5,000.00-10,000.00

Nourse, E.	**25,000.00-50,000.00**
Osthaus, E.	**10,000.00-25,000.00**
Palmer, W.	**5,000.00-10,000.00**
Parker, L.	**10,000.00-25,000.00**
Parrish, M.	**25,000.00-50,000.00**
Paxton, W.	**25,000.00-50,000.00**
Peterson, J.	**10,000.00-25,000.00**
Peto, J.	**25,000.00-50,000.00**
Phillips, B.	**10,000.00-25,000.00**
Picknell, W.	**10,000.00-25,000.00**
Pippin, H.	**25,000.00-50,000.00**
Raphael, J.	**25,000.00-50,000.00**
Redfield, E.	**25,000.00-50,000.00**
Reynolds, W.	**5,000.00-10,000.00**
Rungius, C.	**10,000.00-25,00.00**
Salmon, R.	**25,000.00-50,000.00**
Sawyler, P.	**5,000.00-10,000.00**
Schofield, W.	**10,000.00-25,000.00**
Selden, D.	**5,000.00-10,000.00**
Seltzer, O.	**10,000.00-25,000.00**
Shaw, J.	**10,000.00-25,000.00**
Shulz, A.	**5,000.00-10,000.00**
Shinn, E.	**25,000.00-50,000.00**
Simmons, E.	**10,000.00-25,000.00**
Silva, F.	**25,000.00-50,000.00**
Sontag, W.	**10,000.00-25,000.00**
Stark, O.	**10,000.00-25,000.00**
Steele, T.C.	**10,000.00-25,000.00**
Stewart, J.	**10,000.00-25,000.00**
Tanner, H.	**25,000.00-50,000.00**
Thayer, A.	**25,000.00-50,000.00**
Thieme, A.	**5,000.00-10,000.00**
Tooker, G.	**25,000.00-50,000.00**
Vogt, L.	**5,000.00-10,000.00**
Volkert, E.	**5,000.00-10,000.00**
Weis, J.	**5,000.00-10,000.00**
Wendel, T.	**10,000.00-25,000.00**
Wessell, B.	**5,000.00-10,000.00**
Wessell, H.	**5,000.00-10,000.00**
Whittredge, T.	**25,000.00-50,000.00**
Wiles, I.	**25,000.00-50,000.00**

We are buyers of **original paintings or sketches by deceased artists.** We specialize in Western, wildlife, and Indian subjects. Feel free to send photos (they will be returned).

Sam Kennedy
212 North 4th St.
Couer d'Alene, ID 83814
208-769-7575

Artist	We Pay
A.B. Frost	3,000.00-10,000.00+
Ace Powell	500.00-3,000.00
C.M. Russell, letters & drawings	10,000.00+
C.M. Russell	20,000.00-100,000.00+
Carl Rungus	10,000.00-50,000.00
E.I. Couse	10,000.00+
E.S. Paxson	3,000.00-10,000.00+
Frank Stick	1,000.00-5,000.00+
Frederic Remington	10,000.00+
Grace Hudson	10,000.00+
Hans Kleiber	500.00-5,000.00+
Lynne Boyne Hunt	1,000.00+
Nick Eggenhofer	500.00-5,000.00
O.C. Seltzer	5,000.00-10,000.00
Phillip R. Goodwin	4,000.00-10,000.00+
Richard Bishop	500.00-2,000.00
W.R. Leigh	5,000.00+
William Gollings	10,000.00+

I collect the **works of Joseph Jacinto Mora (a.k.a, J.J. Mora or Jo Mora, 1876 – 1947)**. He was one of California's most versatile artists, a master sculptor, painter, photographer, author, muralist, book illustrator, draftsman, cartographer, cartoonist, linguist, and even did a little jewelry designing — he did it all, and exceptionally well. By the time this book is published, I shall have published my own definitive book on Jo Mora. I am interested in anything in relation to this artist — the acceptable condition of which will depend on scarcity; but in most cases, fine condition or better is desired. I will pay cash or horse trade for items of interest.

Other wants include **a 1930s poster of the ocean liner, Normandie; Art Deco, cowboy-Indian bookends; a Bucking Horse statue and artwork by Till Goodan; and anything by Jo Mora**.

T.J. Ahlberg
1000 Irvine Blvd.
Tustin, CA 92780
714-730-1000 or fax 714-730-1752

Pictorial Posters by Jo Mora (J.J. Mora)	We Pay
Cowboy Rodeo Poster, Salinas	100.00+
Cowboy Rodeo Poster, Levi®	100.00+
Indians of North America Poster	50.00+
Carmel Dairy	100.00+
Animals of Aesop	100.00+

Pictorial Maps (Cartes) by Jo Mora (J.J. Mora)	We Pay
California	50.00+
Los Angeles	100.00+
San Diego (The Marston Co.)	100.00+
Carmel by the Sea	30.00+
Monterey Peninsula	100.00+
Seventeen Mile Drive	100.00+
Central America (The Grace Line)	100.00+
Grand Canyon	25.00+
Yellowstone	100.00+
Yosemite	75.00+

Other Wants by Jo Mora (J.J. Mora)	We Pay
Original Artwork	Call
Sculpture	Call
Authored Books	60.00+
Illustrated Books	25.00+
Carmel Dairy Milk Bottles	Call
Carmel Dairy Calendars & Posters	Call
Christmas Cards	Call
US Half Dollar, California Diamond Jubilee, 1925	300.00
Hotel Del Monte Menu, 12 different, ea	35.00
Pop Ernest's Menu	50.00
Del Monte Bar Recipe Booklet	35.00
Animaldom Cartoon, c 1907, Boston Herald, Sunday	35.00
Sterling Silver Buckles or Jewelry Work, any	Call
Original Photographs by Mora	10.00
Original Photographs of Mora	10.00
Animal Football Calendar, 1903	Call
Other Items	Call

I buy **older original or lithograph drawings by Irene Spencer.** I am particularly looking for an early hand-colored lithograph entitled *First Kiss* which pictures a little boy and girl. The majority of her works were completed in the 1970s.

Beverly Nelson
1010 Lorna St.
Corona, CA 91720
909-373-0977
nelac@earthlink.net

Collector wants to purchase **old art paintings done by well-known artists.** When corresponding please include the name of artist, a clear photo of your item, and your asking price.

R.G. Mulghern
3722 Alabama #130
San Diego, CA 92104

My wife and I are serious collectors from the Hudson Valley. We look for high quality, good, original pieces. We buy one item or entire collections and have twenty years experience. We will assess and evaluate all pieces sent to us free of charge. We buy **large signed oil paintings.** Subjects include abstracts, military themes and battles, landscapes and river views, and scenes with sailing ships. We also buy sketches, watercolors, pastels, and drypoint prints (no dots). Please send a photo with dimensions, a brief history, your asking price, telephone number, and SASE. We respond to all inquiries, even if we do not buy, and certainly try our best to identify and evaluate your items. If we are interested we will ask for a close-up inspection, in which case we will issue a check within 24 hours of delivery.

Other wants include **marked Oriental vases and figurals; Nikon, Canon, and Leica cameras and lenses; any novelty cameras shaped as neckties, cigarette lighters, etc.; Italian violins and some musical instruments; Elvis, Beach Boys, Beatles, Dylan, surf, swing, blues, and rhythm 'n' blues records; and glass negatives, albumen, salt, or silver prints.**

John and Anna Matero
109 Mountain Ave.
Highland Falls, NY 10928
914-446-1032

	We Pay
Artwork, signed, as described	**100.00-5,000.00**
Marked Oriental Vases or Figurals	**50.00-500.00**

Canon, Lecia, or Nikon Cameras & Lenses	**50.00-2,500.00**
Italian Violins	**100.00-3,000.00**
Selmer Mark 6 Alto or Tenor Saxophones	**50.00-500.00**
Fender or Gibson Electric Guitars	**50.00-1,000.00**
Elvis, Beach Boys, Dylan, Other Records	**1.00-10.00**

Art Glass

Houze art glass is usually dark-tinted glass with a humorous saying, a business, a state, or product advertising enameled on the glass. It may/may not be lightly etched 'Houze' on the bottom.

Higgins glass is mostly pastels and marked with either an engraved script 'Higgins' or in gold letters. I am mostly interested in square-like pieces, or ash-tray-type pieces. I am not interested in bowl-type pieces but would consider for trading with others. Some prices I have paid include five pieces (one was chipped) including a piece featuring pocket watches for $210.00 and an irregular triangle-shaped piece for $90.00. What do you have?

Ross Hartsough
R.R. Box 382
Honesdale, PA 18431

Buying art glass: **Steuben, Italian, Fry, Mt. Joy, Loetz, Czechoslovakian, and Locke Art.** We like vases, candlesticks, salts, stemware, tableware, bowls, figures, perfumes, lamps, and jewelry. Send us a photo with good description. Signature is unimportant. Please price your item. Also wanted are **reference books on the above listed glass people.** I'm looking forward to hearing from you. We respond quickly.

Richard Haigh
P.O. Box 29562
Richmond, VA 23242
804-741-5770 (until 9pm EST)

Art Pottery

We are interested in purchasing **fine art pottery.** We will buy single pieces or collections valued into the seven figures. As one of America's premier pottery dealers, we are constantly searching for pieces to add to our inventory. We will travel for large collections and payment is immediate. Below are examples of potters for which we are searching. We will need photos and descriptions sent to us for a more precise estimate. All letters are answered within a few days, or give us a call if that is more convenient for you.

Buffalo Pottery
California Faience
Chelsea Keramic
Clewell
Cowan
Dedham
Fulper
Grueby
Lonhuda
Marblehead
Matt Morgan
Niloak
Newcomb
Norse
Overbeck
Owens
Pewabic
Pisgah Forest
Roseville
Shearwater
Teco
UND
Van Briggle
Vance Avon
Weller

We are buying Rookwood pottery. Prices shown are approximate ranges paid for undamaged artist-decorated Rookwood. For a more precise idea of price, please send photos with complete descriptions.

Cincinnati Art Galleries
635 Main St.
Cincinnati, OH 45202
513-381-2128 or fax 513-381-5727

Rookwood	**We Pay**
Standard Glaze Floral	**200.00-5,000.00**
Iris Glaze Floral	**500.00-20,000.00**
Vellum Floral	**300.00-5,000.00**
Indian Portrait	**1,000.00-20,000.00**
Scenic	**700.00-20,000.00**

I buy **American art pottery.** Please send photo with description, asking price, and condition.

Alan Phair
P.O. Box 30373
Long Beach, CA 90853

	We Pay
Catalina Island	**30.00-600.00**
Catalina Pottery (Gladding McBean)	**12.00-300.00**
G M B	**12.00-300.00**
Brayton Laguna	**10.00-200.00**
Tiles	**15.00-150.00**
Rookwood	**30.00-900.00**
Teco	**60.00-1,200.00**
North Dakota School of Mines	**30.00-700.00**
Clewell	**60.00-900.00**
Grueby	**40.00-900.00**
S.E.G.	**40.00-350.00**
Roseville	**30.00-900.00**
Newcomb	**60.00-900.00**
California Pottery or Dinnerware	**60.00-900.00**

I am interested in purchasing **American art pottery and figurals.** Interests include:

- Abington
- American Bisque
- Sascha Brastoff
- Brayton Laguna
- California Potteries
- Camark
- Ceramic Arts Studios
- Hull
- Kay Finch
- McCoy
- Rookwood
- Roseville
- Watt
- Weller

I will consider just about any pottery or figural if they are in mint condition only! Also wanted are **Art Deco items.**

Gene Underwood
3962 Fruitvale Ave.
Oakland, CA 94602
510-482-2841

I would like to buy **American and European art pottery, ceramics, art glass, paintings, bronzes, copper, dolls, toys, jewelry, and sterling.** Some specifics include:

Amphora
Boch
Cowan
Daum
Deck
Doulton
Fulper
Galle
Lalique
Loetz
Longwy
Majolica
Moorcroft
Moore
Pilkington
Quimper
Rookwood
Roseville
Schneider
Sicard
Tiffany
Weller
Zsolnay
18th-century Delft
Chinese Export Ceramics
European & English Ceramics

The Antique Gallery
8523 Germantown Ave.
Philadelphia, PA 19118
215-248-1700 or fax 215-247-8411
http://membrane.com/chestnuthill/antique_gallery

I am interested in **American, English, and European art pottery.** I will pay from $50.00 to $1,000.00 — depending on condition. I'm also interested in **figural dresser items.** Send photo and SASE.

Katherine Hartman
7459 Shawnee Rd.
N Tonawanda, NY 14120-1367

I love **old art pottery** and took up collecting it. I am interested in all types, shapes, and manufactures (Roseville, Hull, McCoy, and other miscellaneous pottery companies). I especially like Weller. I will pay shipping and insurance. Please send pictures or a description of the items and your asking price. All pieces must be in perfect condition.

Steve Arnhold
3085 F 1/2 Rd.
Grand Junction, CO 81504
970-434-8064

Wanting to buy **Fulper art pottery**, especially Arts & Crafts shapes, cabinet vases, candles, figural flower frogs, bookends, doorstops, wall pockets, porcelain figural perfume lamps, powder jars, and more. Also wanted are **catalogs or reprints, postcards, and other advertising from the Fulper pottery**, particularly book matches. Please send photos with dimensions and describe marks on the bottom.

Bob and Nancy Perzel
P.O. Box 1057
Flemington, NJ 08822
908-782-9631

Pottery wanted includes **Longwy, Boch, Catteau, Keramis, Gein, Vuillard, and related porcelains.**

Jennifer Luna
888-LONGWY-1
guesswho@guesswho.com

Arts and Crafts (Mission Era)

I buy **mission-style furniture and decorative accessories manufactured from 1900 through 1920**. Gustav Stickley, Limbert, Roycroft, L. & J.G. Stickley, and Stickley Brothers all made dark-colored, oak furniture that is plain and heavy in appearance. The furniture often has exposed construction with doweled pegs or wedges that join different boards. I also buy hammered copper and sterling silver accessories made by Jarvie, Roycroft, Kalo, Stickley, Karl Kipp, Dirk van Erp, and others. The metal is frequently a dark brown color and shows hand-hammered workmanship. Leaded glass and reverse-painted hanging and table lamps by such makers as Jefferson, Pittsburgh, Handel, Pairpoint, Bradley & Hubbard, and others are sought for purchase as well as art pottery by such makers as Teco, SEG, Marblehead, Newcomb, Fulper, Grueby, and Walrath. Finder's fee paid for successful leads.

Bruce A. Austin
Rochester Institute of Technology
College of Liberal Arts
Rochester, NY 14623-5604
716-475-2879
baagll@rit.edu

Autographs

We have been paying top prices for **signed letters, photos, books, contracts, sheet music, manuscripts, signed restaurant or store receipts, and canceled bank checks.** Passports and driver's licenses are okay. Other interests include **postcards, movie lobby cards, and posters.** Prices paid depend on content and condition. No Nazi or politican items wanted.

The Movies, Sig Goode
P.O. Box 878
Capt. Cook H
Hawaii, 96704
phone/fax 808-328-8119
(8am to 6pm my time)

	We Pay
The Beatles	up to 5,000.00
Irving Berlin	up to 5,000.00
Humphrey Bogart	up to 5,000.00
Raymond Chandler	up to 5,000.00
James Dean	up to 5,000.00
Ian Fleming	up to 5,000.00
Greta Garbo	up to 5,000.00
Clark Gable	up to 5,000.00
George Gershwin	up to 5,000.00
Jean Harlow	up to 5,000.00
Dashiell Hammett	up to 5,000.00
Ernest Hemingway	up to 5,000.00
Jimi Hendrix	up to 5,000.00
W.C. Fields	up to 5,000.00
Marilyn Monroe	up to 5,000.00
Jim Morrison	up to 5,000.00
John Steinbeck	up to 5,000.00

Automobilia

Automobile books and automobilia of all types purchased. We will buy hard- and soft-bound books, in or out of print, new or used, remainders, surplus stock, large private collections or single copies. Our main interest is in books that deal with auto racing, history of cars and their manufacturers, motorcycles, famous automotive personalities, design, etc. We willingly purchase all automotive books. However, we specialize in European and exotic automobiles such as Ferrari, Maserati, Lamborghini, Mercedes, Porsche, Rolls Royce, etc. We also specialize in domestic manufacturers that are no longer in existence such as Packard, Studebaker, Auburn, Dusenberg, etc. We do not buy ex-library books, sales literature, owners or workshop manuals unless they are appropriate to those types of automobiles previously listed. We purchase automobilia such as race posters, art, period photographs, original design renderings, etc. We are aggressive buyers of top quality items regardless of age and quantity. Prices quoted are for books with dust jackets in top condition.

LMG Enterprises
9006 Foxland Dr.
San Antonio, TX 78230
phone or fax 210-979-6098
102341.142@compuserve.com

	We Pay
Annual Automobile Review 1953/54 #1	**100.00**
Annual Automobile Review 1954/54 #2	**160.00**
At Speed (Alexander)	**80.00**
Autocourse 1964-65	**90.00**
Bentley 50 Years of the Marque (Green)	**60.00**
Boyhood Photographs of J.H. Lartique (Lartigue)	**100.00**
British Light Weight Sports Cars 78 (Japanese)	**140.00**
Cara Automobile (Pininfarina)	**80.00**
Comicar (Bertieri)	**50.00**
Delorean Stainless Steel Illusion (Lamm)	**40.00**
DMG 1890-1915 (German)	**180.00**
Errett Loban Cord (Borgeson)	**120.00**
Ferrari 80, 2nd edition (Italian)	**100.00**
Ferrari Yearbook, 1949-1970, ea	**70.00-400.00**
First Century of Portraits Celebrating Mercedes	**200.00**
Grand Prix Car, Vol. 1 & Vol. 2 (Pomeroy)	**160.00**
L'Art et L'Automobile (Poulain)	**60.00**
La Targa Florio (Garcia)	**80.00**
Les 24 Heures de Mans (Labric)	**160.00**
Piloti che Gente, 4th edition (Ferrari)	**140.00**
Spirit Celebrating 75 Years of Rolls Royce (Dallison)	**60.00**
Ten Ans de Courses (Montaut)	**600.00**

TMC Publications deals in automobile literature for **Mercedes, BMW, Jaguar, Lexus, Porsche, Audi, etc.** We are constantly on the look out for:

Original Workshop Manuals
Owner's Manuals
Parts Catalogs
Sales Brochures
Posters
Old Automobile Toys
Miscellaneous Old Automobilia Collectibles

The prices that we pay depend on condition and originality of merchandise offered.

Jeffrey Foland
TMC Publications
5817 Park Hts. Ave.
Baltimore, MD 21215-3931
410-367-4490 or fax 410-466-3566

I buy **almost anything marked Ford Motor Co.**: books, pamphlets, postcards, coins, tokens, lapel pins, pin-back buttons, glasses, dishes, silverware, factory badges, World's Fair literature, and souvenir items. I am a Ford specialist collector willing to buy collections and offer top dollar for items I need. Prices listed are for items in excellent condition.

Tim O'Callaghan
305 St. Lawrence Blvd.
Northville, MI 48167
248-449-2642

	We Pay
Badge, Ford factory	**15.00-200.00**
Badge, Ford, round picture of factory, WWII	**100.00-250.00**
Books on Henry Ford, or Ford Motor Co	**10.00-50.00**
Dishes or Cups, Ford in large green script	**100.00-200.00**
Gear Shift Knobs, w/various Exposition plates on top	**75.00-200.00**
Lapel Pin, Ford, Lincoln or Mercury	**10.00-35.00**
Salt & Pepper Shaker Set, Ford, from 1924 Chicago Fair	**100.00-200.00**

Aviation

I buy all **pre-1946 airline timetables, brochures, postcards, and airplane (and airplane engine) sales brochures,** especially those with a picture of the Ford Tri-Motor. I specialize in Ford Tri-Motor airplane material and pay premiums on material picturing or featuring the Ford plane from the 1920s. Wanted are World War II Ford aviation items from the Willow Run bomber plant, and the aircraft engine plant at the famous Rouge plant. I also buy most other Ford Motor items. All inquires answered promptly.

Tim O'Callaghan
305 St. Lawrence Blvd.
Northville, MI 48167
248-449-2642

	We Pay
Stout Air Service Timetables, 1926-1929	**25.00-70.00**
Maddux Airlines Timetables, 1927-1929	**20.00-50.00**
Transcontinential Air Transport Timetables, 1929-1932	**20.00-50.00**
TWA Timetables, 1935-1940	**10.00-15.00**
Real Photo Postcards of Ford Tri-Motor Airplanes	**10.00-50.00**
Ford Tri-Motor Sales Brochure, 1927-1929	**125.00-175.00**
Badge, round picture of Ford Factory, World War II	**100.00-200.00**

I buy **items used by airlines as well as the Hindenburg and Graf Zeppelin airships.** My main interest is in dining ware items such as china, glassware, and silver-plate serving pieces such as coffeepots, creamers, and sugar bowls, etc. Of particular interest are butter pats and salt and pepper shakers. Items may be from either domestic or foreign airlines and either old or new.

Also of interest are **airline-issue playing cards, crew wings, junior wings, and metal travel agency-sized airline models.** The only nonairline issue items purchased are the **Aero-Mini brand metal airplane toy models** which are about six inches in length.

Dick Wallin
P.O. Box 1784
Springfield, IL 62705
217-498-9279

Aviation

	We Pay
American Airlines, china w/DC3 plane & flag logo	1,500.00+
American Airlines Flagship, silverware, w/airplane nose handle	15.00
British Airways, butter pat, w/blue & yellow Concorde rim	35.00
Any Airline, butter pat, china w/top logo	20.00+
Cubana Airlines, any china or playing cards	25.00-50.00
Foreign Airlines, cup & saucer set, w/top or side logo	15.00+
Delta Airlines, bowl, w/Flying-D oval logo, Incaware	25.00
Graf Zeppelin (LZ logo), china, blue & gold	1,00.00+
Hindenburg, china w/airship over globe, blue & gold	1,000.00+
Hindenburg, silverware, airship on globe handle	150.00+
Hindenburg, glassware, airship on globe, LZ 129	500.00+
Panagra, any china or playing cards	25.00-50.00
Pan Am, china, w/dark blue winged globe logo	400.00-600.00
Pan Am, teapot, sugar bowl or creamer w/gold eagle & stars	100.00+
TAT-Arrow Logo Joint Air-Rail Service Items, any kind	50.00+

I am always interested in buying **commercial airline items from Pan Am, Panagra, and other domestic and international airlines.** I prefer items from 1927 to 1950, but I will look at all items from 1927 to 1980. So if you have something, please contact me. **Note, I am not interested in any military items.**

William Gawchik
88 Clarendon Ave.
Yonkers, NY 10701
914-965-3010 or fax 914-966-1055
panam314@aol.com

	We Pay
Pilot Wings	25.00+
Pilot Hat Emblems	25.00+
Flight Attendant Wings	25.00+
Flight Attendant Hat Emblems	25.00+
Ground Service Insignia	15.00+
Timetables	3.00+
Playing Cards	1.00+
Anniversary Pins	5.00+
Advertising Pins	50¢+
Uniform Patches	50¢+
Dining Service Items	1.00+
Junior Pilot Wings	1.00+
Junior Stewardess Wings	1.00+

Inflight Safety Cards .... **50¢+**
Ticket Jackets .... **20¢+**
Seat Pocket Information Packets .... **3.00+**
Menus .... **1.00+**
Silverware (silver-plate) .... **1.00+**
Current Issue Insignia .... **12.00+**
International Insignia .... **5.00+**

Wanted to buy: **Charles A. Lindbergh and the Spirit of St. Louis items** including plates, ashtrays, glassware, planes, spoons, pipes, cap guns, pin-back buttons, razors, pocket knives, dolls, Metalcraft hanger for planes, toys, games, etc. Prices will vary depending on condition.

Amelia Earhart memorabilia is also wanted — in particular, a metal lamp in the shape of the parachute. The top of the lamp has open-cut design of stars so that a reflection of stars appears on the ceiling when the lamp is lit. I will consider **other unusual, unique aviation memorabilia.**

Rosemary Zuern
913 Wylde Oak Dr.
Oshkosh, WI 54904

Backscratchers

All types of backscratchers are wanted — especially of unusual materials or from foreign countries. I will pay according to uniqueness or artistic appeal. Please write, thank you.

Manfred S. Rothstein
1308 Medical Dr.
Fayetteville, NC 28304

Badges

I would like **Iowa chauffeur badges for the years 1923, 1925, 1927, and 1928.** I am willing to purchase a complete set of Iowa chauffeur badges or a partial set if these years are included. I will pay $500.00 for a good, complete set in above average condition.

Orrin E. Miller
1920 Franklin St.
Waterloo, IA 50703-5022

Banks

I am interested in buying **any glass or part glass bank I do not have in my collection.** These glass banks include old as well as new glass banks. I will also buy collections of glass banks if there are some I need. I'm also interested in bottle banks, all glass banks, combinations of other materials with glass, bubble banks, fishbowl banks, glass block banks, flask banks, and candy container banks.

Charlie Reynolds
2836 Monroe St.
Falls Church, VA 22042
703-533-1322
reynoldstoys@erols.com

Banks	**We Pay**
Local Order of Moose No 322	**100.00**
Gattuso Rabbit	**100.00**
Dietz Jar w/Lock	**125.00**
Jumbo Peanut Elephant, green or clear	**500.00**
Victory Thrift Jar, more planes/tanks/ships	**225.00**
Kroger Building	**250.00**
Flat Iron Building	**275.00**
Safe w/Raised Diagional Slot, clear	**125.00**
Reddy Kilowatt, bubble bank	**400.00**
I Like Ike, bubble bank	**300.00**
Save for Columbian Missions, bubble bank	**425.00**
Wizard of Oz, glass block bank	**175.00**
Shooting for Savings, fishbowl bank	**200.00**
Change Saver, fishbowl bank	**200.00**
Candy Pay Station Phone, plastic & glass	**225.00**
Mail Box, candy container	**225.00**
Others	**Please Contact Me**

Beanie Babies

I am an avid Beanie Baby collector who is trying to complete her collection. I missed some of the **older Beanie Babies,** since I did not get started until 1996! I am willing to buy Beanies that are played with or even those that do not have swing tags, since I am simply interested in completing my collection. I am also willing to trade extra beanies and/or pay money to obtain them. Please send me a list of which Beanie Baby(ies) you have, photograph(s), as well as your asking price(s). I am looking for reasonable offers only and am willing to help in any way possible to make a fair trade/buy. I will pay $50 for each of the following Beanies and will pay $100 for Humphrey.

Amy Hopper
2161 Holt Rd.
Paducah, KY 42001

	We Pay
Brittania the Bear	**50.00**
Bronty the Dinosaur	**50.00**
Bumble the Bee	**50.00**
Caw the Crow	**50.00**
Chilly the Polar Bear	**50.00**
Chops the Lamb	**50.00**
Digger the Crab, **orange**	**50.00**
Flutter the Butterfly	**50.00**
Garcia the Bear	**50.00**
Happy the Hippo, **gray**	**50.00**
Humphrey the Camel	**100.00**
Inky the Octopus, **tan**, both versions	**50.00**
Lizzy the Lizard, **tie-dyed**	**50.00**
Lucky the Ladybug, 7 felt spots	**50.00**
Lucky the Ladybug, 21 felt spots	**50.00**
Maple the Canadian Bear	**50.00**
Nip the Cat, **all gold**	**50.00**
Nip the Cat, **white face & belly**	**50.00**
Quackers the Duck, **without wings**	**50.00**
Peanut the Elephant, **royal blue**	**50.00**
Peking the Panda Bear	**50.00**
Rex the Dinosaur	**50.00**
Seamore the Seal	**50.00**
Slither the Snake	**50.00**
Sly the Fox, **brown belly**	**50.00**
Spot the Dog, **without spot**	**50.00**
Steg the Dinosaur	**50.00**

Stripes the Tiger, gold & black (1st version) **50.00**
Tank the Armadillo, without shell (1st & 2nd versions) **50.00**
Teddy the Bear, all old & new face versions except new brown face (11 total) **50.00**
Trap the Mouse **50.00**
Web the Spider **50.00**
Zip the Cat, all black or white face & belly **50.00**

Beatnik Collectibles

The 'Beats,' later called 'Beatniks,' consisted of artists, writers, and others disillusioned with traditional mores and values. The Beatniks were nonconformist, Bohemian free-thinkers who expressed their disdain for society from 1960 to 1962. From a collector's point of view, the most highly-regarded Beat authors are William Burroughs, Allen Ginsberg, Jack Kerouac, and Lawrence Ferlinghetti. **Any books, records, posters, pamphlets, or other items** associated with them are desirable.

Richard Synchef
22 Jefferson Ave.
San Rafael, CA 94903
415-507-9933

We Pay

Posters, for poetry readings .... **30.00+**
Leaflets, for anti-nuclear political meetings .... **5.00+**
Significant Poetry Magazines .... **10.00+**
Book, *Howl*, Allen Ginsberg, 1956, 1st printing .... **100.00+**
LP Record, Blues & Haikus, Jack Kerouac, 1959 .... **100.00+**
Life Magazine, Squarsville Vs Beatsville, Sept 21, 1959 .... **25.00**

Beer Cans

I am looking to add to my growing collection of **US cone-top and flat-top beer cans.** I specialize in good condition, 12-ounce cans, but will make offers on other cans of value. I'll pay top dollar for cans I need for my collection! I'm a collector, not a dealer, so I'll pay more!

Steve Gordon
P.O. Box 532
Olney, MD 20830-0632
301-439-4116
gono@clark.net

Black Americana

Wanted to purchase: **Black Americana tin-type toys, especially wind-up types.** Also wanted are **Black Americana books**, such as *Little Black Sambo, Golliwogs, Ten Little Niggers,* etc.

Arthur Boutiette
11724 Fairway
Little Rock, AR 72212

	We Pay
Amos & Andy Taxi	**200.00-650.00**
The Chicken Snatcher	**200.00-750.00**
Jazzbo Jim	**300.00-550.00**
Strauss Coon Jigger	**200.00-650.00**
Spic-n-Span	**300.00-900.00**
Charlestown Trio	**250.00-700.00**
Red Cap Black Porter	**250.00-550.00**
Little Black Sambo Books	**35.00-85.00**
Golliwog Books	**35.00-85.00**
Ten Little Nigger Books	**50.00-225.00**

Seeking **Black memorabilia for historical collection.**

Walt Thompson
P.O. Box 2541-w
Yakima, WA 98907-2541
phone/fax 509-452-4016

	We Pay
Slave Ownership Documents	**50.00+**
Slave Sale Notices	**100.00+**

Slave Manacles, Restraints, Shackles .... **100.00+**
Signs, Colored Only, Whites Only, etc; must be original........................ **50.00+**

Wanted to buy: **original First Day Ceremony Program honoring Booker T. Washington.** Booker T. Washington was the first Black American honored on a United States postage stamp. He was a world famous educator, author, and founder of Tuskegee University, Tuskegee, Alabama, in 1881. The stamp was issued at the Founder's Day Exercises, University Chapel, Sunday, April 7, 1940. The program celebrates the presentation of the stamp to the public. The Order of Service for the Washington stamp includes Scripture Reading and Prayer...Reverend H.V. Richardson; Introductions...President F.D. Patterson; Addresses by President F.D. Patterson; Dr. W.J. Schieffelin, Chairman, Board of Trustees; and Postmaster General James A. Farley. A portion of this event was a radio broadcast. I am willing to pay $75/negotiable if in excellent condition and negotiable if condition is less than excellent.

Lanice P. Middleton
1304 Gregory St.
Tuskegee Institute, AL 36088
334-727-1457

Boats and Boating Memorabilia

Wanted: **rowing boats, boy boats, rowing apparatus, and memorabilia.** I'm interested in classic or newer items.

Bob Gramer
P.O. Box 597
Linden, MI 48451
810-735-7115

I collect all **toy metal outboard boat motors.** These may be electric, tin windup, steam powered, or gas powered. Most of these motors were made in Japan from 1955 to 1970 by KO. I want nice, clean motors with no repaints or chipped paint. No plastic motors are wanted. I will pay 10% extra if you have the original box. Also wanted are **gas-powered race cars.**

Richard Gronowski
140 N Garfield Ave.
Traverse City, MI 49686-2802
616-491-2111

	We Pay
Evinrudes, 40 HP or 75 HP, ea	125.00
Gale Sovereign, 60 HP	200.00
Gale, 30 HP or 35 HP, ea	125.00
Johnsons, 40 HP or 75 HP, ea	125.00
Oliver, 35 HP	200.00
Mercury, black, 100 HP	200.00
Mercury, MK 55, MK 800, MK 78 or MK 75, ea	125.00
All Other Johnsons, Mercurys, Scotts, Evinrudes, Gales, ea	75.00
Sea-Fury	75.00
Sea-Fury Twin	150.00
Fuji or Orkin, ea	125.00
Tin Winups, ea	75.00
Generic's I.M.P, Langcraft, Yamaha, Super Tigre, Speed King, Sakai, New Evince, Le-Page, Swank, Aristocraft, Etc., ea	50.00

Books

We buy **good condition used and out-of-print reference books on antiques**. Particularly need books on art glass, cut glass, silver, R.S. Prussia, toys, furniture, folk art, shaving mugs, dolls, etc. Buy hardcover or paperback; one book or entire library. Send list with title, author, date, number of pages, condition, your phone number, and price wanted. We pay generous shipping allowance. Please list all titles you have available.

Antique and Collectors Reproduction News
Box 71174-WB
Des Moines, IA 50325
515-270-8994

I am interested in purchasing **new or modern signed editions for resale**. I am also interested in **Easton Press and Franklin Press all-leather volumes** both signed and unsigned. I collect the **signed volumes of Ted De Grazia**, a well-known Arizona artist. Some examples of the prices that I pay are listed below. The value of individual volumes is of course dependent on the condition (must be fine or better). I will appreciate any and all quotes. I ask that complete description of the book and its condition be sent with SASE. Thank you for your help.

Al-PAC, Lamar Kelley
2625 E Southern Ave., C 120
Tempe, AZ 85282-7633
602-831-3121 or fax 602-831-3193
alpac2625@aol.com

	We Pay
Easton Press Leather Volumes	**12.00**
Franklin Press Leather Volumes	**12.00**
Easton Press Signed Leather Volumes	**15.00**
Franklin Press Signed Leather First Editions	**15.00-25.00**
First Edition Signed Ted De Grazia	**20.00-25.00**
Modern Signed First Editions	**10.00-40.00**
Other Volumes, older, full leather, by well-known authors	**10.00-1,000.00**

Automobile books and automobilia of all types purchased. We will buy hard- and soft-bound books, in or out of print, new or used, remainders, surplus stock, large private collections or single copies. Our main interest is in books that deal with auto racing, history of cars and their manufacturers, motorcycles, famous automotive personalities, design, etc. We willingly purchase all automotive books. However, we specialize in European and exotic automobiles such as Ferrari, Maserati, Lamborghini, Mercedes, Porsche, Rolls Royce, etc. We also specialize in domestic manufacturers that are no longer in existence such as Packard, Studebaker, Auburn, Dusenberg, etc. We do not buy ex-library books, sales literature, owners or workshop manuals unless they are appropriate to those types of automobiles previously listed. We purchase automobilia such as race posters, art, period photographs, original design renderings, etc. We are aggressive buyers of top quality items regardless of age and quantity. Prices quoted are for books with dust jackets in top condition.

LMG Enterprises
9006 Foxland Dr.
San Antonio, TX 78230
phone or fax 210-979-6098
102341.142@compuserve.com

	We Pay
Annual Automobile Review 1953/54 #1	**100.00**
Annual Automobile Review 1954/54 #2	**160.00**
At Speed (Alexander)	**80.00**
Autocourse 1964-65	**90.00**
Bentley 50 Years of the Marque (Green)	**60.00**
Boyhood Photographs of J.H. Lartique (Lartigue)	**100.00**
British Light Weight Sports Cars 78 (Japanese)	**140.00**
Cara Automobile (Pininfarina)	**80.00**
Comicar (Bertieri)	**50.00**
Delorean Stainless Steel Illusion (Lamm)	**40.00**
DMG 1890-1915 (German)	**180.00**
Errett Loban Cord (Borgeson)	**120.00**
Ferrari 80, 2nd edition (Italian)	**100.00**
Ferrari Yearbook, 1949-1970, ea	**70.00-400.00**
First Century of Portraits Celebrating Mercedes	**200.00**
Grand Prix Car, Vol. 1 & Vol. 2 (Pomeroy)	**160.00**
L'Art et L'Automobile (Poulain)	**60.00**
La Targa Florio (Garcia)	**80.00**
Les 24 Heures de Mans (Labric)	**160.00**
Piloti che Gente, 4th edition (Ferrari)	**140.00**
Spirit Celebrating 75 Years of Rolls Royce (Dallison)	**60.00**
Ten Ans de Courses (Montaut)	**600.00**

I am interested in buying **older, clean, out-of-print bound books and magazines that were printed before 1950 on any subject.** Books wanted include:

Bookman's Wake and *Booked to Die* by John Dunning
Haunted Bookshop, Parnassus on Wheels, and *Tales/Rolltop Desk* by Christopher Morley
Any hardcover books by Anne Rice
Books about bookstores, book people; fiction welcomed
Books about books, such as bibliographies

Books must be bound, in good condition with dust jackets, whenever possible. No ex-library books are wanted. Please note that I am also extremely interested in purchasing any library of books in the states of Florida, Georgia, South Carolina, etc., near the Eastern seaboard. I am interested in any used or antiquarian bookstores that may be going out of business or ones that are looking for a partner. Is there anyone in any Eastern state that would have a large older brick home that can house over 60,000 books and would be interested in starting a bookstore?

Remember, before you donate or give them away, please write. I also buy **old stamps.** Quote first.

Bon Summers
P.O. Box 1167
St. Augustine, FL 32085
904-823-9100

We Pay

Dunning, John; first editions **5.00-25.00**

I am interested in **books that are collections of the cartoons of a single artist.** No general collections of cartoons (Best of Punch), comic books, recent reprints, or storybooks based on cartoons are wanted please.

The marking of first editions varies with different publishers, though a majority of the books by the artists will state a first printing or edition, or have the number one still in the number series. Others will have a date on the title page matching the copyright date. And some give no clue what-so-ever!

Prices are for books in fine to excellent condition — no major tears, coloring, loose pages, bent covers, or broken spines. Prices vary greatly with condition. Listed here are some cartoon anthologies wanted. Publishers for these are Cupples & Leon Publishing Co., Star Co., Ball Pub. Co., and Cartoon Reprint Series (1900 through 1935). **I will pay from $35.00 to $115.00** for these books.

Barney Google
Bringing Up Father
Dick Tracy
Dolly Dimples
Harold Teen
Joe Palooka
Keeping Up With the Jones
Little Orphan Annie
Moon Mullins
Mutt & Jeff
Nebs
Percy & Ferdie
Regular Fella's
Smitty
Tillie the Toiler
The Gumps
Toonerville Trolly
Winnie Winkle

Craig Ehlenberger
Abalone Cove Rare Books
7 Fruit Tree Rd.
Portuguese Bend, CA 90275
310-377-4609 or fax 310-544-6792 (6 am–9 pm PST)
CEhlenberger@worldnet.att.net

Other Early Artists **We Pay**

John McCutcheon .... **25.00+**
Clare Briggs .... **25.00+**
Outcault (Buster Brown) .... **35.00+**

Artist's Collections, First Editions With Dust Jackets **We Pay**

Addams, Charles	**25.00-75.00**
Alain	**15.00+**
Arno, Peter	**15.00-100.00**
Corbean, Sam	**8.00+**
Darrow, Whitney Jr.	**8.00-15.00**
Day, Chon (Brother Sebastion)	**6.00-12.00**
Dunn, Alan	**8.00-15.00**
Fisher, Ed	**8.00-12.00**
Giovannetti, Pericle L.	**8.00-15.00**
Hamilton, William	**12.00-20.00**
Hoff, Syd	**8.00-20.00**
Hokinson, Helen	**10.00-18.00**
Kelly, Walt (Pogo) (most are paperback without dust jackets)	**15.00-75.00**
Ketcham, Hank (Dennis the Menace), all say First, no dust jackets	**10.00-15.00**
Key, Ted (Hazel)	**8.00-25.00**
Kovarsky, Anatol	**8.00-12.00**
Partch, Virgil (VIP)	**5.00-20.00**
Petty, Mary	**10.00-15.00**
Price, George	**12.00-22.00**
Segar (Popeye)	**30.00+**
Shafer, Burr	**10.00+**
Stevenson, James	**10.00-15.00**
Syverson, Henry	**5.00**
Taylor, Richard	**8.00-15.00**
Wilson, Gahan	**8.00-20.00**
Other Newspaper & Magazine Cartoonists	**Contact Me**

I have been a serious buyer for over 30 years (a fact that collectors, dealers, pickers, and lay people all over the US can attest to). I do repeat business with most sellers and always welcome a chance to do business with someone new. The 'secret of my success' is quite simple: (1) my offers are very fair and generous; (2) I don't 'pick and choose,' I take the bad with the better; and (3) I pay promptly! Same day as arrivals! If there is anyone who is not familiar with me (or my reputation), I can offer trade and bank references. My policy always has been that no deal is complete until everyone is 100% satisfied. If you have any questions, phone me.

Wanted items include:

Big Little Books: 1933 through 1950 only. These mainly comic-character (Flash Gordon, Dick Tracy) based books were little and fat (3½" x 5", 300 to 400 pages). They were published by Whitman and Saalfield mostly; other companies such as Dell and Fawcett produced some. Books with missing spines, pages, and covers are not wanted.
Walt Disney: 1928 through 1950s books, magazines, comics, watches, and

other items. Book publishers include Whitman, McKay, Blue Ribbon, plus many more. If in doubt, just describe as best you can.
Pop-Up Books: circa 1930s by Blue Ribbon, etc.

Other wants include: **comic books, Sunday newspaper comic strips and pages; radio, TV, and cereal premiums; nonsports cards; movie posters; animation cels; popular music; jazz and song magazines; Lone Ranger; Lionel train materials; Korlix and Tarzan ice cream promotions of the 1930s** — plus anything you have that you feel is remotely related to any item on this list, just describe.

The post office is the best method of sending parcels, but UPS may be suitable in some instances. To speed delivery, please put **Value of $25.00 or less, per parcel.** Indicate 'printed matter' and do not put any invoice in parcels. Pack well. The mails are very reliable and provide reasonably quick service (anywhere from six to 10 days). Finder's fee will be paid to anyone who puts me in touch with someone who I do business with.

Ken Mitchell
710 Conacher Dr.
Willowdale, Ontario
Canada M2M 3N6
416-222-5805 (anytime)

We want to buy **children's series books from 1900 to 1970**. These books are popular literature for children. Each series, or set, has a continuing main character or group of characters, e.g., Nancy Drew, The Five Little Peppers, etc.

Until 1960, all of these books were published with a paper cover, called a dust jacket. If the series book has a copyright date prior to 1960, the book **must** have its dust jacket to be considered for purchase. After 1960, most series were published in a format called 'pictorial cover.' The binding is an embossed cardboard with a picture printed on the front cover. Often the book cover has a listing of other books in the same series. Also the spine of the book usually has a number somewhere mid-span (1, 25, 33, 47, etc.) showing where your particular title falls in the series.

We only buy very good, tight books. Dust jackets must be in good condition too. We do **not** buy Bobbsey Twins (except with paper doll dust jacket) or Happy Hollisters (except for numbers 30 through 33). Prices also depend on condition; feel free to inquire about others not listed here. We are happy to answer all questions (SASE). Please do not quote or ask about any books which have damp stains or have a musty odor.

We also are interested in the **Limited Editions Club** begun in 1929 by George Macy. These books go mostly to collectors, and must be in as-new condition. Almost all of them were boxed, and came with a 'monthly letter.' There are over 500 titles. Some are worth very little — $5.00 to $15.00 others are worth many hundreds. See some sample prices listed below for fine copies. We are also very interested in the original artwork and all of the ephemeral material from the

Club. Ephemeral material consists of letters, shipping statements, prospectus volumes, etc. — anything that was meant to be thrown out, but was saved.

Heritage Press books are mostly classics and are well illustrated. They come boxed and have a letter included (called a 'Sandglass'). We usually buy these books in lots, as they are only worth $2.00 to $3.00 each, with some exceptions. Some exceptions are listed below.

We are also interested in the **Beat Generation** period-modern first editions, fine in dust jackets of Kerouac, Ginsberg, etc. Some interesting items were done in very small printings by private presses, and only came in a pamphlet style. If unsure, contact us.

To sum it all, we specialize in series books. We have over 20,000 books in stock and pay the highest prices. We buy books in all fields except medicine and law. We **do not buy** book club editions, paperbacks, encyclopedias, or any book in poor condition. We are always in the market for nicely illustrated children's books and will consider books in any language.

Lee and Mike Temares
50 Heights Rd.
Plandome, NY 11030
516-627-8688 or fax 516-627-7822
Tembooks@aol.com

Author, Children's Series	**We Pay**
Appleton, Tom Swift Jr., #31 through #33	**50.00+**
Keene, Nancy Drew, w/dust jacket	**4.00+**
Dixon, Hardy Boys, w/dust jacket	**4.00+**
Cherry Ames, w/dust jacket	**4.00+**
Sutton, Judy Bolton, #30 through #38	**20.00+**
Rich Brant, w/dust jacket	**4.00+**
Chip Hilton, w/dust jacket	**4.00+**
Ken Holt, w/dust jacket	**4.00+**

Heritage Press Books	**We Pay**
Most Titles, fine in fine box	**2.50**
Ink & Blood, Heritage Press Special, fine in fine box	**100.00**
Living Talmud, Heritage Press Special, fine in fine box	**10.00**
Gone With the Wind, Heritage Press Special, fine in fine box	**20.00**

Limited Edition Club	**We Pay**
Most Titles	**5.00-15.00**
Lysistrata	**400.00-800.00**
Ulysses	**400.00-1,400.00**
Alice	**300.00**

Shakespeare, 37 volumes	**250.00**
Sherlock Holmes, 8 volumes	**75.00**
Other Titles	**10.00-200.00**

We are purchasing **children's books having from four to thirty-two pages with color plates by such publishers as Raphael Tuck and McLoughlin Brothers.** Books must be pre-1925 and not torn. Also we are looking for **Black Americana books** such as Little Black Sambo, etc. They can be on linen, linenette, or common paper.

We also collect **leather-bound, pre-1800 books and book sets.** We will pay top dollar if in good condition, complete, and written in English. We are interested in purchasing **medical books with subjects such as surgery, diseases of children, gynecology, and midwifery.** Send a list of your books for sale.

Melanie Boutiette
410 West Third St.
Little Rock, AR 72201

	We Pay
Common Paper	**5.00-75.00**
Linenette	**10.00-85.00**
Linen	**20.00-125.00**
Black	**5.00-200.00**
Ethnic or Negro Stories	**30.00-225.00**
Full Leather	**20.00-60.00**
Half Leather	**10.00-50.00**
Civil War, leather	**30.00-100.00**
Medical Books	**35.00-100.00**

One day my husband brought home a small book; he explained that it was a tradition of his company, R.R. Donnelley & Sons (Lakeside Press), to give these out at Christmas time to each employee and special customers. This was my first encounter with a Lakeside Classic. The title of the first one was *A Frontier Doctor* by Henry F. Hoyt — the biography of a doctor who had an encounter with Jesse James. Other books followed through the years; all are biographies, autobiographies, or diaries of people who helped shape the history of our country. I was hooked; and I've looked forward to getting a new book each Christmas.

Lakeside Classic books originated in 1903 as a project for apprentice printers to learn the trade. The books are small (6⅞" tall by 4¼" across) with very plain fabricoid covers. The spine has a gold stamped title and author's name at the top and 'The Lakeside Press' in gold at the bottom. The front cover has only the gold-stamped R.R. Donnelley & Sons Company/Lakeside Press logo (Indian Chief's head in full headdress). Each twenty-five years the color of the binding is changed. There have been red, green, and blue bindings with current releases in brown.

As R.R. Donnelley & Sons has factories all around the world, these little books may be found anywhere. I would like to find some earlier books that I haven't read. Please look for red, green, or blue bindings; brown covers are not wanted. Please send a good description of condition, your asking price, and SASE. Feel free to contact me for more information or with questions about this series. I also have mint examples in brown binding (many in original shrinkwrap) that I am willing to trade. Price range paid in the past has been from $5.00 to $25.00 per book.

Linda Holycross
109 N Sterling Ave.
Veedersburg, IN 47987

Some titles that are wanted along with their copyright dates include:
A True Picture of Emigration, by Rebecca Burlend, 1936
Absaraka, Home of the Crows, by Mrs. Margaret I. Carrington, 1950
Across the Plains in Forty-Nine, by Reuben Cole Shaw, 1948
Adventures of the First Settlers on the Oregon or Columbia River, by Alexander Ross, 1923
Advocates and Adversaries, by Robert R. Rose, 1977
Alexander Henry's Travels and Adventures in Years 1760-1776, 1921
Alexander Mackenzie's Voyage to the Pacific Ocean in 1793, 1931
Among the Indians, by Henry A. Boller, 1959
Army Life in Dakota, by Philippe deTrobriand, 1941
Autobiography of Benjamin Frankin, 1903
Autobiography of Gurdon Saltonstall Hubbard, 1911
Bark Covered House, by William Nowlin, 1937
Bidwell's Echoes of the Past — Steele's in Camp and Cabin, 1928
Border and the Buffalo, by John R. Cook, 1938
Colorado Volunteers in New Mexico, 1862, by Ovando J. Hollister, 1962
Commerce of the Prairies, by Josiah Gregg, 1926
Conquest of Illinois, by George Rogers Clark, 1920
Dakota War Whoop, by Harriet E. Bishop McConkey, 1965
Death Valley in '49, by William L. Manly, 1927
Early Day of Rock Island and Davenport, by J.W. Spencer and J.M.D. Burrows, 1942
Excursion Through America, by Nicolaus Mohr, 1972
Frenchman in Lincoln's America, I & II, by Ernest Duvergier deHauranne, 1974, 1975
Forty Years a Fur Trader, by Charles Larpenteur, 1933
Fruits of Solitude, by William Penn, 1906
Fur Hunters of the Far West, by Alexander Ross, 1924
Growing Up With Southern Illinois, by Daniel Harmon Brush, 1944
Hardtack and Coffee, by John D. Billings, 1960
History of Illinois, by Gov. Thomas Ford, 1945, 1946

Honolulu, by Laura Fish Judd, 1966
Inaugural Addresses of the Presidents, 1904, 1905
Indian Captivity of O.M. Spencer, 1917
John D. Young and the Colorado Gold Rush, 1969
John Long's Voyages and Travels in Years 1768-1788, 1922
Kendall's Texan Santa Fe Expedition, 1929
Kit Carson's Autobiography, 1935
Life of Black Hawk, 1916
Memorable American Speeches, 1907, 1908, 1909, 1910
Milford's Memoir, by Louis Leclerc deMilford, 1956
My Experiences in the West, by John S. Collins, 1970
My Life on the Plains, by General George A. Custer, 1952
Narrative of the Adventures of Zenas Leonard, 1934
Narrative of Colonial America, 1704-1765, 1971
Narratives of the American Revolution, 1976
Outlines From the Outpost, John Esten Cooke, 1961
Pattie's Personal Narrative, 1930
Pictures of Illinois One Hundred Years Ago, 1918
Pictures of Gold Rush of California, 1949
Pioneers by Noah Harris Letts and Thomas Allen Banning, 1825-1865, 1972
Private Smith's Journal, 1963
Reminiscences of Chicago, 1912, 1913, 1914, 1915
Six Years With the Texas Rangers, by James B. Gillett, 1943
Southwestern Expedition of Zebulon M. Pike, 1925
Three Years Among the Indians and Mexicans, by General Thomas James, 1953
Three Years in the Klondike, by Jeremiah Lynch, 1967
Truth About Geronimo, by Britton Davis, 1951
Two Views of Gettysburg, by Sir A.J.L. Fremantle and Frank Haskell, 1964
Two Years' Residence on the English Prairie of Illinois, by John Woods, 1968
Uncle Dick Wootton, by Howard Louis Conrad, 1957
Vanished Arizona, by Martha Summerhaves, 1939
Voyage to the Northwest Coast of America, by Gabriel Franchere, 1954
War on the Detroit, by Thomas Vercheres deBoucherville and James Foster, 1940
Wau-Bun, The Early Day in the North-West, by Mrs. John H. Kinzie, 1932
War-Path and Bivouac, by John F. Finerty, 1955
Western Country in the 17th Century, by Lamothe Cadillac and Pierre Liette, 1947
Woman's Story of Pioneer Times, by Christiana Holmes Tillson, 1919

We are interested in **used books, hardcover only, no college text books, and antique clocks.** Condition is everything! We buy all categories of books with special interest in the following:

- Children's books
- North Beach Peninsula
- 19th-century cookbooks
- Books on trains
- Long Beach Peninsula
- 18th-century English-language

Travel and exploration to 1939
Western Americana
Military
Metaphysical

Norma and Milt Wadler
The Whale's Tale
P.O. Box 1520A
360-642-3455 or fax 360-642-2626
whalesta@willapabay.org

We are buying **children's series and illustrators, horse and dog stories, aviation, and magic.** Let us hear about the books you are interested in selling.

Bob and Gail Spicer
1250 Ashgrove Rd.
Cambridge, NY 12816-9801
phone/fax 518-677-5139
ashtrestrv@aol.com

Wanted: **Dick and Jane readers.** All early edition readers from primary grades in good or better condition, published by Scott Foresman are wanted. I'm also looking for flash cards, workbooks, and large teacher portfolios. I will pay $10.00 and up. I also trade or sell.

Sue Samuels
831-484-9272

Advanced collector wishes to buy **Sherlock Holmes** items, i.e., pre-1960 books, sculpture, posters, photos, prints, dolls, toys, games, pins, etc. Anything associated with Sherlock Holmes or Dr. Watson, i.e., Victorian Gasogene, dark lantern, tantalus, and 221B Baker Street furnishings as well as items associated with Sir Arthur Conan Doyle (Watson's literary agent) are wanted. Prices vary according to condition and rarity. Antiques should be circa 1880 to 1910.

Richard D. Lesh, B.S.I.
1205 Lory St.
Ft. Collins, CO 80524
970-221-1093

Sherlock Holmes Items	We Pay
Books, 1st editions by Doyle	**300.00+**
Books by Other Authors, pre-1960	**30.00+**
Sculpture of Sherlock Holmes or Dr Watson	**100.00+**
Posters of Movies or Plays, pre-1960	**100.00+**
Cigarette Cards	**10.00+**
Autographed Letters, Books or Photos	**100.00+**
Dr Watson's Service Revolver, Adams .450, circa 1880	**150.00+**
Gasogene (seltzer bottle)	**100.00+**
Tantalus (2, 3 crystal decanters)	**100.00+**
London Police Dark Lantern, tin	**200.00+**

Wanted to purchase for private collection: **first edition books of famous authors with limited distribution.** Also wanted are **maps, atlases, and any old, old books.** Send as much information as you have and price you desire.

Mr. R.G. Mulhern
3722 Alabama #130
San Diego, CA 92104

Bottle Openers

I am interested in buying **any figural bottle opener not in my collection.** Openers I am looking for must be three-dimensional standing figures or wall-mount figures. I will also buy examples that will upgrade the condition of openers in my collection.

Charlie Reynolds
2836 Monroe St.
Falls Church, VA 22042
703-533-1322

	We Pay
Boots, brass	**50.00-75.00**
Boy w/Books, cast iron	**2,000.00**
Cardinal, cast iron	**325.00**
Dragons, cast iron	**125.00**

Drunk on Lamppost or Signpost, aluminum **15.00**
Eskimo Holding Bottle, pot metal **350.00**
Indian, Syroco Wood **350.00**
Knight, Syroco Wood **450.00**
Monk, Syroco Wood **350.00**
Nudes, brass or cast iron, ea **40.00-75.00**
Rhino, cast iron, Japan **350.00**
Roadrunner, opener in beak & tail **350.00**
Turtle, pot metal or brass, opener at beak & tail **200.00**
Others .... **Top Dollar**

Bottles

Before 1900 all bottles were handmade. These can usually be distinguished from modern, machine-made bottles by looking at the seams on the sides. On a machine-made bottle they go all the way to the top of the lip. If they end lower, if there are perpendicular seams (3-piece mold), or if there are no seams at all, the bottle is probably handmade.

I will consider purchasing **almost any type of handmade bottle.** Most machine-made bottles have no value as collectibles. The most desirable have one or more of the following characteristics:

Embossed lettering, design, or picture
Pontil mark (round, rough gouge on underside of bottle where glassblowing rod was broken off)
Unusual shape or color

Bottles without any of the above are probably of no value. Presence of a label or a crudely-made appearance (such as bubbles or a 'whittled' surface) adds to the value. I will not buy bottles with cracks, scratches, chips, bruises, iridescence, or with a condition known as 'sick glass' (a milky haze, usually on the inside, that will not clean off).

The more detailed the description of your bottles the better, but state at least what it is embossed on the front and sides (not the bottom), and indicate size and color. If the bottle is labeled or pontiled, include that information. I will respond promptly to all communications whether I buy or not (please include a reply card or envelope). If I don't buy your bottles, I will give you an informal appraisal. The huge variety of collectible bottles makes it hard to give a general estimate of prices, but the prices below will give you some idea of the price ranges for the more collectible bottles in each category.

Michael Engel
43 Bryan Ave.
Easthampton, MA 01027
413-527-8733
IWWlives@aol.com

Type	We Pay
Bitters	15.00-500.00+
Cosmetic (hair, perfume, cologne)	2.00+
Food or Household (unusual embossing, shape, or color)	2.00-10.00
Ink (unusual shape or color only)	10.00-100.00+
Medicine (especially cures)	2.00-100.00+
Mineral Water (blob-tops & squat shapes only)	5.00-100.00+
Peppersauce/Pickle (elaborate design)	10.00+
Poison (especially cobalt or unusual shape)	5.00+
Soda or Beer (blob-tops or squat shapes only)	5.00-20.00
Whiskey	2.00+

We purchase **perfume bottles of all types**: miniatures, Czechoslovakian crystal bottles, Baccarat, Lalique, DeVilbiss atomizers, and commercial perfume bottles. Commercial bottles are these that originally contained perfume when they were sold, such as Matchabelli Windsong in a small crown-shaped bottle. Commercial bottles should, if possible, have a label and the original box.

Monsen and Baer
Box 529
Vienna, VA 22183
703-938-2129 or 703-242-1357

Minatures	We Pay
Solid Perfume, Estee Lauder, Avon, etc	25.00+
Dior, Schiaparelli, Guerlain or Coty	5.00+
Ceramic, metal crown top	40.00+

Atomizers	We Pay
DeVilbiss, 6"	100.00+

Volupte, 5" .... **75.00+**

Lalique **We Pay**

Most 1930s or before .... **500.00+**
D'Orsay, black glass Ambre d'Orsay .... **500.00+**
Molinard Calendal Nudes .... **500.00+**
Roger & Gallet Le Jade, green glass .... **1,500.00+**

Commercial Bottles **We Pay**

Vigny Le Golliwogg .... **100.00+**
Hattie Carnegie, bust of woman .... **100.00+**
Ciro Chevalier, knight, black glass, in box .... **150.00+**
Schiaparelli, Zut, woman's torso, in box .... **600.00+**
Schiaparelli, Success, Fou, green leaf, in box .... **800.00+**
Lucretia, Vanderbilt, blue glass, in box .... **750.00+**
Many Others, original label & box .... **50.00-100.00+**

Baccarat **We Pay**

Elizabeth Arden, It's You, hand .... **800.00+**
Houbigant, Buddha, in box .... **200.00+**
Ybry, green square .... **200.00+**
Ybry, purple or orange square .... **500.00+**
Christian Dior, Diorissimo, in box .... **2,000.00+**
Christian Dior, dog .... **5,000.00+**

Perfumes by Bourjois Perfume Company are wanted. I buy unusual presentations or rare single bottles of any fragrance produced by the Bourjois Company. I also buy **paper items such as catalogs, display stands, and any other promotional material from the company.** I am also buying **their compacts, lipsticks, and other cosmetic items.** The Bourjois Company produced the famous blue bottles of Evening in Paris. They also produced about one hundred other fragrances.

Beverly Nelson
1010 Lorna St.
Corona, CA 91720
909-737-0977
nelac@earthlink.net

Bottles and stoneware from Michigan cities listed below are wanted and must be in very good condition. No chips, cracks, or sick glass please. Paying reasonable prices for items I need. Common milk bottles are not wanted. Mainly looking for **early beer, soda, pharmacy, and stoneware.** Also wanted are **any House of David bottles.** Send photo or photocopy and price. Wanted are bottles from Michigan towns of:

Benton Harbor (House of David)
Benton Harbor
Bridgman
Coloma
Derby
Dowagiac
Eau Claire
Hartford
Keeler
Millburg
Sawyer
Sister Lakes
Stevensville
St. Joseph
Watervliet

Gred Marquart
P.O. Box 8615
Benton Harbor, MI 49023
616-926-7080

Bottoms-Up/Down

Bottoms-up cups were made by McKee in the 1940s. The nude is draped over the cup with her bottom 'up,' so that you must finish your drink before setting it down! These have a pattern number under the feet. The cups were sold with or without a coaster. Bottoms-down mugs are footed with her bottom hidden under the foot. Her legs form the handle and the pattern number is under the foot.

April and Larry Tvorak
P.O. Box 94
Warren Center, PA 18851
570-395-3775
april@cpix.net

	We Pay
Bottoms-Up Cup, Jade-ite	**40.00**
Bottoms-Up Cup, any other color	**35.00**

Coaster, Jade-ite	**75.00+**
Coaster, any other color	**65.00+**
Coaster, crystal or crystal w/fired-on color	**10.00-15.00**
Bottoms-Down Mug, Jade-ite	**150.00**
Bottoms-Down Mug, any other color	**135.00**

Boxes

We collect **Victorian era boxes** which held collars and cuffs; gloves; brush, comb, and mirror sets; shaving sets; neckties; etc. Also wanted are photograph albums and autograph albums. The items we collect have lithographs affixed to the front or top of the piece. The lithographic prints usually show scenes or people. We prefer those which show close-up views of children or ladies, but will consider others. The print (or in some cases the entire album) is covered with a thin layer of clear celluloid. In other instances, part of the box or album will be covered with an abstract or floral print paper or colorful velvet material.

We are interested only in pieces in top condition: no cracked celluloid, split seams, or missing hardware. Condition of the interior of these boxes and albums is not as important as the condition of the outside. We are *not* interested in French Ivory celluloid boxes or solid celluloid dresser sets. If you see an exceptional celluloid box or album, but are uncertain about buying it for resale, please put us in touch with the owner. If we can buy it, we will pay you a finder's fee. Request our illustrated want list, or view our want list and examples of celluloid boxes on our website.

Mike and Sherry Miller
303 Holiday Dr.
Tuscola, IL 61953
217-253-4991
miller@tuscola.net
http://www.tuscola.net/~miller/

	We Pay
Boxes, sm, ea	**40.00-75.00**
Boxes, med, ea	**50.00-100.00**
Boxes, lg, ea	**85.00-200.00**
Autograph Albums, ea	**25.00-75.00**
Photograph Albums, ea	**75.00-175.00**
Photograph Albums, musical, ea	**100.00-250.00**

Bronzes

I am buying **all bronze figures of people and animals, vases, inkwells, and lamps made before 1940.** I also collect **Art Deco, Art Nouveau bronzes, ivory, and marble items.** Wanted: single bronzes or an entire collection. Send photos and your price to:

Arthur Boutiette
11724 Fairway
Little Rock, AR 72212

Bronzes	We Pay
Bookends	**20.00-150.00**
Statues, 24" or taller	**250.00-2,500.00**
Statues, 24" or smaller	**150.00-1,500.00**
Animals, lg	**250.00-7,500.00**
Animals, sm	**50.00-1,000.00**
Vases	**50.00-3,500.00**
Inkwells w/Figures	**100.00-300.00**

Buffalo Pottery

We wish to buy **Buffalo Pottery: Deldare, Blue Willow, jugs and pitchers, as well as their advertising and identified commercial ware.**

Deldare is easily distinguished by the masterful use of hand-tinted scenes on the natural olive-green color of the body of the ware and generally portrays village and hunting scenes. Emerald Deldare, made with the same olive-green (and generally employed the same body shapes) depicts historical scenes and is highlighted with an Art Nouveau border or decoration.

Additionally, Buffalo Pottery produced Blue Willow ware, a series of jugs and pitchers, and served the needs of industry and its fine line of commercial ware for hotels, restaurants, railroads, steamships, and various government agencies.

Fred and Lila Shrader
2025 Hwy. 199 (Hiouchi)
Crescent City, CA 95531
707-458-3525

Buttons

I am a collector of **clothing buttons, old and new.** Of new buttons, I collect snap-togethers which have at least two pieces. These come apart and snap back together. Of the older buttons, china stencils and calicos are wanted; glass, realistics, ornamental shell, Bakelite, Lucite, celluloid, Victorians, and many others as well. No military, clay, or plain shirt buttons, please. I prefer to buy batches of buttons as opposed to singles.

Trisha J. Price
4815 W Clearwater #70
Kennewick, WA 99336
509-783-0920
Trisha@awt.co

I want to buy **singles or collections of old, interesting sewing buttons.** I will also try to help anyone identify their buttons if they send a close-up picture and a self-addressed, stamped envelope. My main button collecting interests are Bakelite, animals, insects, realistics, Chinese and Japanese, and other unusual types. I pay top prices for rare or interesting buttons.

Gwen Daniel
18 Belleau Lake Ct.
O'Fallon, MO 63366
314-987-3190
SlimGirl200@aol.com

Calculators

I collect **1970s-vintage pocket/portable calculators with an LED or type-type number display.** In case you're not familiar with the phrase, this is the type that 'lights up' usually in red, green, blue, or orange. I'm not interested in the modern LCD (liquid crystal) type of display (silver-gray background with black numbers).

I have most models from Texas Instruments, Sears, Lloyds, Unisonic, Rockwell, Bohsei, and Casio. However I do want pocket calculators from companies like Aries, Colex, General, ICI, Hermes, Hewlett Packard, Master,

Mintron, Sinclair, Summit, Universal Data, Verax, Vito, and many, many more.

I do not care if they work. Please contact me with a model number and condition. In addition, sending a photocopy or e-mailing a scanned picture of the calculator would be helpful. Generally, I am paying $15.00 to $30.00 for most models that I want; however, I am paying the following prices for these calculators in very good condition.

Guy 'Mr Calculator' Ball
P.O. Box 345
Tustin, CA 92781-0345
phone/fax 714-730-6140
mrcal@usa.net
http://www.oldcalcs.com

	We Pay
Bowmar MathMate	**80.00**
Busicom 80A	**120.00**
Busicom 120A	**100.00**
Calcu-pen, red display	**70.00**
Master MiniMaster	**75.00**
National Cash Register 1844	**95.00**
PRA Wisp	**50.00**
Sanyo ICC-804D	**60.00**
Sinclair Sovereign	**80.00**
Vito Elektron 2000	**140.00**

I collect a variety of things, but special interests are **1970s LED watches and calculators.** I also want **old computers and related materials, old video game stuff from the 1970s and 1980s, and pre-1990s metal trash cans featuring advertising or comic characters.**

Robb Sequin
P.O. Box 1126
Dennisport, MA 02639
508-760-2599
rsesquin@capecod.net

California Items

Mount Shasta, California, is my home town. I would be interested in buying **souvenirs or memorabilia items from Mount Shasta or McCloud, California.** I'm interested in single items or entire collections — large or small. Please write and let me hear about your item(s). Below is a sample of items wanted and prices paid. Thank you very much.

Jennie Krause
530 Butte Ave.
Mount Shasta, CA 96067

	We Pay
Postcards, real photo	**1.00+**
Watercolor Art	**20.00+**
Oil Paintings	**20.00+**
Advertising Items	**5.00-100.00**

California Perfume Company and 'Go-Withs'

In New York City, New York, in 1886, Mr. D.H. McConnell, Sr., founded the California Perfume Company (C.P.C.). These toiletries continued to be manufactured with the C.P.C. label until 1929 when 'Avon Products Inc.' was added. Both names appeared on the label until about 1939 when 'C.P.C.' was removed, and the labeling continued as 'Avon Products.' The name 'Perfection' was used on the household products issued by these companies.

Prior to the C.P. Company, another company called Goetting & Company (1871–1896) existed that was founded by Adolph Goetting. In 1896 it was bought out by the C.P. Company and Mr. Goetting became their chief chemist. Another French perfume company, Savoi Et. Cie labeling, was marketed by the C.P.C. in retail outlets. Lastly the 1918 C.P.C. packaged Marvel Electric Silver cleaner (patent Jan. 11, 1910) and Easy Day or Simplex Automatic Clothes Washer (patent July 4, 1916).

I am a collector of these items and the additional items listed below. Items are wanted for my collection and research. I have listed a pay and up price; I am seeking the ones of interest to me that I do not have. A description, condition, price, and notes of importance are helpful. A large SASE is required for information seekers only. I **do not want any 'Avon' or 'Perfection' marked items**.

Mr. Richard G. Pardini
3107 N El Dorado St., Dept. W
Stockton, CA 95204-3412
209-466-5550 (early am hours or leave message)

Go-Withs	We Pay
Goetting & Company Products	10.00+
Savoi Et Cie Products	10.00+
Marvel Electric Silver Cleaner, patent Jan. 11, 1910, boxed	25.00+
Easy Day or Simplex Automatic Clothes Washer, patent July 4, 1916, boxed	25.00+

C.P.C. Items	We Pay
Natoma Rose Fragrances Items, circa 1920	20.00+
Gift Sets, 1886 to 1929	25.00+
Catalogs, 1886 to 1914	20.00+
Outbooks, 1905 to 1929	2.00+
Items w/CP or Eureka Trade Marks	10.00+
Items w/126 Chambers St., New York USA address	20.00+

Cameras

We are looking to purchase **all types of photographic equipment and photo related items.** We are in the market for cameras, lenses, tripods, toys, figurines, photos, and books. Any item that relates to photography is wanted. Prices will vary due to condition and working order. Send make, model, condition, and a brief description about your item. Photographs are helpful and will be returned. SASE envelope will receive quicker response. Send information to:

HM Collectibles
3457 Julington Ck. Rd.
Jacksonville, FL 32223
hforsythe@ilin.com

Items wanted include:

Aerial cameras
Agfa
Aires
Ansco
Argus
Bolex
Bolsey
Box cameras

- Braun
- Brownie
- Burke & James
- Canon
- Character cameras
- Contax
- Contessa
- Exacta
- Folding cameras
- Fuji
- Goerz
- Graflex
- Hasselblad
- Kodak
- Konica
- Leica
- Lenses of all types
- Light meters
- Linhof
- Lumiere
- Mamiya
- Miniatures
- Minolta
- Mouse
- Worm & Surprise cameras
- Nikon
- Olympus
- Ornamental
- Panoramic cameras
- Pentacon
- Pentax
- Photographs
- Photographic advertising items
- Pixie
- Plaubel
- Polaroid
- Premo
- Reflex
- Retina
- Ricoh
- Rollei
- Spy cameras
- Stereo cameras
- Still cameras
- Tower
- Twin Reflex
- Underwater cameras
- Universal
- Vest Pocket
- Voiglander

I buy **classic, collectible, and usable cameras** of many types; prices paid may range from a few dollars to thousands for some rare cameras. Send list with complete descriptions (including model, lens name and size, shutter type, film size, cosmetic and mechanical condition, and other pertinent information); or call for estimate or general information. We also buy **old lenses of many types.** We **do not buy** Polaroid cameras or the modern 'Point and Shoot' types of cameras. We are primarily collectors and traders of the cameras of yesteryear that are in good, usable condition. Some examples of both classic and user cameras and more recent vintage cameras with prices paid are listed here. We pay shipping charges for all cameras purchased.

Gene's Cameras
2614 Artie St., SW, Suite 37
Huntsville, AL 35805
205-536-6893
genecams@aol.com

Cameras

Classic/Collectible Cameras

Classic/Collectible Cameras	We Pay
Alpa, by Pignons, AG	**100.00-1,000.00**
Ashi, Asahiflex	**100.00-300.00**
Canon Rangefinder, by Canon, many models	**100.00-300.00**
Exakta, Exa, Other Ihagee Kamerwerk Co Models	**25.00-250.00**
Kodak Retina, many models	**25.00-250.00**
Leica Cameras, Leitz Lenses, many models	**100.00-5,000.00+**
Minolta Rangefinder, early folding type or 35mm	**50.00-300.00**
Nikon Rangefinder, Other Models by Nippon Kogaku	**200.00-3,000.00**
Sears Tower, Types 3, 16, 19, 22, 26, 29, 32, 33, 34, 45, 46	**30.00-200.00**
Voigtlander & Sohn	**25.00-200.00**
Canon, Hansa	**1,000.00**
Leitz, Lecia, 1930-1945	**200.00**
Other Early Cameras	**Contact Me**
Zeiss Ikon (as Contaflex, Contax, Contessa, Ikonta)	**25.00-400.00**
Others: Konica, Olympus, Lordomat, etc	**25.00+**

Modern or User Cameras	We Pay
Canon Series A, F, T, EOS; many models	**25.00-250.00**
Contax II, III, 137, 159, 167, RTS, etc	**100.00-300.00**
Mamiya Twin Lens Reflex (C220, C33, C330, etc	**50.00-200.00**
Minolta SR, SRT Series, X-Series, Ma, AF	**25.00-250.00**
Nikon F, F2, F3, FE, FG, FA, FM, S, S2, SP, etc	**100.00-500.00**
Nikkormats, various models	**35.00-125.00**
Olympus OM Series, many models	**50.00-200.00**
Pentax Spotmatic, ME, K1000, LX, P Series, etc	**40.00-300.00**
Rolleicord & Rolleiflex Twin Lens, Rollei SLR	**50.00-500.00**
Yashicamat Twin Lens Reflex, many models	**25.00-200.00**
Fujica AX Series	**40.00-150.00**
Subminiatures: Minox, HIT, Steky, Expo, Petal, Atoron, etc	**10.00-200.00**
Others: Konica, Topcon, Hasselblad, some novelties	**10.00-500.00**

Camera collecting has been my hobby for some forty years. I am a charter member of one of the oldest collecting societies in New England. I am also an avid photographer and have recently had two of my photos selected by jury to hang in a local prestigious not-for-profit gallery.

At eighty-seven and in good health, my interests are varied — but I still like the pursuit and thrill of discovering real camera oldies. I am especially fond of the **early all-wood cameras** because of the workmanship in putting these beauties together. I will pay at least $200.00 for good examples, more for the earliest ones.

I am also seeking models of the **early 35mm camera such as the Canon 'Hansa'** for which I will pay $1,000.00 if in good to excellent working condition. Another early precision 35mm camera I am looking for is the **Leitz 'Lecia' of the 1930–1945 period.** For any of these in reasonable appearance and working condition, I will pay $200.00 and more, much more, for certain models.

Warren S. Patrick
3143 Vt. Rd. 100 S
Jamaica, VT 05343
802-874-4087

Early Cameras	**We Pay**
All-Wood Types	**200.00+**
Canon, Hansa	**1,000.00**
Leitz, Lecia, 1930-1945	**200.00**
Other Early Cameras	**Contact Me**

I collect wooden, detective and stereo cameras. Also old brass lenses.

John A. Hess
P.O. Box 3062
Andover, MA 01810

Capo-Di-Monte

I am interested in purchasing all relief-styled Capo-Di-Monte pieces including figurines. I prefer the older blue crown pieces. Some pieces may also be called Ginori, Docchia, or Royal Naples. Send picture and price requested. I am interested in single pieces as well as complete collections and will purchase from individuals as well as dealers. I will reimbuse all shipping fees. I am the largest buyer of older Capo-Di-Monte in the country! It should be noted that some pieces have Meissen Crossed Sword mark or Made in France markings.

James R. Highfield
1601 Lincolnway E
S Bend, IN 46613
219-288-0300

	We Pay
Box, 11"	500.00-2,500.00
Cup & Saucer	75.00-200.00
Ewer, 16"	10,000.00
Figurine, lady, 6"	60.00-175.00
Plaque, 10x13"	200.00-450.00
Stein, 1-liter	500.00-1,200.00
Urn, 20", pr	2,500.00
Urn, 35", pr	4,000.00
Vase, 12", pr	500.00-1,000.00
Vase, 20", pr	3,000.00

Carnival Chalk Prizes

I buy **old carnival chalkware prizes that were given away at carnivals from about 1915 to 1950.** I am not interested in animals unless they were in the comics, such as **Felix the Cat, Spark Plug the horse from Barney Google, or Disney's Pluto.** Some of the early prizes were Kewpie types, often found with original wigs and dresses. I look for **old radio lamps made of plaster**. Examples of lamps would be Art Deco nudes or cowboys on bucking horses. I am also looking for **pre-1950s movie magazines, especially with Ginger Rogers on the cover.**

Tom Morris
P.O. Box 8307
Medford, OR 97504
541-779-3164
chalkman@cdsnet.net

	We Pay
Alice the Goon, from Popeye, 6" or 10", ea	65.00+
Amos & Andy, single or pr, 12" (varies)	85.00+
Betty Boop, 14½"	200.00+
Eugene the Jeep, from Popeye, 14"	295.00+
Felix the Cat, 12½"	120.00+
Hula Girls, 10" or larger	55.00+
Ma & Pa Yokum, 12½", ea	55.00+
Mae West, 13" to 14"	70.00+
Maggie & Jiggs, 8½" or larger, pr	95.00+

Miss America, 15¾" .... [illegible]
Moon Mullins, from Barney Google, 7" .... [illegible]
Nudes or Semi-Nudes, various sizes, ea .... 5[illegible]
Nude Art Deco Lamp, various sizes, ea .... **125.00+**
Olive Oyl, from Popeye, 7" or 12+", ea .... **65.00+**
Pirate Lady, 13½" .... **90.00+**
Popeye, 12" or larger, ea .... **65.00+**
Sea Hag, from Popeye, 8" .... **45.00+**
Shirley Temple, 9" or larger .... **45.00+**
Spark Plug, the horse from Barney Google, 7" .... **195.00+**
Sugar, marked Jenkins, 13" **75.00**
Superman, 15" .... **145.00+**
Uncle Sam, 12 to 15", ea .... **85.00+**
Wimpy, from Popeye, 7" to 16", ea .... **35.00-95.00+**

Cast Iron

I am buying cast iron as well as other collectibles listed below. I will purchase one item or an entire collection. Top, confidential prices paid for items I want. Please describe fully and include SASE with a phone number with your correspondence. Photos are appreciated and make dealing much easier. Original paint is very important on the figural cast iron. It effects the value greatly. No damaged or new pieces in all categories are wanted. I am a dealer/collector with 27 years of satisfied customers and collector friends. Thanks.

Craig Dinner
Box 4399
Sunnyside, NY 11104
718-729-3850

Figural Cast Iron — **We Pay**

Advertising **10.00-3,000.00**
Advertising Paperweights **10.00-250.00**
Architectural **10.00-650.00**
Bottle Openers **10.00-1,000.00**
Curtain Tie Backs **10.00-65.00**
Door Knockers **40.00-750.00**
Doorstops **40.00-3,000.00**

Cast Iron

Governor Weights	25.00-1,500.00
Locks	5.00-400.00
Pencil Holders	10.00-75.00
Sad Irons	100.00-750.00
Shooting Gallery Targets	25.00-1,500.00
Windmill Weights	25.00-3,500.00
String Holders	75.00-500.00
Windmill Weights	25.00-3,500.00

Cast Iron	We Pay
Advertising	25.00-1,000.00
Architectural Items	10.00-300.00
Children's Cookware	15.00-1,500.00
Coin Vending	75.00-750.00
Cookware (includes Griswold, Filley, Wagner & unmarked muffin pans)	10.00-2,500.00
Other Unusual Cookware	25.00-2,000.00
Match Holders	20.00-175.00
Pencil Sharpeners, pre-1920	25.00-1,000.00
Sad Irons	10.00-450.00
Signs	25.00-500.00
Toy Sad Irons	10.00-600.00

Eclectic Pieces	We Pay
Advertising Match Holders, tin	25.00-600.00
Condom Tins	2.00-500.00
Lux Pendulette Clocks	10.00-500.00
Early Battery Clocks	25.00-550.00
Early Fans, ceiling & desk styles	25.00-1,000.00
Laundry Sprinkler Bottles	10.00-300.00
Stoneware Advertising	10.00-200.00

I also will buy **cast-iron cookware** — especially pieces marked Wagner, Griswold, Filley, Davis, or other manufacturers (also want unmarked items). Unusual pieces are preferred, and items must be in good or better condition with no damage. **Other figural cast-iron items are also wanted; please let me hear about what you have.**

	We Pay
Buster Brown Waffle Iron	250.00
Filley Muffin Pan	400.00
Griswold Muffin Pan, #13	500.00+
Griswold Muffin Pan, #2800	1,000.00
Griswold Muffin Pan, #2700	100.00
Griswold Muffin Pan, other numbers	50.00-1,000.00
Griswold Skillet, #20	300.00
Griswold Vienna Roll Pan	450.00+
Griswold Waffle Rack, 3-tiered	600.00
Griswold or Wagner Skillet Rack, ea	175.00
Wagner Muffin Pan	75.00

Cat Collectibles

I collect many cat figurines, but specialize in **quality cat items such as Goebel, Hagen-Renaker, Freeman-McFarlin, Brad Keeler, Josef Originals, and Border Fine Arts.** I love the Goebel utilitarian pieces which include salt and peppers, ashtrays, creamers, bookends, mustard pots, etc. I collect mostly figurines for all other cat makers. Please send photos with markings and asking price — I respond to all phone calls and letters. There are many more I'm searching for to complete my collection, so call or write anytime!

Renae Giles
1033 Sunny Ridge Dr.
Carver, MN 55315-9355
612-448-7046

Goebel	We Pay
32-901, black cat paperweight	40.00
CK 40, black cat sitting on white base, by Armin Muller	70.00
CK 301, gray & white cat standing on base, 6"	80.00
CK 318, 2 sm cats playing, 1-pc, 2½"	40.00
EUL 370, plate, black cat holding mouse in mouth	60.00
EX 134, oval plaque w/cat	55.00
G 117, cat jam jar (green, yellow or orange)	60.00
KZ 628, cat trump card indicator	70.00

Cat Collectibles

KZ 770, Art Deco cat planter....60.00
M 90 A, mustard jar....60.00
P 181 A&B, stylized cat & dog salt & pepper shakers....50.00
P 391 I&O, cat & dog salt & pepper shakers....50.00
P 394 I&O, kittens salt & pepper shakers....50.00
S 194, white sitting cat creamer, loop at tail is handle, 5"....55.00
S 636, match holder, black cat standing w/green box, 2"....60.00
S 701, cat & dog creamer, 3""....65.00
Schau 114, cat leaping....100.00
Schau 115, cat stretching....100.00
VP 107, yellow cat wall pocket, 6"....65.00
VT 28, cat vase, black or white, 6½"....60.00
XP 47, yellow arch w/2 black cats as stoppers w/cork bottoms....70.00
Many Others Wanted....**Call or Write**

Freeman-McFarlin **We Pay**

Cats, call or write for wants....**15.00-40.00**

Josef Originals **We Pay**

Cats, call or write for wants....**15.00-40.00**

Hagen-Renaker **We Pay**

Cats, call or write for wants....**25.00-150.00**

I'm a collector/dealer/trader of **Kliban cat items.** I am looking for cookie jars, teapots, salt and pepper shaker sets, Christmas ornaments, mugs, candy dishes, bowls, banks, ceramic picture frames, bookends, trinket jars, etc. In paper and plastic, I would like framed pictures, check book covers, rubber stamps, photo LP's, lunch boxes, puzzles, wastebaskets, serving trays, posters, cat feeders, letter holders, clocks, ice buckets, etc. Wanted in cloth items are stuffed pillows, aprons, towels, place mats, sheets, etc. There are also metal ornaments, candles, and store displays. The list goes on and on. Please give a detailed description. There are many different cat scenes depicted on the same item.

Please give honest condition and price you are asking, as you are the seller. You may write or call.

Sue Lucente
115 Marbeth Ave.
Carlisle, PA 17013-1626
717-249-9343
Sooloo@webtv.net

I collect **cat collectibles in all areas of interest**: ceramic, wood, metal, paper, glass, etc. — cookie jars, salt and pepper shakers, dolls, planters, statues, creamers, sugars, Black Cats, Kitty Cucumber, unusual items — anything with a cat! What do you have to sell or trade? Please send photo or proper description, the price, and SASE.

Jean R. Ehrlich
Rt. 2, Box 147-A4
Grand Saline, TX 74140
903-963-3212

Serious cat collector seeking **old, unusual cat items.** I am looking for (but not limited to) prints, lithographs, postcards (I like photo ones best), toys, games, stuffed animals with glass eyes, bottles, coins, metal items (cast-iron figurals, spoons, pewter, bronzes, etc.), fine figurines (Goebel, Royal Copenhagen, Bing & Grondahl, Shafford, Beswick), and more! I also like advertising banks and Victorian pieces. I will consider all offers. I have a very large collection, but I am sure that there are items out there that I haven't seen so a picture would be ideal. If calling or writing, please provide detailed information and condition of pieces. I would be interested in buying collections or parts of collections. I will pay shipping for all purchases. **No reproductions please!** Thank you!

Melissa Arbogast
35162 Dolphin St.
Princeton, MN 55371
612-389-0849

Catalina Island Pottery

I buy pieces marked **Catalina Pottery made by Gladding McBean**, shells, and some pieces marked with blue ink Made in USA. **G.M.B., Franciscan, Catalina Pottery advertising items, and price lists** as well as **some Franciscan dinnerware** pieces are wanted. All pieces must be in excellent condition. Send description or photo and price of your item or call and leave message.

Catalina Island Pottery

Alan Phair
P.O. Box 30373
Long Beach, CA 90853
310-983-7020

Catalina Pottery/G.M.B	We Pay
Samoan Lady Holding Baby	up to 250.00
Fan Lady	up to 350.00
Hat Lady	up to 350.00
Reclining Lady	250.00
Mermaid	up to 400.00
Polynesian 'Painted Pieces'	up to 300.00
Encanto	up to 300.00
Ox Blood	up to 400.00
Signs for Franciscan, G.M.B., Etc.	up to 250.00
Shells	up to 150.00

Franciscan Dishes	We Pay
Wild Flower	up to 250.00
Twilight Rose	up to 250.00
Contours	up to 250.00
Ivy	up to 200.00
Small Fruit	up to 200.00

Ceramic Arts Studio

Ceramic Arts Studio was a pottery in Madison, Wisconsin, from 1940 to 1956. Beginning with hand-thrown pottery, the studio was particulary famous for highly-detailed figurines. The following is a list of Ceramic Arts Studio creations I hope to add to my collection. Please call with offers of mint-condition items only.

Tim Holthaus
P.O. Box 46
Madision, WI 53701-0046
608-241-9138
e-mail: ceramicart@aol.com

	We Pay
Any Hand-Thrown Pottery, especially signed Rabbit	50.00+
Swirl & Swish Fish, swimming, 3½", pr.	60.00+
Ram, stylized, 2"	40.00+
Spaniel, Honey, 6"	75.00+
Chick (nesting, 1½") and Nest (snuggle, 1"), pr.	60.00+
Colonial Man, blue, 6½"	60.00
Colonial Woman, green, 6½"	60.00
Hans & Katrinka, chubby boy and girl, blue trim, pr.	120.00+
Dutch Dance Boy & Girl, 7½", pr	175.00+
Egyptian Man & Woman, 9½", pr	250.00+
Harem Girl, lying w/feet behind, 6"	60.00+
Zulu Man & Zulu Woman, black, 5½" & 7", pr	180.00+
Zulu Man #2 & Zulu Woman #2, 5½" & 7¼", pr	180.00+
Zulu Man & Zulu Woman, white, 5½" & 7", pr.	220.00+
Macabre Dance Man & Woman, pr	250.00+
Encore Woman, pink or black, ea	80.00+
Fire Man, burgundy & red, 11¼"	90.00+
Fire Woman, gray & brown, 11¼"	90.00+
Hamlet (plaque), 8"	90.00+
Water Woman, chartreuse, 11½"	80.00+
Swan Lake Man & Woman, pr	200.00+
Bird on Birdbath, for St. Francis, 4¼"	40.00+
Warter Well for Rebekah	40.00+
Madonna, w/Bible, 9½"	95.00+
Madonna, w/child, pink, 6½	95.00+
Madonna, w/halo, 9½"	95.00+
Our Lady of Fatima, gold trim, 9"	95.00+
St. Francis, w/birds, brown or white, 7", ea.	80.00+
Chubby St. Francis, w/birds, brown, 9"	80.00+
Sleeping Girl Angel, 3¼"	50.00+
Angel w/candle, 5"	50.00+
Black Bobby, 3¼"	90.00+
White Willy/Ball Down (shelf sitter), 4½"	90.00+
White Winnie, 5½"	90.00+
White Woody, 3¼"	90.00+
White Rabbit, standing, 6"	90.00+
Goosey Gander (plaque), 4½"	75.00+
Jack Be Nimble (plaque), 5"	80.00+
Piper's Girl Praying, 3"	60.00+
Devil Imp w/Spear, 5"	75.00+
Devil Imp Sitting, 3½"	75.00+
Devil Imp Lying, 3½"	75.00+

Adult Band	We Pay
Accordion Lady, standing, 8½"	95.00+

Flute Lady, standing, 8½"	**95.00+**
Violin Lady, standing, 8½"	**95.00+**
Cellist Man, sitting, 6½"	**95.00+**
French Horn Man, sitting, 6½"	**95.00+**
Guitar Man, sitting, 6½"	**95.00+**

Balinese Dancers	We Pay
Lao, topless, standing, 8½"	**95.00+**
Bali-Lao, standing, green, 8½"	**70.00+**
Bali-Gong, croutched, green, 5½"	**70.00+**
Balinese Girl, shelf sitter, 5½"	**75.00+**
Balinese Woman, brown or pair in blue	**60.00+**
Chinthe, 4"	**50.00+**
Burmese Temple	**150.00+**

Indian Group	We Pay
Seagull, fits on canoe, 2½"	**50.00+**
Birch Wood Canoe, blue trim	**75.00+**
Minnehaha, blue trim, 6½"	**75.00+**

My collection of **Ceramic Arts Studio pottery** (Madison, Wisconsin) has a few gaps I hope you can help me fill. The studio was particulary famous for highly-detailed figurines, but also made metal pieces to hang on the wall for displaying their ceramic work. The following is a list of Ceramic Arts Studio creations I hope to add to my collection. Please call with offers of mint-condition items only.

Jim Petzold
P.O. Box 46
Madision, WI 53701-0046
608-241-9138
e-mail: ceramics@execpc.com

	We Pay
Salome, 14"	**25.00+**
Spring Leaf, green, 2" long	**40.00+**
Gremlin, standing, 4"	**75.00+**
Gremlin, sitting, 2"	**75.00+**
Mermaid, lying, 2½"	**75.00+**
Mermaid, sitting, 3"	**75.00+**
Sprite/Fish Down (plaque), 4½"	**95.00+**
Peek-A-Boo Pixie, 2½"	**50.00+**

Pixie Girl, kneeling, 2½" ....50.00+
Pixie Riding Snail, 2¾" ....50.00+
African Man (plaque), white trim....................130.00+
African Woman Head Vase, white trim....................150.00+
Skunky Bank, 4"....................95.00+
Modern Jaguar, stylized, 5" ....80.00+
Leopard Baby ....75.00+
Leopard, fighting, 6" or 8", ea." ....125.00+
Panther, fighting, 8" ....150.00+
Panther, fighting, crouched....................150.00+
Dachshund, lying, 3½" ....40.00+
Sassy & Waldo Dachshunds, 3¼"....................80.00+
Modern Dog, stylized, 5" ....95.00+
Donkey, 3¼" & 3", pr ....90.00+
Elephant, bisque, w/trunk down, 5" ....75.00+
Horse Mother & Spring Colt, 4¼" & 3½", pr....................150.00+
Zebra, amber & black, 5"....................150.00+
Mouse, realistic, 3" ....40.00+
Seal Mother, 6"....................75.00+
Seal Pup, 3" ....75.00+
Seal on Rock, 5", pr ....160.00+
Tortoise w/Hat, crawling, 2½" ....60.00+
Kitten Washing, w/bow, 2" ....40.00+
Kitten Sleeping, 1"....................40.00+
Bird of Paradise A & B, 3", pr. ....80.00+
Canary, left & right (shelf sitters), 5", pr ....80.00+
Cockataoo Male, wings spread (F), 5"....................60.00+
Cockatoo Female (shelf sitter), 5" ....60.00+
Duck Mother & Duckling, 3¼" & 2¼", pr....................70.00+
Budgie & Pudgie Parakeets (shelf sitters), 5"....................70.00+
Rooster & Hen, 3"....................60.00+
Swans, neck up & neck down, 6" & 5", pr"....................90.00+
Straight Tail Fish, lg & sm, pr....................60.00+
Striped Fish Mother (plaque), 5" ....50.00+
Striped Fish Baby (plaque), 3" ....50.00+
Barber Shop Quartet Mug, 3½" ....75.00+
Moutain Goat Caddy, oval, 5¼" ....75.00+
Paul Bunyan Plate, 6" dia....................60.00+
Buddah Pitcher, Wedgwood, bisque, 3½" ....60.00+
Grapes Teapot, 2"....................50.00+
Miss Forward WI, Wedgwood, 4" ....80.00+
Toby Mug, 2¾"....................60.00+

Metal Pieces **We Pay**

Arched Window /Cross, 14"....................50.00+
Beanstalk for Jack, w/ladder, 13" ....40.00+
Bird Cage, w/perch for parakeets, 14" ....50.00+

Corner Web, w/spider, 4" .... **40.00+**
Pyramid Shelf .... **50.00+**
Sofa for Maurice & Michelle .... **40.00+**
Staircase for Angel Trio .... **50.00+**
Triple Ring, left & right, 15" ea. .... **50.00+**
Triple Ring w/Shelf, left & right, 15", ea. .... **60.00+**

Cereal Boxes

Pre-1960 cereal boxes and panels, including backs are wanted. All brands such as Kellogg's, General Mills, Post, Quaker, etc. are wanted. I am most interested in boxes, panels, and backs with cutouts, activities, or offers. My mom never would buy the 'good' cereals when I was a kid, so now I am forced to get them as an adult! I prefer uncut pieces, but would like to hear about anything you have. Postage will **always** be reimbursed. As with any collectible, condition is the most important consideration when figuring out a price. These amounts are only estimates.

Bruce Cervon
10074 Ashland St.
San Buenaventura, CA 93004
805-659-4405 or fax 805-659-4776

We Pay

Complete Boxes **8.00-25.00**
Pieces of Boxes **2.00-15.00**

Character and Promotional Drinking Glasses

We are paying the following prices for mint examples of these glasses (no fading, cracks, or poor registration).

Collector Glass News
P.O. Box 308
Slippery Rock, PA 16057
724-946-2838 or 724-794-2540
fax 724-946-9012
cgn@glassnews.com
http://www.glassnews.com

	We Pay
1930s & 1940s Characters (Disney, Popeye, Warner Bros.), ea	**10.00-100.00**
Pepsi or Canadian Jungle Book, ea	**20.00-50.00**
Pepsi Mighty Mouse, ea	**200.00**
Pepsi Callahans Characters, ea	**40.00**
Pepsi Walter Lantz Characters, ea	**10.00-100.00**
Pepsi Warner Bros. Interactions, ea	**3.00-25.00**
1962 Hanna-Barbera Cindy Bear, Yogi Bear or Huckleberry Hound, ea	**30.00**
Canadian Pepsi Glasses, ea	**2.00-25.00**
Al Capp, ea	**5.00-25.00**
Coke Collegiate Crest, ea	**5.00-25.00**
McDonald's Manager & Regional Glasses, ea	**3.00-100.00**
Dr. Pepper Star Trek, ea	**5.00-10.00**
Super Hero Glasses,ea	**3.00-50.00**
Monster Glasses, ea	**10.00-35.00**
Sports Glasses, especially glasses that feature professional players	**3.00-25.00**
Elby's Columbus Clippers, ea	**10.00**
Kentucky Derby, Preakness & Other Horse Racing Glasses, ea	**5.00-500.00**
Frosted Iced-Tea Glasses Featuring Indians, State Themes, Etc., ea	**2.00-10.00**

Character, TV, and Personality Collectibles

We buy all types of **Beatles memorabilia but specialize in toy or 3-D type**. We are basically interested in original '60s items. There are many reproductions out there, so give us a call if you have any questions on an item. We aren't really interested in records or paper items unless they are out of the ordinary. **Yellow Submarine items from 1968** are of special interest, so please give us a call or drop a line. All prices below are for excellent to near-mint items, and we are seldom interested in good or lower quality items unless rare. Remember these are just a *few* examples.

Bob Gottuso
BOJO
P.O. Box 1403
Cranberry Twp., PA 16066
724-776-0621

Beatles	**We Pay**
Apron, white paper w/black & white pictures	**130.00**
Ball, black rubber w/white photo	**400.00**
Banjo, complete only	**600.00+**
Binder, vinyl, various colors	**80.00**
Bongos, by Mastro	**800.00+**
Bowl, by Washington, pottery	**90.00**
Brunch Bag, oval vinal bag w/zipper	**250.00**
Bubble Bath, Paul or Ringo (condition is important)	**75.00**
Bubble Bath, Paul or Ringo, MIB	**150.00**
Candy Sticks Box, complete only	**75.00**
Carrying Case, by Airflight, square vinyl	**300.00+**
Clutch Purses, various styles, ea	**125.00+**
Colorforms, complete only	**350.00+**
Comb, by Lido Toys, 14", excellent condition	**100.00**
Compact, UK, complete & excellent condition	**150.00**
Concert Tickets, complete w/photo & name (other than Suffolk Downs)	**90.00+**
Ticket Stubs	**45.00+**
Corkstopper, 1 of ea Beatle, ea	**250.00**
Disk-Go-Case, plastic 45rpm record carrier, many colors, ea	**100.00+**
Doll, Remco, Ringo or Paul, w/instrument & life-like hair, 4", ea	**40.00+**
Doll, Remco, George or John, ea	**70.00+**
Dolls, Remco, set of 4	**250.00**
Doll, blow-up style, set of 4 (must hold air well)	**80.00**
Doll, bobbin' head, 8", set of 4, mint condition	**300.00**
Doll, bobbin' head, 8", set of 4, MIB	**550.00**
Drinking Glasses, many styles, ea	**70.00+**
Drum, by Mastro (hardest to find), complete	**650.00**
Drum, other manufacturers	**Wanted**
Guitars, many styles, ea	**250.00+**
Hair Bow, on sealed original card	**225.00+**
Hair Spray	**600.00+**
Halloween Costume, MIB	**400.00**
Halloween Costume, mint, missing box	**140.00**
Handbags, different styles & sizes available, ea	**190.00+**
Lamps, wall or table styles, ea	**325.00+**
Lunch Boxes, metal or vinyl, prices vary widely, mint condition	**260.00+**
Models, plastic, sealed contents, w/mint original box	**160.00+**
Paint by Number Kit, 4 portraits, unused	**475.00+**
Pencil Case, various styles & colors	**90.00+**

Pennants, felt, many styles & colors (many fakes) .... **30.00+**
Pillows, any of 3 different styles, w/tag, ea .... **90.00+**
Puzzles, different ones available, complete, ea .... **80.00+**
Record Player, mint condition **2,200.00**
School Bag **500.00**
Tennis Shoes, unused w/paper insert, MIB **500.00**
Thermos, for lunch box **110.00**
Wallets, various styles & colors, complete **70.00**

Radio premiums, box top and cereal giveaways, and comic character items wanted by collector. Items wanted (but are not limited to) include:

Badges
Decoders
Manuals
Pin-back buttons
Cereal boxes
Paper items
Maps
Rings

Others wanted

Characters sought are:
Buck Rogers
Captain America
Captain Midnight
Dick Tracy
Doc Savage
Don Winslow
Flash Gordon
Green Hornet
Hop Harrington
Jack Armstrong
Jimmie Allen, Jr.
Justice Society
Lone Ranger
Orphan Annie
Operator 5
Ralston Straight Shooters
Sgt. Preston
Shadow
Sky King
Space Patrol
Spider
Straight Arrow
Superman
Tarzan
Tom Mix

Also wanted are **Cracker Jack items and items marked Checkers (no plastic items).**

Richard J. Gronowski
140 N Garfield Ave.
Traverse City, MI 49688-2802
616-941-2111

I would like to buy **Barney Google and Spark Plug** items from the comic strip. Barney is a wooden man and his horse, Spark Plug, is felt and cloth. They were made in the 1920s. Price depends on condition.

Barb Farber
Rt. 1, Box 44
Reeder, ND 58649
701-563-4418

I buy, sell, trade **anything to do with California Raisins, Garfield, and Smurfs.** Items include but are not limited to the following: figurines, plush toys, kitchen items, mugs and cups, bath items, general household items, collector plates, music boxes, bells, banks, telephones, jewelry, holiday items, foreign items. Other interests include **Holly Hobbie and Kewpie items.**

Wilma Schiebel
HCR 63 Box 116C
Yellville, AR 72687
870-436-5874

Dionne Quint items are wanted. If you have any other items or dolls not listed, send your list, pictures, and prices. The prices listed here depend on condition.

Marcia Kessler
4477 Olive Branch Rd.
Greenwood, IN 46143

	We Pay
Doctor Bag, for doll, black w/tag	**up to 90.00**
Baby Dress, actually worn by a Quint, w/tag	**up to 150.00**
China Pieces, no chips, especially with picture of Marie	**up to 100.00**
Furniture (play pen, high chair, etc) for 7" doll	**up to 150.00**
Quint Doll, 23", open mouth, tongue & teeth, original clothing, M	**up to $500.00**
Quint Doll, 11½" toddler, single or set	**up to 2,000.00**

I'm looking for **Dr. Seuss and Hanna-Barbera character items.**

Jim Rash
135 Alder Ave.
Egg Harbor Twp., NJ 08234-9302
609-646-4125

	We Pay
Bullwinkle & Rocky Flicker Rings, 1961, ea	**100.00**
Bullwinkle Coins: 9, 11, 25, 27, 34, 42, 52, 58, ea	**15.00**
Dr Seuss Merry Menagerie, duck, giraffee (curved neck), woodpecker, Poynter, 1968, ea	**350.00**
Hanna-Barbera Squeeze Toy, Wally Gator, Touche Turtle,Top Cat, Quickdraw, Scooby Doo, Wilma Flintstone, Pebbles, Dino, latex, Spain, 1967, ea.	**100.00**
Hanna-Barbera Peter Potamus Wagonwheel, ea	**100.00**
Underdog Gumball Rings, Sweet Polly Purebread	**200.00**
Wham-O Bendies, Nell Fenwick, 1972	**100.00**
Wham-O Bendies, Inspector Fenwick, 1972	**100.00**

I need **metal trash cans (pre-1990) with advertising, comic characters, TV show and movie characters, and entertainers.** I started collecting these (mostly made by Cheinco) and have no idea how many different designs exist. Help me add to my collection with cans in nice shape and/or salesman's brochures. Since this is a new area of collecting, prices range from $15.00 to $50.00 for interesting cans in fine to mint condition.

I also need **video game stuff from the 1970s and 1980s.** I love **Pac Man, Donkey Kong, and Tron stuff as well as the old PONG-type and Atari TV games.** I also want to buy **hand-held video games and toys related to older video games.** Other wants include **1970s LED watches and calculators, old computers and related materials, commercial art, advertising, toys, tennis ball cans, and Nike sneakers.**

Robb Sequin
P.O. Box 1126
Dennisport, MA
508-760-2599
rsequin@capecod.net

Metal Trash Cans	**We Pay**
1970s to 1990s, ea	**15.00-25.00**
1960s to 1970s, ea	**25.00-50.00**
Specialty Cans, ea	**up to 80.00**

Video Game Stuff **We Pay**

Video Game Stuff	We Pay
Hand-held Game, w/box	**10.00-75.00**
TV-based Game, w/box	**15.00-50.00**
Vectrex, w/box	**100.00**
Other Games, w/box	**15.00**

I am looking to buy any and all types of **Dick Tracy memorabilia** including any strip-related characters such as Sparkle Plenty and Bonny Braids. Collectible interest include all toys, games, premiums, ephemera, posters, books, comics, guns, puzzles, dolls, figures, original art, store signs and displays — anything. I also have hundreds of Dick Tracy items to offer in trade or sell. (Send $2.00 and LSASE for 21-page list if interested.) I also do **free** appraisal of Tracy items. Send a photo or very good description of the item you want appraised.

Larry Doucet
2351 Sultana Dr.
Yorktown Hgts., NY 10598
914-245-1320

Disneyland souvenirs and memorabilia wanted — anything from the California amusement park before 1970. My collection of Disneyland items is considered the world's best! I'm always looking for maps, guidebooks, tickets, food wrappers, brochures, jewelry, ceramic items, special events programs, posters, passes, postcards and postcard folders, personal black and white or color photos, pin-back buttons, and any other type of souvenir. I love Disneyland and have been there more than once a month since the park opened in 1955! I would like to add your items to my collection and will give them a good home. **No** Walt Disney World in Florida, please. Prices depend on condition and age as per Tomart's *Disneyana Price Guide.*

Linda Cervon
10074 Ashland St.
San Buenaventura, CA 93004
805-659-4405 or fax 805-659-4776

Disneyland Souvenirs	We Pay
Guidebooks & Pictorial Souvenirs	**3.00-25.00+**
Tickets & Ticket Books	**50¢-5.00+**

Maps	5.00-20.00+
Postcards & Postcard Folders	50¢-4.00+
Brochures & Folders	1.00-10.00+

We buy **Ginger Rogers** memorabilia. Items in good to fine condition only are wanted. We're not interested in reproduction or poor quality posters, window or lobby cards. Please describe if applicable: title, size, and condition. We will pay for shipping and insurance.

If you have a large amount of sheet music or magazines, please send SASE for our want list. If you have questions, we'd like to hear from you.

Tom and Yvonne Morris
P.O. Box 8307
Medford, OR 97504
541-779-3164
chalkman@cdsnet.net

	We Pay
Autographs, pre-1950	50.00+
Book, *The Films of Ginger Rogers*	20.00+
Buttons/Pins, advertising	5.00+
Cigarette Cards	8.00+
Commemorative Plates	25.00+
Dixie Cup Lids	5.00+
Greeting Cards, autographed	10.00+
Standee Figure, full size	95.00+
Lobby Cards	15.00+
Magazines, complete w/Rogers on cover	15.00-30.00
Play Programs	5.00+
Posters, Inserts, One-Sheets, Two-Sheets or Three-Sheets	50.00-500.00
Sheet Music, American or foreign	5.00-25.00
Song Books or Song Magazines	15.00
Window Cards	25.00+

Wanted are any items, recent or from the 1950s, dealing with the **Howdy Doody Show or Buffalo Bob.** Other items wanted include memorabilia from the **Popeye the Sailor or King Features Syndicate family of cartoon characters.** I also have items to trade.

Jeri Findlay
422 Congress St.
Ottawa, IL 61350-3014

I am looking for **Howdy Doody show hand puppets of Clarabell, Princess Summerfall Winterspring, and Flub-A-Dub.** These are painted plastic and 5" tall with a small lever on the back that moves the mouth. Also wanted are **children's character spoons.** These would be silver plate and show such characters as Buster Brown, Tige, Batman, Boy Scout, Clamity Jane, Captain Video, etc.

Linda Morrissey
24 Cliff St.
East Haven, CT 06512
203-466-6970

We buy all toys depicting **the KISS rock group** in full-painted faces and costumes. We stay away from most paper and records but may be interested in tour programs or picture discs. Most of the items we are looking for were licensed by Aucoin and are from the 1977 to 1980 period. We are only interested in excellent or better condition items as they are not that old and are not that hard to find in this condition. All prices below are given for excellent to mint condition only. Please call if you have any questions. Thank you. Bob Gottuso

BOJO
P.O. Box 1403
Cranberry Twp., PA 16066
474-776-0621

KISS	**We Pay**
Costume Jewelry	**3.00-20.00**
Backpack	**50.00**
Backpack, MIP (sealed)	**100.00**
Bedspread, MIP (sealed)	**120.00**
Colorforms, complete	**50.00**
Halloween Costume, MIB, ea	**55.00**
Cup, 7-11, by Majik Market, ea	**15.00**
Cup, Megaphone-Scream Machine	**35.00**
Curtains, MIP (sealed)	**100.00**
Doll, Paul or Gene, complete clothing, ea	**60.00**
Doll, Paul or Gene, MIB, ea	**110.00**

Doll, Ace or Peter, complete clothing, ea....65.00
Doll, Ace or Peter, MIB, ea....115.00
Game, On Tour, complete....40.00
Guitar, plastic....75.00
Guitar, MIP....150.00
Halloween Make-Up Kit, Kiss Your Face, MIP (sealed)....75.00
Jacket, paper w/flames....45.00
Lunch Box w/Thermos....90.00
Microphone, MIB....70.00
Model, Kiss Van, 100% complete in opened box....45.00
Model, Kiss Van, MIB (sealed)....70.00
Notebook, various photos on cover, ea....20.00
Pencils, set of 4, MIP (sealed)....30.00
Pens, any group member, MOC (sealed), ea....30.00
Poster Art, MIP (sealed)....45.00
Puzzles, group photo, MIP (sealed), ea....25.00
Puzzles, group photo, 100% complete, opened package, ea....15.00
Puzzles, any group member photo, MIP (sealed), ea....35.00
Puzzles, any group member photo, 100% complete, opened package, ea....20.00
Radio, MIB....75.00
Radio, missing box....50.00
Record Player, MIB....400.00
Record Player, missing box....200.00
Remote-Control Van, MIB....125.00
Remote-Control Van, missing box....65.00
Rub 'n' Play Set, unused....45.00
Sleeping Bag, MIP....100.00
Sleeping Bag, missing package....50.00
View-Master Reel Set, w/booklet....20.00
View-Master Double-View on Card, ea....35.00
Wastebasket....100.00

I am a big **Land of the Giants** fan. I am currently collecting toys and other items of interest from this great Irwin Allen TV show. Here is a list of the toys I am looking to buy.

Ronald Morini
714 Frankford Rd.
W Babylon, NY 11705
516-321-0577

We Pay

Costume, Steve Burton, by Ben Cooper....**150.00+**

Costume, Dan Erickson, by Ben Cooper .... **150.00+**
Costume, Giant Cat, by Ben Cooper .... **150.00+**
Costume, Giant Witch, by Ben Cooper .... **150.00+**
Display Box, gum or candy .... **200.00+**
Flashlight, Mystery Nite-Glo, by Bantam Lite .... **75.00+**
Frisbee, Flying Spaceship Spindrift Saucer, by Remco .... **125.00+**
Motorized Flying Rocket Plane, by Remco .... **200.00+**
Oil Paint by Number, by Remco .... **200.00+**
Spaceship Control Panel, by Remco .... **300.00+**
Signal Space Gun, by Remco .... **200.00+**
Target Gun Set, by Hasbro .... **150.00+**
Double-Action Bagatelle (pinball) Game, by Hasbro .... **200.00+**
Paperback Book, *Mean City,* British issue .... **25.00+**

I am always interested in purchasing good quality **Lone Ranger** memorabilia. Each item may be just that special piece I'm missing. I would like to have early items from the late 1930s through the early 1950s, but sometimes a brand-new item is needed for my collection. I need 1938 pulps, 1940 gum cards, Tonto dolls, and much more. I do not care if the item is a newspaper article about some Lone Ranger/Tonto facts or a premium from some cereal company. I am after puzzles, pin-backs, toy guns, watches, etc., of our hero. Also of interest are **International Harvester** items. I love paper stuff of old tractor ads, tools, and miscellaneous items.

The Silver Bullet
Terry V. Klepey
P.O. Box 553
Forks, WA 98331
360-374-5717 or 360-327-3726

Pogo was a daily newspaper comic strip character drawn and illustrated by Walt Kelly. Wanted are:

Comic strip paperback or hardback cartoon books
Pogo comic books published by Dell Comics
Small figures as Pogo Possum, Albert Alligator, Churchy Turtle, or Howland Owl
Pin-back buttons
Stamps
Records, 33 rpm or Canadian storybooks with small 78 rpm records
Other Pogo items

Because these items are usually subjected to hard use by children, prices will be according to condition. Also wanted are *Walt Disney Comics and Stories* by Dell Comics about Donald Duck and dated November 1947 through

November 1951; *Walt Disney, the Wonderful Adventures of Pinocchio,* Dell Comics, January 1946; *Walt Disney's Snow White and the Seven Dwarfs*; *Walt Disney's Story of Pinocchio*; and children's books by Tony McClay: *Trouble on the Ark, The Downy Duck,* and *Raffy Uses His Head.* I will answer all letters that include a SASE.

David P. Norman
Normans Enterprises
542 Gettysburg Rd.
San Antonio, TX 78228-2058

Chewing Gum Memorabilia

This collector is looking for **anything and everything connected with gum.** Wrigley wartime gums such as Orbit, K Ration, and PK (Packed tight — Keep right!) Gum are wanted as well as Wrigley premium gift items and advertisements. Collector would love to find Fleer Funnies starring PUD and Bazooka Comics, packages of Topps celebrity and movie cards, Topps Goofy Groceries, Wacky Packages, and Crazy Spray Can series, gumball tubes with novelty toppers (filled or empty), and all flavors, makers, and styles of bubble gum dispensers.

Old or new, if it's GUM, I'm the One! Reach in your 'pack' and share or sell a 'piece' of gum with me. I'd love to 'chew' on fun facts and history too! Any Wrigley, Topps, or Fleer workers out there? Don't let the puns fool you — this collector is very serious! Please write or surf the net and e-mail me.

Chewing Gum Chronicles
10115 Greenwood Ave N, #M157
Seattle, WA 98133
e-mail: tmgum@worldnet.att.net

Children's Glass and China

I am looking for **miniature dishes in marigold carnival or Depression glass.** Items as butter dishes, creamers, sugar bowls, spoon holders, and a miniature punch bowl with cups are sought. Also wanted is a **regular size marigold carnival bell in any pattern.**

Gladys Norton
2208 South College
Ft. Collins, CO 80525
970-484-0071

Collector wants **Walt Disney Productions** children's china tea sets or individual cups, saucers, teapots, sugars, creamers, etc. Most items are tan, blue, or green luster with painted designs of Donald Duck, Mickey or Minnie Mouse. I am also interested in **pieces of sets made by Marx** for Walt Disney Productions. These have a white background with gold at the edge and a multicolor transfer design. I will purchase one piece or an entire set. Prices range from $10.00 per item to $500.00 and up per set. Prices depend on design, age, etc. Please send a picture of the item offered and specify your asking price. Also wanted are **pieces of early American pattern glass in the Hawaiian Lei pattern.**

Cal Hackeman
8865 Olde Mill Run
Manassas, VA 20110-6132
703-368-6982

I am interested in buying **children's tea sets made of china or glass.** I prefer older sets made before 1950 that are decorated with floral patterns, small children, Blue Willow, etc. I'm also collecting **children's spice and canister sets.** Photos and descriptions would be helpful when you reply.

Diane Genicola
25 E Adams Ave.
Pleasantville, NJ 08232
609-646-6140

China and Porcelain

I have a special interest in Chintz-style china — an allover floral transfer design pattern — frequently sold by English companies such as Royal Winton. I particularly need serving pieces, so incomplete sets or single pieces are fine. Most important is that there be few or no scratches on the items. Chips or cracks destroy the item's value, but I can buy a cup and saucer if the saucer is cracked or a tureen with a chip. Please send me the following information and I guarantee a reply: pattern name (very important), pattern number (if listed and readable), manufacturer, color, and your name and address.

Also list items and what you'd like to be paid for them; or, I'll make you an offer if you're more comfortable with that. And thank you for your consideration.

Harriet Myers
1132 Woodview Rd.
Burr Ridge, IL 60521

Wanted: **all fine china from England, France, Germany, Japan, etc.** Pieces must be in mint condition. For offers, send name of manufacturer, pattern, pieces, and quantity for sale; or, use photocopy of both sides of a dinner plate. The best time to call is 7pm to 11pm EST.

Jay Adams
248 Lakeview Ave, Suite 208
Clifton, NJ 07011
973-365-5907 or fax 973-471-5325

We are buying **pottery and china from the following list** for resale. Please send pictures and description of items including any marks and **your asking price. All pieces must be in mint condition,** free of all nicks, chips, cracks, bruises, glaze crazing, or other damage.

Blue Willow
Currier & Ives by Royal China
Franciscan
Hall
Liberty Blue by Staffordshire
Memory Lane by Royal China
Coors
Fiesta
Friar Tuck Monks by Goebel
Hull
McCoy
Roseville

The Glass Packrat
Pat and Bill Ogden
3050 Colorado Ave.
Grand Junction, CO 81504

I am interested in **fine items in mint condition** from items listed here. I am paying high prices for quality items. Send photo and SASE. Also wanted are **figural dresser items.**

Aynsley
Chelsea
Flow Blue
Limoges
Minton
Nippon
Paragon
Picard
Royal Winton
Shelley

Katherine Hartman
7459 Shawnee Rd.
N Tonawanda, NY 14120-1367

I am interested in **several different lines of pottery and dinnerware.** Please contact me with information about your items. If you call, evenings only please. Pottery wanted includes:

Brayton Laguna
Catalina Island
Gladding-McBean/Catalina
Homer Laughlin, children's ware
Red Wing, Raymor Modern Artware
Salem China, Free Form shape
Vernon Kilns, art pottery and dinnerware
Russel Wright, metal, glass, pottery and wood
Eva Zeisel, Bay Ridge Specialty, Hyalyn, Riverside China, and children's ware

Ray Vlach, Jr.
5364 N Magnet Ave.
Chicago, IL 60630-1216
312-225-5692 (evenings only)

Buying **T.G. Green's Cornish Kitchenware.** It is sky blue with a white stripe. The company made dinnerware as well as lots of accessory pieces such as rolling pins, canister sets, spice jars, and serving pieces. Many of the pitchers and jars have the name of the contents in square black letters. The company also made a pattern called Domino. It is the same blue color and has recessed white dots. There is also a dark blue wide stripe pattern. Let me know what you have.

I love anything **blue or blue and white: mixing bowls, canister sets, graniteware, utensils, glass, pottery, appliances, linens, dish towels, dishes.** Also wanted are **any kitchen advertising items, Hall or Universal crockery in sky blue or navy blue.** I also need **70" or larger round tablecloths.**

Flow Blue in the Regent pattern by Alfred Meakin is also wanted. The price will depend on the piece and the condition.

Deborah Golden
3182 Twin Pine Rd.
Grayling, IL 49738
517-348-2610

	We Pay
Rolling Pins	**20.00-40.00**
Canisters, lg	**30.00-40.00**
Spice Jars, sm	**10.00-14.00**
Platters	**15.00-35.00**
Mugs	**5.00-10.00**
Cereal Bowls	**5.00-10.00**
Pitchers, depending on size	**Call or Write**
Soup Plates	**5.00-15.00**

I am looking to buy items and accessory pieces in the following patterns: **Red Apple by Harker and Calico Fruit by Universal.** Red Apple has a decal of a large apple and pear with the pear leaning on the apple. There is a blue or gray shadow trailing off to the right side of the fruit. Calico Fruit has a decal that looks like a bunch of fruit that has been covered in different cloth materials. The banana is speckled and the other fruits are checked or striped. Some pieces have the fruit in a blue bowl while other pieces do not. Several pieces have a gold stamp on the bottom which reads 'Calico Fruit, Universal Cambridge.'

Please send a list of the pieces you have. I am willing to pay up to 90% of book price and postage, depending on the piece and condition.

Jason Marks
118 E Walnut
Herrin, IL 62948
618-988-8565

Phoenix Bird dinnerware is a very busy blue and white, Japanese-made porcelain of the late 1890s and early to mid-1900s. Its main design depicts three phoenix (or sometimes two, depending on the piece) that resemble eagles — its wings are spread wide and its head faces back over one wing while its feet face forward! Accompanying the phoenix is a three-leaf design, a chrysanthemum, and a trailing vine with little leaves.

While the majority of its pieces are of Japanese manufacture, a minority of its pieces and varied shapes were made in England by Moytt & Son during the early 1930s.

Since the collecting of Phoenix Bird has been going on for so many years now, most of today's collectors are now on the lookout for the unique, the unusal, and the hard-to-find shapes — as is this collector and author of the pattern's four books, *Phoenix Bird Chinaware.*

I am interested in hearing from owners and/or sellers of a soap dish with its drain and cover; a boat-shaped, five-piece castor set; a washbowl and pitcher; a cracker jar and cover; a cracker trough; and pieces of Phoenix Bird that have the less-often-found heart-like border instead of the horseshoe-like border. Thank you for your interest. For information or questions answered, please send SASE.

Joan Collett Oates
685 S Washington
Constantine, MI 49042
616-435-8353

Wanted: **Phoenix Bird China,** a blue and white china depicting the phoenix bird. Both wings reach out and upward and there are usually five or six dots on the chest; most often the bird's head faces back towards the tail. Various backstamps are found from Japan. Measurements, pictures, or photocopies appreciated. Any and all pieces considered, but especially any on the following list. Mint condition items only are wanted.

Nancy Young
128 Mohican Rd.
Blairstown, NJ 07825
908-362-8757

Phoenix Bird China	**We Pay**
Butter Tub, w/drain	**35.00-50.00**
Chocolate Pot	**40.00-125.00**
Coffee Pot	**40.00-125.00**
Condensed Milk Holder	**40.00-75.00**
Cracker Jar, w/lid	**50.00-125.00**
Gravy Boat	**25.00-50.00**
Mustard Pot	**25.00-50.00**
Pitcher, lg	**40.00-125.00**
Tureen, w/lid	**50.00-125.00**

Wanted: Japanese dinnerware/kitchenware called **Rooster & Roses.** It was made in the '40s and '50s by PY, UCAGCO, and Early Provincial. I am interested in any of the unusual pieces and there are many! Please write, call (nights or weekends), or e-mail telling me of your item. Thank you!

Dianne Marsh
2209 20 1/2 St.
Rice Lake, WI 54868
715-236-7525
marshins@chibardun.net

We wish to buy **Shelley china** to better accommodate our Shelley china replacement service. We particularly wish to buy the 6-flute Dainty shape in full dinner sets as well as individual pieces. Additionally, we seek Shelley figurines (Mabel Lucie Attwell's children, animals, and particularly characters), chintz wares, advertising, and other items. Early Shelley wares marked with an intertwined 'CW' (Charles Wileman) are also of interest.

Fred and Lila Shrader
2025 Hwy. 199 (Hiouchi)
Crescent City, CA 95531
707-458-3525

	We Pay
Advertising Pieces, as signs, brochures, figures, pre-1967	**please inquire.**
Bell	**45.00+**
Butter Pat, various shapes	**25.00+**
Coffeepot, various sizes	**95.00+**
Cup & Saucer, various sizes & shapes	**35.00+**
Cup & Saucer, Chintz; various sizes & shapes	**40.00+**
Cup & Saucer, miniature, various shapes	**85.00+**
Festival of Empire Series	**95.00+**
Intarsio Ware	**100.00+**
Mabel Lucie Attwell Wares, Figures, Etc.	**85.00+**
Napkin Ring	**50.00+**
Pitcher & Bowl Set	**155.00+**
Place Settings, 5-pc or more, various shapes	**55.00-80.00+**
Plate, Dainty shape, various sizes	**15.00-65.00+**
Platter, Dainty shape, various sizes	**75.00+**
Salt & Pepper Set	**50.00+**
Teapot, various sizes and shapes	**95.00+**

I would like to purchase a **gold Tea Leaf (ironstone) water pitcher and will pay up to $100.00. for this.** Also wanted is a **chocolate pot**. I will pay up to $100.00 for this also.

Sharon Peterson
330 N Linden
Northfield, MN 55057

I collect **Wallace China.** This 'cowboy' china was produced from 1945 to 1962. The pieces are hotel weight vitrified china and vary in price depending on condition and piece. I will only buy those pieces or sets that are in good to mint condition. Call me and we can determine the condition of your pieces. Some pieces have a stamp depicting a Conestoga wagon with the words 'Westward Ho,' the pattern name, and 'Wallace China.' Others just have a stamp stating 'Wallace China, Los Angeles.' The following are patterns wanted and their descriptions.

Rodeo: Cattle brands border in brown on each piece with a background color in buckskin (tan). Most pieces have a center motif of a western rodeo scene.
Longhorn: Cattle drive border in brown on white background or buckskin background. Center motif is the Longhorn Steer head. Some pieces state on the plates: 'Texas — The Lone Star State' along with steer head.
Boots & Saddle: Cattle brands border in the brown or buckskin background. Center motif is western saddle and cowboy boots in brown.
Pioneer Trails: Covered wagon train border with center motifs depicting the early history of the pioneer west. This pattern came in two styles: one with pattern in blue on white background and the other in brown with buckskin background.

T.J. Ahlberg
1000 Irvine Rd.
Tustin, CA 92780
714-730-1000 or fax 714-730-1752

Christmas and Other Holidays

We are actively seeking **older Christmas items from the 1900s through the 1940s and other holiday collectibles produced before 1950**. If you have one item or a collection of older Christmas, Halloween, Valentines, Fourth of July, Uncle Sam, etc., items to sell, please contact us. We love it all! Condition, size, color, age, and country of origin are important to note because prices paid vary greatly. Due to the vast amount of Christmas items produced over the years, it is most helpful if you include a photo and description of what you are selling. Please call us any time if you prefer.

The Murphy's
216 Blackhawk Rd.
Riverside, IL 60546
708-442-6846

Christmas	We Pay
Bubble Lights, old, ea	**4.00+**
Matchless Star Wonder Lights	**22.00+**
Light Stand, electrified & plastic	**10.00+**
Ornament, figural glass	**35.00+**
Ornament, figural glass, Italian	**22.00+**
Ornament, wire-wrapped figural	**30.00+**
Postcards, featuring Santa, stamped pre-1914, ea	**5.00+**
Revolving Musical Key-Wound Tree Stand	**250.00+**
Feather Trees, wooden stand, stamped Germany	**95.00+**
Santa or Reindeer, key-wound clockwork	**400.00+**
Santa, old	**25.00-35.00+**

Holidays Other Than Christmas	We Pay
Halloween Items, pre-1950, ea	**10.00+**
Fourth of July Items	**5.00+**
Thanksgiving Items	**10.00+**
Uncle Sam Items	**5.00+**
Valentines, ea	**5.00+**

Collector looking for plastic **Halloween and Christmas items from the 1950s through the 1960s**! Let me know what you have.

Daryl
Box 2621
Cedar Rapids, IA 52403
319-365-3857

I'd like **Christmas and Halloween items** such as cookie jars, noisemakers, paper decorations, candles, snow globes, bowls or candy dishes, pumpkins, witches, Halloween cats, Christmas tree fences, small aluminum trees, and anything weird and unusual — the older the better. I love this stuff! Please, **no Christmas ornaments.** Send description, your address, and phone number.

Harriet Myers
1132 Woodview Rd.
Burr Ridge, IL 60521

Clocks

I buy **American-made wall and shelf clocks manufactured prior to 1915**. Especially wanted are weight-driven wall clocks, calendar clocks, double-dial clocks, and other interesting clocks. Finder's fee paid for successful leads. Other interests include **Stickley Mission oak furniture as well as other arts and crafts-styled furniture, copper, pottery, etc.; American art pottery such as Rookwood, Teco, Grueby, and others; reverse-painted and leaded lighting and lamps by Pairpoint, Jefferson, Handel, Tiffany, and others. Again, finder's fee paid for successful leads.**

Bruce A. Austin
Rochester Institute of Technology
College of Liberal Arts
Rochester, NY 14623-5604
716-475-2879; baagll@rit.edu

I buy **antique clocks, especially clocks made before 1890**. Single pieces or entire collections are wanted. Travel distance is not a problem. Send photos or call 1-800-277-5275. Listed below are prices for mint, original clocks.

Mark of Time
24 South Lemon Ave.
Sarasota, FL 34236
800-277-5275

Maker's Name or Type of Clock	We Pay
Welch Spring & Co.	up to 3,000.00
S.B. Terry	up to 1,500.00
Eli Terry	up to 4,000.00
English Weight-Driven Wall Clocks	up to 4,000.00
American Weight-Driven Wall Clocks	up to 10,000.00
German Weight-Driven Wall Clocks	up to 4,000.00
English Grandfather Clocks	up to 7,500.00
American Grandfather Clocks	up to 30,000.00
China Clocks	up to 1,200.00

Fancy Repeating Carriage Clocks	**up to 3,000.00**
F. Kroeber	**up to 1,000.00**
Ansonia	**up to 5,000.00**
Seth Thomas	**up to 9,000.00**
Waterbury	**up to 4,500.00**
French Statue Clocks	**up to 7,500.00**
American Fusee Clocks	**up to 2,500.00**
English Fusee Clocks	**up to 7,500.00**

I collect **novelty clocks and am especially looking for Mi-Ken moving-eye wind-up wall clocks** that are approximately 5" to 6" tall. Their eyes move back and forth as a pendulum would swing. They were made in Japan. The earlier clocks had wooden faces while the later ones were plastic. Some of the clocks were made to reflect different Disney characters. Price depends on condition and rarity. I am also interested in **clocks missing parts and other novelty clocks such as Lux, Keebler, Poppo, etc.** Lux clocks may be animated, wall or shelf types, or heart-beat style. We buy only clocks in excellent condition. Only original clocks are wanted, *no reproductions or clocks that have been repainted.*

Carole Kaifer
P.O. Box 232
Bethania, NC 27010
336-924-9672
carolek@ols.net

	We Pay
Mi-Ken (Japan), plastic	**15.00-50.00**
Mi-Ken (Japan), wood	**45.00-125.00**

American-made, key-wound, clocks with chimes are preferred. These must be made before 1932. Please send photos with ruler showing the height and depth. Photos should show front, sides, and back and include all available information. We have special interest in **carriage clocks.** Other interest includes **antiquarian books.**

The Whale's Tale
Norma and Milt Wadler
P.O. Box 1520A
620 S Pacific
Long Beach, WA 98631
360-642-3455 or fax 360-642-2626
whalesta@willapabay.org

Clothing and Accessories

I'm looking for **teens to ladies leather clothing made from the 1960s through the 1980s.** Items wanted include mini-skirts, micro minis, hot pants, dresses, bras, and panties. **No suede or vinyl items are wanted.** Please check your closets. I will pay from $8.00 to $100.00 for items I need. I am listed in other publications as well.

Steve Hannan
141 East Central St
Natick, MA 01760-3625

Coca-Cola

We buy **pre-1965 Coca-Cola advertising memorabilia** in excellent to mint condition. Areas of interest include calendars; tin, porcelain, cardboard, and paper signs; diecuts and window displays; festoons; light-up signs; playing cards; clocks; thermometers; trays; salesman's samples and miniatures; trucks and toys. Our experience includes over ten years of collecting soda-pop memorabilia, editors for several antique and advertising price guides, and writers of a monthly column dedicated to Coca-Cola and soft drink collectibles. As collectors we can offer top dollar for quality pieces and collections. Condition and rarity are important factors that must be taken into consideration when determining the value of an item. We are willing to travel to purchase items or pay for shipping and handling. Besides purchasing for our collection, we assist in determining the authenticity, age, and value of items at no charge. Please feel free to call us or write with your inquiries. A clear photograph is always helpful for a quick response.

Craig and Donna Stifter
P.O. Box 6514
Naperville, IL 60540
630-789-5790

Coca-Cola	**We Pay**
1924 Calendar, complete pad	**900.00+**
1936 Calendar, complete pad	**500.00+**
1937 Sign, cardboard w/running girl	**350.00**
1938 Sign, cardboard, signed	**700.00+**

1922 Window Display, cardboard w/aquaplane girl ....**1,000.00+**
1950s Porcelain Button Sign, shows bottle, 24" dia ....**250.00+**
1930s Tin Sign, Take Home a Carton, shows 6-pack, 19x54" ....**200.00+**
1950s Tin Sign, Drink Ice-Cold Coca-Cola, bottle on right, 20x28".......**175.00+**
1960s Tin Tire Rack Sign, Enjoy Coca-Cola While We Check Your Tires..**500.00+**
1950s Porcelain Fountain Service Sign, shows ribbon, 12x28" ....**350.00+**
1920s Paper Hanger Sign, shows boy eating hot dog, 12x20"...............**350.00+**
1944 Cardboard Cutout, service girl, 17"..**200.00+**
1953 Cardboard Santa Cutout, The Gift For Thirst...............................**150.00+**
1958 Festoon, sports cars, 5 pieces...**350.00+**
1928 Playing Cards, Bobbed Hair Girl, complete deck w/jokers & box.**300.00+**
1951 Playing Cards, Girl at Party, complete deck w/jokers & box...........**50.00+**
1950s Light-Up Sign, 2-sided plastic, Shop Refreshed.........................**250.00+**
1960s Light-Up Sign, plastic & tin, rotating lantern style ....**85.00+**
1942 Serving Tray, Roadster Girls ....**200.00+**
1930 Serving Tray, Telephone Girl...**250.00+**
1941 Thermometer, shows 2 Coke bottles...**200.00+**
1950s Clock, lights up, shows bottle ....**250.00+**
1939 Salesman Sample Floor Cooler, closed front style, w/carrying case...**2,000.00+**
1960s Buddy L Truck, yellow w/cases & dollies ....**90.00+**

Coin-Operated Machines

I collect and buy **jukeboxes, pinball machines, slot machines, soda machines (particularly Pepsi, R.C., Seven-Up, and Dr. Pepper), and items relating to or advertising such items.**

Also collected are **Catalin or mirrored radios. Novelty radios** such as Charlie McCarthy, Coca-Cola, Pepsi, and Hopalong Cassidy are wanted. **Radio-shaped items such as banks or product-shaped radios such as Rario Beer, Radio Perfume, etc.** are wanted. **Catalin clocks, barometers, desk sets, etc.** are sought as well.

Richard O. Gates
P.O. Box 187
Chesterfield, VA 23832
804-748-0382 (day) or 804-794-5146 (night or weekends)

Wanted: **jukeboxes, jukebox speakers, jukebox selector units (wall boxes), slot machines, and cast iron coin-operated games.**

Also wanted are **musical devices such as horn phonographs, disc and cylinder music boxes, Victorolas, Automatons, etc.**

Jim Allen
420 S 46th
Lincoln, NE 68510
402-483-5789

I wish to buy **any kind of older bulk vending equipment** — whole routes or one machine, dead or alive. **Also wanted are counter-top games.** Send prices.

Bob Ward
7723 Arlington Ave.
Cincinnati, OH 45255
513-231-9236

Coins

We buy **all coins — U.S., foreign, or gold; and paper currency of the Civil War, etc.** We have been in business since 1953; thirty-five of our years in business have been in the same location. We are also very interested in **anything pertainning to Paducah, Kentucky:** books, magazines, post cards, jugs, dishes, etc. Send your items by registered mail for our appraisal. We also buy **stamp collections, old post cards, fountain pens, jewelry, gold, silver, and costume jewelry.**

Hoskins Coins, Stamps & Jewelry
120 S. Third St.
P.O. Box 368
Paducah, KY 42002
(502) 442-4531

We are major buyers of **all types, designs, and denominations of copper, silver, and gold coins of the United States minted prior to 1965**. A few of these issues were minted in very small quantities and command very high prices today. Others are quite common in low grades but command substantial premiums in new or near-new condition. All US gold coins are collectible and quite popular. As always, condition is everything. Prices listed are for circulated coins with all designs and lettering complete and clearly readable. Cleaned or damaged coins are worth substantially less. A few examples are listed below. Please call or write about any examples not listed.

Glenn G. Wright
P.O. Box 311
Campellsport, WI 53010
800-303-8248
'Our 38th Year'

US Coins	We Pay
Half Cent 1793	750.00+
Half Cent 1794 to 1797	100.00+
Half Cent 1800 to 1857	10.00+
Large Cent 1793	500.00+
Large Cent 1794 to 1795	80.00+
Large Cent 1796 to 1814	12.00+
Large Cent 1816 to 1857	4.50+
Flying Eagle Cent 1857 to 1858	7.00+
Indian Cent 1859 to 1909	50¢+
Two Cent Piece 1864 to 1873	4.00+
Three Cent Piece (nickel) 1865 to 1889	4.00+
Three Cent Piece (silver) 1851-1873	6.00+
Shield Nickel 1866 to 1883	3.50+
Liberty Nickel 1883 to 1912	40¢+
Half Dime 1829 to 1836	9.00+
Half Dime 1837 to 1873	3.00+
Dime 1809 to 1836	8.00+
Dime 1837 to 1891	3.00+
Dime 1892 to 1916	55¢+
Twenty Cent Piece 1875 to 1878	25.00+
Quarter 1838 to 1891	4.50+
Quarter 1892 to 1916	1.50+
Half Dollar 1796 to 1797	7,000.00+
Half Dollar 1807 to 1838	18.00+
Half Dollar 1839 to 1891	8.00+
Half Dollar 1892 to 1915	3.00+
Silver Dollar 1794 to 1797	250.00+
Silver Dollar 1798 to 1803	200.00+
Silver Dollar 1836 to 1873	65.00+
Silver Dollar 1878 to 1935	5.00+
All US Gold Coins	**Call or Write**
Tokens & Medals	**Write & Fully Describe**
Old Foreign Coins	**Write & Fully Describe**

I am interested in purchasing **foreign coins as well as United States coins, tokens, and medals**. I am **not** interested in parking tokens, sales tax tokens, or transportation tokens. I am especially interested in Western states 'Good For' tokens. I am interested in all foreign coins, but special areas of interest are Japan, Germany, and China.

My interests in US coins are mainly **proof and mint sets from 1936 to the present as well as coins prior to 1920.** While it is difficult to advertise a price that will be paid a year or so in advance, the following can be used as a guide. Normally, I will pay high or higher than any advertised price for US coins. This does not include the *Red Book*, or other non-weekly guides. I will be glad to make an offer on any and all coins.

Fred Hopkins
P.O. Box 2263
Peoria, AZ 85380
602-848-9229
fax 602-848-6055
e-mail: FECoins@earthlink.com

	We Pay
German 5 Marks, 1951 to present	**2.25-1,200.00+**
German Silver Coins, (1,2,3,5 Marks), before 1912	**2.00-5,000.00+**
German Minor Coins	**up to 500.00+**
German Gold Coins	**50.00-1,000.00+**
Japan 1 Yen (silver dollar size), 1870-1914	**5.00-3,000.00+**
Japan Gold Coins, 1870-1932	**200.00-40,000.00+**
Other Foreign Coins (must see to evaluate)	**up to 5,000.00+**
Good For Tokens(depends on state)	**10¢-500.00**
Foreign Coins (**no Mexican or Canadian**), per lb.	**2.00-5.00**

I am a coins buyer with 53 years of experience. All offers entertained. Please note time zone when calling.

Clarence Francis Chun
dba Eastern Spring
P.O. Box 22512
Honolulu, HI 96823
808-597-2270

Comic Books

I have been a serious buyer for over thirty years (a fact that collectors, dealers, pickers, and lay people all over the US can attest to). I do repeat business with most sellers and always welcome a chance to do business with someone new. The 'secret of my success' is quite simple: (1) my offers are very fair and generous; (2) I don't 'pick and choose,' I take the bad with the better; and (3) I pay promptly! Same day as arrivals! If there is anyone who is not familiar with me (or my reputation), I can offer many trade and bank references. My policy always has been that no deal is complete until everyone is 100% satisfied. If you have any questions, phone me. Wanted items include:

Comic Books: Published from 1897 into the 1960s. Most of these have 10¢ and 12¢ cover prices, although 1950s Giants may have a 25¢ price. If in doubt, ask me. The value of comics are determined by title, issue number, and condition — so this is the information I require. (If list making is too much trouble, just send the lot for a free, no-obligation appraisal.) Comics must have all pages and covers. Duplicates are okay. Bad-condition comics are of little, if any, value.

Sunday Newspaper Comic Sections and Pages: Color only, dating from 1890 through 1963. The 'Funnies' are a little harder to evaluate, as the interest to me depends on the content (name of characters), number of pages, year, and condition. (Most people seem to find this a lot of work, and usually 'shoot the works' to me for fair payment. Either way, okay.) I can't use brittle, soiled, dirty, or poor condition comics.

Pulp Magazines: 1930s through 1950s. These were made on cheap paper and had titles like The Shadow, The Spider, Doc Savage, G-8, and other 'hero' types, plus spicy and detective titles. I can't use any others.

Walt Disney: 1928 through 1950s books, magazines, comics, watches, and other items. Book publishers include Whitman, McKay, Blue Ribbon, plus many more. If in doubt, just describe as best you can.

Original Comic-Book, Comic-Strip Art: 1890 through 1960s. Other illustrations considered.

The post office is the best method of sending parcels, but UPS may be suitable in some instances. To speed delivery, please put **Value of $25.00 or less, per parcel.** Indicate 'printed matter' and do not put any invoice in parcels. Pack well. The mails are very reliable and provide reasonably quick service (anywhere from six to 10 days). A finder's fee will be paid to anyone who puts me in touch with someone who I do business with.

Other wants include: **Big Little Books and pop-up books; radio, TV, and cereal premiums; nonsports cards; movie posters; animation cels; popular music; jazz and song magazines; Lone Ranger; Lionel train materials; Korlix and Tarzan ice cream promotions of the 1930s** — plus anything you have that you feel is remotely related to any item on this list, just describe.

Ken Mitchell
710 Conacher Dr.
Willowdale, Ontario
Canada M2M 3N6
416-222-5805 (anytime)

Compacts

We collect **figural compacts** (powder compacts with cases in the shape of various objects such as a guitar, globe, or binoculars). Generally we do not purchase conventional round, square, or rectangular compacts even if they have an embossed, engraved, or three-dimensional figure on the lid.

One of those exceptions we **would** like to find is a round, square, or rectangular compact enameled mint green or orange with the 1933–1934 Chicago World's Fair 'A Century of Progress' theme and comet logo on top. We also collect **mesh vanity bags**. See our listing under purses in this book for descriptions and prices.

Only mint or near-mint compacts will be considered. Scratches, dents, or excessively-worn finishes will cause us to eliminate even the most sought-after pieces from consideration. The condition of the mirror is important, but in some cases we may still be interested in the piece even if the mirror is discolored or broken. Highest prices paid for compacts in mint condition complete with puff and original box. Below are just a few examples of figural compacts we're trying to find. Request our more complete, illustrated want list or view our want list and examples of figural compacts on our website.

Other wants include: **advertising and ephemera about mesh purses (circa 1920 through 1935), glass bead purses (18–20 beads per inch), Victorian autograph and photo albums (with lithographed print on cover), photographs of women carrying purses (circa 1925), Art Deco picture frames with reverse-painting, jewelry catalogs (circa 1920 through 1935), Bakelite jewelry,** *Moulin Rouge* lobby card dated 1934, Moxie 'Doll House' bottle carton, and sheet music titled *Maid of Mesh* by Irving Berlin and dated 1923.

Sherry and Mike Miller
303 Holiday Dr.
Tuscola, IL 61953
217-253-4991
miller@tuscola.net
http://www.tuscola.net/~miller/

Figural Compacts	We Pay
Bird, by Elgin (signed Dali)	**750.00+**
Jockey's Cap	**100.00-150.00**
Christmas Ornament Ball	**75.00-100.00**
Padlock	**60.00-80.00**
Fox (face), marked Italy	**100.00-150.00**
Cat (face), marked Italy	**100.00-150.00**
Cat, by Schuco	**650.00-750.00**

Book, by Raquel, red or green	**40.00-55.00**
Beach Umbrella	**150.00-175.00**
Binoculars, by Wadsworth	**300.00-350.00**
Guitar, by Samaral	**150.00-200.00**
Drum, by Charbert	**125.00-150.00**
Piano, by Pygmalion, musical	**175.00-225.00**
Hand w/Black Glove, by Volupte	**175.00-200.00**
Navy Officer's Cap, blue & white	**40.00-50.00**
Roulette Wheel, by Majestic	**65.00-80.00**
Hand Fan, by Wadsworth, engraved blades	**40.00-50.00**
Globe, by Kigu, musical	**275.00-350.00**
Hot Air Balloon	**175.00-225.00**

We are serious buyers of **vintage compacts** and have written several books on the subject including *Vintage Purses at Their Best,* and *Vintage Compacts and Beauty Accessories,* as well as having appeared on The Discovery Channel.

We are especially interested in compact collections and individual compacts. We buy all fine quality compacts and especially like figurals (those in the shape of something else) and French celluloid novelty powder containers like those that appear on the cover of our book. Generally, we pay better prices for those in top condition. Being collectors and dealers, we usually purchase more than those who purchase exclusively for their collection. We especially like rare and unusual compacts. You may send photos, photocopies, or scanned images by e-mail.

Lynell Schwartz
The Curiosity Shop
P.O. Box 964
Cheshire, CT 06410
203-271-0643
PURSES@aol.com

	We Pay
Bird in Hand, signed Dali	**500.00+**
Robert Chair	**200.00+**
Artist's Palette	**200.00+**
Figural Musical Instrument (guitar, drum, tambourine, etc)	**300.00+**
Powder Patters (puffs on sticks)	**35.00+**
Vanity Purses	**200.00+**
Postcards, showing people applying makeup	**Market Price**

Cracker Jack Items

I am an advanced Cracker Jack collector looking for **all early marked Cracker Jack items**. I look for pre-1940s prizes, boxes and display signs, and salesman's promotional items. I also look for the same items in **Checkers**. I am *not* interested in plastic items or items marked Borden.

Other wants include:

Angelus Marshmallow Items
Radio Premiums: Rings, decoders, manuals, maps, etc. — from Buck Rodgers, Capt. Midnight, Green Hornet, Orphan Annie, Lone Ranger, Tom Mix, Shadow, Sgt. Preston, Sky King, Superman, and Space Patrol
Miniature Irons: Swans, Wood Grip, Potts, Sensible, two-piece styled, and advertising
Tin Windup Toys and Tin Toys: Featuring comic strip characters or marked Occupied Japan, Marx, Structo, Chein, Girard, Kingsbury, Lehmann, Lindstrom, Strauss, Unique, Bing
Iron Toys: Marked Arcade, Hubley or Kenton
Still and Mechanical Banks
Old Dells Souvenir Items: Marked Kilbourn (plates, cups, postcards, photos, etc.)

Phil Helley
629 Indiana Ave.
Wisconsin Dells, WI 53965
608-254-8659

Cracker Jack	We Pay
Advertising Mirror	50.00
Bank, tin book	35.00
Baseball Card	20.00-75.00
Baseball Score Keeper	55.00
Calendar, paper, 1928, round	55.00
Cracker Jack Box, 1930s	65.00
Jack at Chalkboard, arm moves, paper	35.00
Jigsaw Puzzle, paper w/zepplin, 1930s	75.00
Train Engine, No 512	65.00
Train Car, any of 3 circus animals, ea	85.00
Horse-Drawn Wagon, pot metal	125.00
License, Model T Ford, 1916	250.00
Orphan Annie Stand-Up, tin, oval	45.00
Pencil Clip	130.00
Pin-Back Button, w/Cracker Jack Boy, tin	100.00
Pin-Back Button, celluloid	35.00
Sign, Cracker Jack, cardboard, 1920s	300.00

Cracker Jack prizes, premiums, and related items wanted. Also wanted are **early French fashion doll accessories or 19th-century doll clothing and accessories up to circa 1915.**

Larry White
108 Central St.
Rowley, MA 01969-1317
978-948-8187

Credit Cards

Seeking **all old charge-related cards,** from airlines, hotels, restaurants, oil companies, bank credit account cards, specialty stores, etc. Travel and entertainment cards such as American Express, Carte Blanche, and charge tokens are wanted. These may be made of paper, plastic, metal, celluloid, or fiber. I wish to purchase undamaged cards only that date before 1960. I'm also looking for **Black Americana**.

Walt Thompson
P.O. Box 2541
Yakima, WA 98907-2541
phone/fax 509-452-4016

	We Pay
American Express, specimen cards, pre-1960	**380.00**
American Express, cardboard, 1958	**120.00**
American Express, violet cards	**23.00**
Diners' Club, cards and booklets, pre-1960	**25.00**
Diners' Club, cards and booklets, pre-1950	**750.00**
Hotels, pre-1950	**5.00**
Metal Charge Cards, pre-1965	**10.00**
Playboy Cards, pre-1970	**5.00**
Playboy Cards, pre-1980	**4.00**
Playboy Keys, w/logo	**10.00**
Oil Company, paperboard, pre-1960	**5.00**
Oil Company, pre-1940	**10.00**
Oil Company, pre-1920	**25.00**

Cuff Links

I am always buying **cuff links**; no quantity is too large or too small. Several factors determine my offers: *condition*, age, and whether in original box. Naturally, I also pay more for precious metal than for costume jewelry. Size and unusual designs are also factors in my evaluations. The mass-produced SWANK, Anson, and Hickok Cuff Links of the '40s, '50s, and '60s are generally worth much less than the older and hand-crafted pairs. Typically, my offers range from 50¢ to $10.00 per pair. But unusual designs or superior workmanship can be worth more.

In addition to cuff links, I also buy **tie tacks, collar buttons, shirt studs, money clips, stick pins, and lapel buttons**. Many people are surprised to learn that I also buy single cuff links; they need not be in pairs!

I have earned an excellent country-wide reputation for fair and prompt offers. That is why people send me their merchandise and I mail them a check or an offer (whichever the seller prefers). And, unless you are sending precious or rare items, there is probably no need to incur the high cost of insurance. Other wants include **shoe button covers and money clips.**

Eugene R. Klompus
P.O. Box 5700
Vernon Hills, IL 60061
847-816-0036

Czechoslovakian Collectibles

At the close of World War I, Czechoslovakia was declared an independent republic and developed a large export industry. The factories produced glassware, pottery, and porcelain until 1939 when the country was occupied by Germany. I am especially interested in **Peasant Art pottery**. Pieces must be marked 'Made in Czechoslovakia.'

Delores Saar
45 Fifth Ave. NW
Hutchinson, MN 55350
320-587-2002

Peasant Art Pottery	**We Pay**
Bowl, footed	**95.00**

Creamer **25.00**
Chocolate Pot, 8¼" **75.00**
Egg Cup, 3½" **25.00**
Cup & Saucer **45.00**
Candle Holder **45.00**
Lamp **125.00**
Pitcher, w/lid, 7" **95.00**
Vase, 7½" **50.00**

Dairy Bottles

I will pay $15.00 per dairy creamer with a dairy name on it. These are individual serving creamers used by restaurants, etc. I will pay a little more for dairy creamers from Northern Illinois. Also wanted are **typewriter ribbon tins. I pay $5.00 for plain tins and more for tins with pretty pictures. Please send photo of what you have.**

Jerry Dobyns
4222 E 2551st Rd.
Sheridan, IL 60551
815-496-2605

Depression Era Glassware

I am interested in buying **buying patterns of Depression glass** (such as American Sweetheart, Mayfair, Miss America, Cameo, etc.) and **elegant glassware** (such as Fostoria, Cambridge, Heisey, Morgantown, etc.) whether a single piece or an entire set or collection. I will generally pay 50% to 60% of current book value, but for more desirable pieces I will consider paying more. I am interested in mint condition pieces only — no chipped or cracked pieces or pieces with major manufacturing flaws, please.

Larry D. Cook
P.O. Box 211
Walnut, IA 51577-0211
fax 712-784-2224
walmerch@netins.net

Depression Era Glassware

	We Pay
American Sweetheart, cream soup bowl, monax, 4½"	**70.00**
Cameo, vegetable bowl, oval, yellow, 10"	**25.00**
Cameo, dinner plate, green	**12.00**
Floral (Poinsettia), lemonade pitcher, pink, 10¼"	**150.00**
Mayfair, decanter w/stopper, pink	**140.00**
Mayfair, dinner plate, pink	**36.00**
Miss America, butter dish w/lid, pink	**350.00**
Miss America, dinner plate, pink, 10½"	**18.00**
Miss America, iced tea tumbler, pink	**55.00**

I am buying **pink Depression glass in the following patterns:**

Adam
American Sweetheart
Florentine #1
Florentine #2
Mayfair (by Hocking)
Princess
Royal Lace (also cobalt)
Sharon

I am also buying **elegant glassware in pink made by Cambridge and Fostoria** (pattern pieces are preferred). In **pink kitchen items,** I am looking for juice reamers, canister sets, mixing bowls, refrigerator boxes, measuring cups, spice sets, salt and pepper shakers, etc. (Salt and pepper shakers are also wanted in other colors.) All items should be in perfect condition. Photos and descriptions would be helpful when you reply.

Diane Genicola
25 E Adams Ave.
Pleasantville, NJ 08232
609-646-6140

We are buying **Depression glass for resale.** We buy most patterns and colors. All glass must be in perfect condition — free of chips, nicks, cracks, and scratches. We also buy **elegant glass of the Depression** such as Heisey, Fostoria, Cambridge, Fenton, Duncan Miller, Paden City, Westmoreland, Indiana, and Imperial. Also wanted are **glass kitchen items** from this time such as juice reamers, canisters, mixing bowls, measuring dishes, etc. We also buy **glassware of the '40s, '50s, and '60s.** Please send a list of what you have for sale and your asking price. Pictures are also helpful. **Mint condition glass only, please!** Other wants include, but are not limited to the following:

Willow Ware (red and blue, other than dinnerware items)
Children's glassware and china dishes
Liberty Blue Pattern 1976 by Franciscan

Staffordshire
Marx Toy Trains, 027 gauge
Coors
Hall
Roseville
Goebel Friar Tuck Monks
Royal China (Currier & Ives)
Fiesta
Hull
Memory Lane

The Glass Packrat
Pat and Bill Ogden
3050 Colorado Ave.
Grand Junction, CO 81504

Amber Madrid rare pieces wanted: gravy boat, platter, footed salt and pepper shakers, 6" square ashtray, wooden lazy Susan, jam dishes, hot dish coasters, etc.

Tonia Sheppard
4605 W Lincoln Circle
Knoxville, TN 37918
tonia@esper.com

Dog Collectibles

I am interested in buying **any or all dog-related items.** Items include such things as collectibles, advertising, figures, toys, statues, stuffed dogs with glass eyes, ashtrays, lamps, luggage, books, games, jewelry, dishes, bottles, prints, tins, linens, and quilts. I'm especially interested in Pomeranians and 'Peteena' by Hasbro or Peteena-related items. Please call or write. Thank you very much.

Other wants include **Planet of the Apes, Jetsons, Poppin' Fresh, and Flintstones character items.**

Carole Csernyk
317 Montague Ave.
Caro, MI 48723
517-673-1880

I began collecting **Royal Copley dogs** to display with a yard-long print that shows a puppy/kitten tug of war. As not all Royal Copley dogs are marked, refer to *Royal Copley* and *More About Royal Copley* published by Collector Books for good information and photos.

The cocker head wall pocket/planter is marked with raised letters and will be easy to identify. There is also a 7" dog with a string bass standing on a stump. This one had paper label which may not be present and may be harder to identify. Dogs with a basket, instrument, etc., are more desirable as I already have plain Shawnee dogs. Please note that poodles are not wanted.

If you have dogs other than Royal Copley, you might contact me. Chic made some cute ones as did Lefton and Shawnee. I am especially fond of Shi-Tzus, and I would also like to have a cat wall pocket. What are you looking for? We might be able to trade. Please send photos and your asking price. I have paid a range of $2.00 to $25.00 each for my dogs. Thank you.

Linda Holycross
109 N Sterling Ave.
Veedersburg, IN 47987

Wanted are **books and figurines on border collies.** You may write or fax information. Thank you.

Nancy O'Brien
15475 Pohez Rd.
Apple Valley, CA 92307-4634
fax line only 760-242-3171

I collect **figural dachshunds.** I have listed what I need to complete my collection. Please list what you can. Thank you.

Carol Allen
1307 Fourth St. SW
Altoona, IA 50009-1208

	We Pay
Dachshund, by Hull, 6x14"	**100.00**
Dachshund Liquor Bottle	**25.00**

Dolls and Doll Houses

Wanted to buy: **boudoir dolls of the 1920s through early 1930s** for my collection. Flapper type, movie stars, smokers, French, silk mask faced, musical, glass or sleep-eyed, male, Blossom Co., and unusual-sized dolls are wanted. I'm interested in very pretty or unusual dolls and prefer excellent condition over all, but I also do repair so I will consider dolls that need work for a reasonable price. Also wanted are high heeled shoes and outfits for boudoir dolls that are in excellent condition. Please send price, description, and a clear photo of the doll.

Bonnie Groves
402 N Ave. A
Elgin, TX 78621
512-281-9551

	We Pay
Dolls	35.00+
Outfits	5.00+
Shoes	5.00+

I am a serious collector of **hard plastic dolls produced from the late 1940s to the mid-1950s by US companies** such as Ideal, Effanbee (F&B), Arranbee (R&B), Madame Alexander, and Vogue. I am especially interested in buying mint dolls with original clothing and accessories, including box if available. I also buy dolls in lesser condition for parts or rehabilitation.

Diane Francis
148 King St.
Wadsworth, OH 44281
330-335-3717 or fax 330-335-3617
fphadv@bright.net

	We Pay
Hard Plastic Dolls, needing work	20.00+
Hard Plastic Dolls, MIB	250.00+
Nancy Ann Storybook Dolls, mint condition, no box	15.00
Nancy Ann Storybook Dolls, MIB	25.00
Doll House Furniture, plastic, 1940s-1950s, ea piece	2.00-8.00

Dolls and Doll Houses

Wanted are **Nancy Ann Storybook dolls.** I prefer mint-in-the-box dolls with original brochure and gold I.D. tag that are bisque or hard plastic and circa 1930s or later. I will pay $25.00 to $100.00 and am willing to trade. I also sell these dolls.

Sue Samuels
831-484-9272

I buy **dolls from the 1950s and older**. Price paid depends on condition. I belong to a local doll collector's club, so even if I don't want to buy your particular doll, I will know someone who will be interested.

Annette Nichols
5732 Edward Ware Circle
Garden Grove, CA 92845-2624
714-898-7407
gtn@webtv.net

Composition	We Pay
Shirley Temple, 1930s	**100.00+**
Buddy Lee	**100.00+**
Baby Dolls, 24" & taller	**50.00+**
Miscellaneous Girl or Mama Dolls	**50.00+**

Hard Plastic	We Pay
Buddy Lee	**75.00+**
Terri Lee, 16" (also Black)	**100.00+**
Jerri Lee (boy version of Terri Lee), 16"	**100.00+**
Terri Lee Family, Linda Baby, Connie Lynn, Gene Autry	**100.00+**
Terri Lee Clothing, most are tagged	**10.00+**
Terri Lee Furniture, Suitcases, Etc	**25.00+**

Vinyl	We Pay
Shirley Temple, 1957, 12"	**35.00+**
Shirley Temple, 1957, 17"	**50.00+**
Shirley Temple, 1957, 19"	**75.00+**
Shirley Temple, 1957, 36"	**500.00+**

I am buying **old dolls, doll parts — wigs, heads, eyes, and bodies**. My special wants are mint-in-box hard plastic dolls and 30-inch tall or larger antique bisque dolls. Please look in your attics, basements, and sheds to find the lost dolls of yesteryear. I will pay according to condition.

Sue Fishwick
523 West Osage
Pacific, MO 63069
314-271-6269

I buy **dolls and doll parts from 1900 to the 1960s** for my collection and doll repair business. I specialize in composition dolls that crack and craze. I would like mint condition, but would consider others. I also need wigs, eyes, stands, cases, and wardrobes. I pay top prices for original clothing and dolls that are mint.

Clara Louthan
HC 64 Box 58
Coldwater, KS 67029
316-582-2850

I am a collector of **old bisque and composition dolls** (especially Bye-Lo babies and Dream babies in bisque). I am also interested in **old doll clothes, baby clothes, and christening gowns.** Please send photo, detailed description, and asking price.

Other interests include: **cat collectibles, children's books, prints (old), Victorian collectibles, Virginia Rose by Homer Laughlin, and lace, linens, and needlework items.**

Eunice Gentry
604 Prairie Ave.
Cleburne, TX 76031-6236
817-556-3746

Barbie doll collector seeks vintage dolls and accessories pre-1966. Will pay top dollar for quality items. Sell your items to a collector instead of a dealer. Send a good photo along with price wanted to:

Lois Burger
2323 Lincoln St.
Beatrice, NE 68310
402-228-2797

Barbie Dolls	We Pay
#1	500.00-5,000.00
#2	500.00-5,000.00
#3	100.00-1,000.00
American Girls	100.00-1,000.00
Color Magic	100.00-1,000.00
Bubble Cut	50.00-250.00

Accessories	We Pay
Car	35.00-150.00
Plane	100.00-1,000.00
Vinyl Items	20.00-500.00

Barbie dolls of all kinds are wanted — especially Happy Holidays and others. Dolls should be reasonably priced, please. Also wanted are doll clothes and other dolls such as 'Kimberly' — Tomy's 18" doll made in the 1980s. All 'American Girls' dolls are wanted. I am also buying **advertising tins (old and new) and cardboard product boxes**. Thank you.

Judy Pender
126 E Wilburn Ave.
Greenville, SC 29611

Private collector will pay top dollar for **any Barbie collectibles made before 1988.** This includes dolls, clothing, houses and structures, pets, or anything related to Barbie. I am also interested in any friends of the Barbie family. These items may be with or without the original packaging.

I also would like to have **Dawn items made by Topper.** This includes the Dawn family and any related items as clothes and accessories.

Denise Davidson
7321 Seymour Rd.
Owosso, MI 48867
517-723-4611
davidson@tir.com

I am paying up to thousands of dollars for **vintage (circa 1959 through the early 1970s) Barbie collections**. This includes Barbie, Francie, all her other family and friends, their clothing, accessories, structures, etc. Condition, scarcity, and desirability affect the price of any given item, but in general I pay higher prices for mint and complete or mint-in-original box items.

Susan Anderson
410 N Hayford Ave.
Lansing, MI 48912
517-484-7069

Doll	**We Pay**
#1 Barbie	**2,000.00+**
#2 Barbie	**1,500.00+**
Other Ponytail Barbies	**125.00+**
Francie (twist & turn)	**60.00+**
Black Francie	**400.00+**
No Bangs Francie	**300.00+**
American Girl Barbie	**200.00+**
Long Haired American Girl Barbie	**600.00+**
Side Part American Girl Barbie	**1,000.00+**
Bubble Cut Barbie (redhead or brunette)	**60.00+**
Twist & Turn Barbie, Stacey or Casey, ea	**60.00+**
Other Barbie & Family Dolls, Clothes, Related Items	**Contact Me**

I want to buy **mint-in-the-box, never-removed-from-the-box Barbie dolls.** Send your list to the address below. Sample prices are listed. I also want to buy **Lionel and American Flyer Trains.**

Ivan Patnick
2506 Cliffmont Ave.
Bluefield, WV 27401
iandm@inetone.net

	We Pay
#1703, 1988 Happy Holidays	**350.00**
#3523, 1989 Happy Holidays	**100.00**
#4098, 1990 Happy Holidays	**50.00**
#1871, 1991 Happy Holidays	**60.00**
#1429, 1992 Happy Holidays	**40.00**
#14056, 1995 Bob Mackie Goddess of the Sun	**100.00**

I am looking for **Barbie dolls made between 1959 through 1966.** I want a complete **Color 'n Curl set** and will pay up to $4,000.00 for this. I need some boxes as well. Please call. Other wants include a platinum ring with 1-carat or ½-carat diamonds.

Lorraine
208-347-2554

I am a devoted collector of **anything and everything in the Betsy McCall line** from dolls to accessories — anything with the Betsy McCall name! A complete description of your item(s) and a SASE would be helpful along with your asking price, or please feel free to call me. I also collect **1960s trolls, Sandra Sue, and American Character's 10½" tall Toni.**

Marci Van Ausdall
P.O. Box 946
Quincy, CA 95971
530-283-2770
dreams@psln.com

Betsy McCall	**We Pay**
Doll, nude, 8", EX	**100.00+**
Doll, all original clothing, any size, EX	**100.00+**
McCall's Sewing Patterns for Betsy McCall, any size doll	**10.00+**
Outfit, any size doll	**25.00+**
Outfit, MIP	**45.00+**
Designer Studio Boxed Set	**200.00+**
At the Ranch Boxed Set	**250.00+**
A Day With Betsy McCall Boxed Set	**200.00+**
Original Pamphlets	**15.00+**
Carrying Case, w/bed & bureau, Standard Plastics	**50.00+**
Frame-Tray Puzzle, Fairchild	**20.00+**
Record Albums	**15.00+**
Children's Dish Set, china	**50.00+**
Cookie Cutter	**15.00+**
McCall's Magazine Paper Dolls, per pg	**2.50**
Trunk, for 14" doll	**50.00+**
Betsy's Dog Nosey or Lamb, stuffed plush, by Knickerbocker	**20.00+**
Original Wrist Tag for Ideal or American Character Dolls	**10.00+**
Little Golden Book #559	**10.00+**
Empty Doll or Clothing Boxes, ea	**10.00+**
Any Unusual or Rare Betsy McCall Item	**Your Price**
Always Buying Anything & Everything Betsy McCall Related	**Contact Me**

I am wanting to buy **shoes for a Horsman airline hostess doll marked Horsman 82 on her neck.** The shoes are marked NEE and the doll is 17" tall. She came with a two-piece navy suit trimmed with red and a headpiece with red trim. Please describe or send photo of your shoes and asking price.

I also have the **father of the Sunshine Family who needs a left eye.** Send your price or call. Thank you.

Flora Belle Allen
26 S Prospect
Liberal, KS 67901
316-624-3910

I received a 21" toddler-size Dionne Quintuplet and would like to find original clothing for my doll. I would like to find the original organdy dress in any pastel color and/or coat and hat to complete the outfit. I will pay up to $200.00 for a complete outfit.

Barbara M. Kuta
14061 James Ave.
Maple Heights, OH 44137

Dionne Quint items are wanted. If you have any other items or dolls not listed, send your list, pictures, and prices. The prices listed here depend on condition.

Marcia Kessler
4477 Olive Branch Rd.
Greenwood, IN 46143

	We Pay
Doctor Bag, for doll, black w/tag	**up to 90.00**
Baby Dress, actually worn by a Quint, w/tag	**up to 150.00**
China Pieces, no chips, especially with picture of Marie	**up to 100.00**
Furniture (play pen, high chair, etc) for 7" doll	**up to 150.00**
Quint Doll, 23", open mouth, tongue & teeth, original clothing, M	**up to $500.00**
Quint Doll, 11½" toddler, single or set	**up to 2,000.00**

Mattel's Liddle Kiddles — whole collections or one doll — I want it all. I am collecting all small vinyl dolls from the '60s and '70s including **Upsy-Downsys, Dolly Darlings, Tiny Teens, Flatsys, and more.** Also wanted are **Hasbro Showbiz Babies.** These are small bendable celebrity dolls.

Other wants include **Yardley cosmetics from the 'Mod Era' of the '60s and '70s such as lipsticks, eye shadows, nail polish, and accessories.** Please send SASE for information.

Paris Langford
415 Dodge Ave.
Jefferson, LA 70121
504-733-0667

Cash paid for **Liddle Kiddles.** I will buy collections or loose items. I'm also buying **1960s dolls such as Chatty Cathy, Small Talks, Barbie and family, etc.** Please call. If I'm not at home, leave a message on machine and I will return your call.

Linda Carlson
6 Still Quarters Rd.
Ellabell, GA 31308
912-823-9042

Raggedy Ann and Andy are truly American dolls. These dolls, originated by Johnny Gruelle, have been loved by children and adults alike who are charmed by their saucy, pert expressions. They were made by the Gruelle family prior to 1918. Volland Manufacturing acquired the manufacturing rights from 1918 through 1934, and in 1935, Exposition Doll & Toy produced Raggedys. Mollye Goldman also made them in 1935, but because she did not obtain the manufacturing rights, she had to discontinue making the dolls. Her dolls have multi-striped legs and the words 'Manufactured by Mollye Doll Outfitters' across their chests. In 1938 Georgene Novelties began making the dolls; they continued production until 1963.

I buy good condition Raggedys made prior to 1950 including early handmade Raggedys, Raggedy books, and books about other characters. I also buy **teddy bears, Lulu and Tubby, Nancy and Sluggo, Howdy Doody, and early Barbies.**

Gwen Daniel
18 Belleau Lake Court
O'Fallon, MO 63366
417-978-3190
GWENDANIEL@aol.com

	We Pay
Early Volland Raggedy Anns & Andys, dated or undated	**300.00-600.00**
Beloved Belindy, by Volland	**300.00-600.00**
Beloved Belindy, by Georgene	**300.00-600.00**
Pirate Chieftain, Percy Policeman, Uncle Clem or Eddie Elephant, by Volland	**100.00-400.00**
Exposition Raggedy	**250.00-400.00**
Black-Outline Nose Raggedy, by Georgene	**100.00-250.00**
Raggedy Ann, Andy or Baby, by Mollye	**400.00-600.00**
Raggedy Ann or Andy, by Georgene	**30.00-100.00**
Books by Volland, Donahue or Gruelle	**5.00-25.00**

I am buying **old Raggedy Ann dolls that were made before the 1960s.** Also wanted are **miscellaneous Raggedy Ann items.** Fair prices paid. One piece or an entire collection is wanted.

Raggedy's and Teddy's Co.
6337 Nightwind Circle
Orlando, FL 32818-8834
phone/fax 407-884-5483

The Little Falls Railroad and Doll Museum Ltd. is constantly looking for **dolls and railroad memorabilia** to enhance and expand the museum. We are looking for primarily porcelain dolls or heads to place on display. We appreciate histories with the dolls and especially desire dolls from the 1880s to early 1900s. We are able to give recognition for donations on a tax-exempt basis.

We can be reached by phone, fax, or mail. All contacts will be answered.

The Little Falls Railroad and Doll Museum Ltd.
P.O. Box 177
Cataract, WI 54620-0177
608-272-3266
www.wi.centuryinter.net/Raildoll/

Private collector of **high quality dolls, toys, and antiques** is willing to pay from $5.00 to $5,000.00 for the following items:

Vogue Dolls from the 1950s: Crib Crowds, Crib Crowd Bunny, Black Ginny, Ginny (mint in original box), Strung Ginnys, Ginette (mint in original box),

Baby Dear (mint in original box), Musical Baby Dear (mint in original box), and anything else mint in original box.
Other dolls: Orsini dolls, Playmates' Talking Jill dolls and accessories, WOW Talking Julia doll voice cards, all-bisque Mildred the Prize Baby, Hilda Baby, Gene Dolls, and Hollywood Babies.
Other items: baby rings, baby necklaces, baby bracelets, old baby paper dolls, buggies, doll furniture, etc.

If you have a wonderful doll from the '50s and early '60s, please contact me. I haven't listed everything I'm looking for!

S Ogilvie
P.O. Box 59434
Shaumburg, IL 60159-0434
sloest@megsinet.net

Egg Timers

I would like to hear from anyone having **figural egg timers** for sale. I answer all correspondence. I will consider all figurals made of china or bisque, glass, plaster, or plastic. Please, **no advertising types.** These figurals will average 3" to 4" in height. They might be people, animals, birds, etc. They might be quite detailed or plain. The figural itself must be in very good condition. Normal wear is acceptable. Please, **no** damaging cracks or severe chips. Expertly repaired pieces can be considered. Missing sand tubes are not a problem, although a missing original tube devalues the piece. A photo or rough drawing is helpful. Prices reflect timers in mint condition with original sand tube.

Jeannie Greenfield
310 Parker Rd.
Stoneboro, PA 16153

	We Pay
German (person, animal, etc)	**25.00-75.00**
Goebel (single or double)	**40.00-135.00**
Occupied Japan or Japan (person, animal, etc)	**25.00-70.00**
Miscellaneous Figure (plaster, glass, plastic, etc)	**10.00-25.00**

Erich Stauffer Figures

These Japanese-made, Hummel-look-alike figures are all marked 'Designed by Erich Stauffer' on the bottom. They are all products of Arnart Imports, Inc., whose address was once Fifth Avenue, New York; their warehouse was in Port Newark, New Jersey. Although Arnart was incorporated in 1952, production began somewhere around the latter part of the 1950s up to sometime in the middle 1970s. By the early 1980s, their copyrighted 'royal crown' mark was being used.

These child-like figures range in size from 4½" up to 10" tall. Besides the Erich Stauffer identification, there is always a style number on the base and sometimes a pair of crossed arrows. A style number can sometimes be part of a series of six to eight different boy or girl figures — all having the same number but having a different prop from the others!

More often than not, time has taken its toll on Arnart's gold-colored stickers that were found on the bottom of these figures; they are usually missing today. Often lost as well are the small paper titles that were once on the lower front part of each figure, i.e., 'Farm Chores,' 'Music Time,' etc.

As a collector of these lovable children, besides wanting to give them a good home, I'm always interested in knowing what figures were made and what their style numbers are. This enables me to catalog them for their future — whatever it may be.

I am especially looking for an angel, four nuns (each displaying a seasonal activity), sitting dog figures that wear small brass chains and collars (such as 'Champion Boxer'), or small porcelain Southern belles that are Josef-look-alikes. These all carry the 'Designed by Erich Stauffer' indentification and a style number.

Depending on the uniqueness of a figure's size, activity, and its props (goose, dog, rooster, doll, etc.), I can offer from $3.00 to $4.00 per inch; if a figure is outstanding, perhaps $5.00 would be offered per inch and possibly even more for a Stauffer wall plaque.

Please send a complete, overall description of the figure, its condition, style number, measurements (height and base), and note if the paper title is still intact. A photo is helpful, if available, but not necessary. No need for an SASE, if I can use it, I will respond quickly. Thank you for your interest.

Joan Oates
685 S Washington
Constantine, MI 49042
616-435-8353

Fast-Food Collectibles

We are looking to buy any/all of the following **McDonald's®** items: Ronald telephones; Ronald and other McD character older wall clocks; paper and/or plastic kites; wall plaques/pictures made by SetMakers; Ronald comic books by Charleton; any items with Archy, Speedy, or Slash-Arch; older Happy Meal boxes from the late '70s to early '80s; Ronald coloring books from the early '70s; paper items, pictures, letters, etc., from the '50s, '60s, or '70s which have anything to do with McDonald's® and/or Ray Kroc; owner, operator, manager, convention crystal wine glasses or goblets with a specific event given on them; and regional items like the My Little Pony Charms or Southeast Florida Metrozoo sets — all items must be mint condition or mint in original package. We are also interested in large playground character statues in excellent to mint condition. If you have any of the items mentioned and want to get the best deal on it/them, please contact us.

Bill and Pat Poe
220 Dominica Circle E
Niceville, FL 32578-4068
904-897-4163 or fax 904-897-2606
McPoes@aol.com

World's largest collector of **Big Boy** memorabilia is buying all unusual and older items with the Big Boy logo. This could include ashtrays, salt and pepper shakers, menus, matchbooks, nodder heads, china, counter displays, children's lamps, employee items and awards, cookie jars, buttons, puzzles, games, lunch pails, comics — just about anything else with the Big Boy logo. I do not buy duplicates unless I can upgrade my collection. Items must be in good or better condition (no reproductions). I do not buy any vinyl banks or trading cards. The older the item, the better. I will pay shipping charges. For my highest buying price, send me two or three photos of the item and include a complete description as to age, condition, size, colors, and where it came from (if possible).

Steve Soelberg
29126 Laro Dr.
Agoura Hills, CA 91301
818-889-9909

Big Boy	**We Pay**
Ashtray, figural, green or maroon	**300.00**

Bank, ceramic, full color glaze	**300.00**
China or Glassware, w/logo	**20.00+**
Comic Book, Bob's Big Boy #1	**100.00**
Counter Display, plaster, 18"	**1,000.00**
Counter Display, papier-mache, 14"	**1,000.00**
Employee Awards & Trophies, ea	**100.00+**
Promo Items, Buttons, Jewelry, Pins, Pamphlets	**10.00+**
Decals or Anything Unusual w/Big Boy Logo	**10.00+**
Hamburger Wrappers, early	**10.00+**
Lamp, ceramic figural w/shade	**1,500.00**
Matchbooks	**10.00+**
Menu #1, showing original location	**100.00**
Other Menus, early only	**100.00+**
Nodder/Bobbin' Head Dolls	**800.00**
Cookie Jar, ceramic, 1994 edition	**400.00**
Transistor Radio	**200.00**
Ashtray, white ceramic w/Big Boy figure on rim	**200.00**
Lunch Pail, metal	**200.00**

I have been collecting **M&M's promotional items** since 1972. I buy, sell, and trade! I have no specific wants and am looking for other collectors.

Fred Kraut
120 Covington Dr.
Warwick, RI 02886
401-738-2277
Uki845@aol.com

Fiesta

I am interested in buying **old Fiesta for resale.** All pieces must be in mint condition — free of all chips, cracks, nicks, or other damage. Please send a list of pieces that you have for sale and your asking price. I'm also looking for **large, hand-painted Picard items (not dinnerware).** Other dinnerware wanted for resale includes:

- Bauer Ringware
- Franciscan Apple (USA)
- Franciscan Ivy
- Franciscan Starburst
- Liberty Blue (Staffordshire)
- Coors Rosebud
- Franciscan Desert Rose (USA)
- Other Hand-Painted Franciscan
- Harlequin
- Metlox California Provincial (Rooster)

Metlox California Freeform	Mexicana by Homer Laughlin
Mobile and Contempra	Riviera
Vernon Kilns (no plaids)	Vistosa

Neat Stuff
Carolyn Brooks
7808 Scotia Dr.
Dallas, TX 75248-3115
972-404-1951
fax 972-404-1870
Neatstuff@aol.com or Carolyn@neatstuff2.com

Figurines and Flower Frogs

We are interested in buying **cast-brass, bronze or silver-plated bells that have human, animal, or other figures as the entire bell or forming the handle of the bell.** Details of the metal casting should be distinct and any identifying marks as to subject, artist, country of origin, and year cast are important. Also, the tone of a good bell is clear and lasts for some time after being rung. We prefer older bells, but do not polish away the patina. Newer bells are also of interest to us if the quality is good. We do not buy cheap reproductions, rolled metal bells, or badly damaged bells. Send detailed description with drawing or photograph along with your asking price.

Donald Matthews
3215 Garner Ave.
Ames, IA 50010-4225

Ballantyne Bells	**We Pay**
Becky Thatcher, 1977	**200.00+**
Robin Hood, 1981	**200.00+**
Hopi Kachina Dancer, 1993	**150.00+**
Blackbeard, 1992	**125.00+**
Ponce de Leon, 1990	**125.00+**
Aladdin's Genie, 1989	**125.00+**
James Bridger, 1985	**180.00+**

Other Bells **We Pay**

Roman Centurion, Huddy Bells .... **175.00+**
Welch Lady, w/spinning wheel .... **50.00+**
Sally Bassett, w/2 feet for clappers .... **80.00+**
Martha Washington .... **75.00+**
Turtle Bells, wind-up type from Toledo, Spain **95.00-140.00**
Interesting Bells .... **Write**

I collect **figural chickens and dachshunds.** I have listed what I need to complete my collection. Please list what you can. Thank you.

Carol Allen
1307 Fourth St. SW
Altoona, IA 50009-1208

We Pay

Fighting Cock, by LE Smith Glass Co, butterscotch slag (brown to red swirls), 9" **100.00**
Hen, by Royal Copley, black & white w/white base, 7¼" **50.00**
Hen Wall Pocket or Plaque/Planter, by Royal Copley, 6¾" **35.00**
Hen & Rooster, by Royal Windsor, 10" & 10¼", pr. **200.00**
Rooster, by New Martinsville Glass Co, crystal w/crooked tail, 7½" **65.00**
Dachshund, by Hull, 6x14" **100.00**
Dachshund Liquor Bottle **25.00**

I am interested in child-like figures that resemble the Hummel figures, but are imposters! (However, they are good imposters and can pass for Hummels from a distance.) The figures **must have 'Designed by Erich Stauffer'** on the bottom and a style number; some numbers will be preceded by an S or a U. Some of these figures will also have two crossed arrows on the base and some will still retain their maker's sticker: 'Arnart Imports,' from Japan. Originally a paper label was on the front of each figure giving a title to each boy or girl and/or its activity such as 'Farm Chores,' 'Music Time,' etc.

Most especially I'm looking for an angel figure as well as the figures of four nuns that I'm aware of. I'd also like the small perfume bottle girls, and china animals, and a rectangular wall plaque of a clipper ship, Great Republic; all will have 'Erich Stauffer on the base.

Depending upon the uniqueness of the figure's activity and the uniqueness of its props (goose, dog, rooster, chicken, doll, etc.), I will offer $3.00 to $4.00 per inch tall but perhaps up to $5.00 per inch for those items mentioned. I'd pay $15.00 to $20.00 for the wall plaque; postage is extra, of course.

I'd need a good, overall description of the figure and its condition, number, height and base measurements, paper title, and asking price. Of course, there is nothing like a photo, if one is available. No need for a SASE; if I can use it, I will respond quickly. Thank you for your interest.

Joan Oates
685 S Washington
Constantine, MI 49042
616-435-8353

I am interested in purchasing **quality retired Pendelfin rabbit figurines and display pieces made prior to 1970**. Quality and condition are extremely important. Please send picture and/or description along with price desired. I will respond to all inquiries.

George Sparacio
P.O. Box 791
Malaga, NJ 08328
609-694-4167 or fax 609-694-4536
mrvesta@compuserve.com

Royal Bayreuth figurals are wanted: Santa Claus, Rabbit, Mouse, Kangaroo, Platypus, Snake, Clowns, Devil and Cards, People, flower pitchers, bowls, and candlesticks.

Dorothy Earle
15 Burning Tree Dr.
Newburgh, NY 12550
914-562-8139 or 954-946-3284

Member of a pack-rat family wishes to start a collection of **Royal Doulton Middle Earth characters.** Please send SASE with a list of any pieces you may have. With SASE, all pictures will be returned. I can also be reached by e-mail at paxton71@gte.net. Thanks and God bless.

Harold M. Paxton, III
5800 58th St. N
Kenneth City, FL 33709
727-544-8974
paxton71@gte.net

Wanted by a Florida dealer: **all Royal Doulton dog figurines and Middle Earth series figurines.** I do wish to hear from you if you have **Elegant Ladies and/or Handsome Gentlemen** too. If you have a large collection, please mail list with HN numbers from the bottom of the pieces along with color descriptions. Please call for free quote. Buying quality figurines seven days a week! Thanks and have a wonderful day.

Bill Stenger, Collector/Appraiser
Gas Plant Antique Arcade
1246 Central Ave.
St. Petersburg, FL 33709
727-544-2431
Billantq@get.net

I would like to find **glass flower frogs** that are used for flower arrangements. I am looking for flower frogs of the 1920s through 1950s. Especially wanted are those of colored glass. All shapes wanted.

Sue Murphy
29668 Orinda Rd.
San Juan Capistrano, CA 92675

Fire-King

We like **all unusual Fire-King. We do not buy white, white with gold trim, or peach lustre.**

April and Larry Tvorak
P.O. Box 94
Warren Center, PA 18851
570-395-3775
april@epix.net

	We Pay
Batter Bowl, turquoise blue	**35.00-150.00**
Batter Bowl, white w/red band	**20.00**
Batter Bowl, fruit design	**20.00**
Bowl, basketweave, turquoise blue	**35.00+**
Bowl, teardrop, Jade-ite, depending on size	**12.00-45.00**
Bowl, mixing; swirl, Jade-ite, 5"	**20.00**
Bowl, splash proof, Jade-ite, depending on size	**15.00-25.00**
Any Jade-ite Sheath of Wheat Piece	**8.00+**
Any Ivory Jane Ray Piece	**8.00+**
Demitasse Cup & Saucer, Jade-ite	**40.00**
Butter Dish, Jade-ite base w/clear lid	**30.00**
Casserole, Philbe, ivory	**50.00+**
Serving Pieces for Anniversary Rose, Honeysuckle or Gamebird, ea	**5.00+**

Want to sell your **Fire-King?** Call us if you think we would be interested or e-mail. We buy only good quality Fire-King with no chips, cracks, worn marks, or color defects. We also like to stay away from buying peach lustre and white with gold trim Fire-King.

Unless it's a very unusual piece, we can not afford to buy only one because of shipping costs. The following list gives you an idea of pieces we're seeking. Keep in mind that we can only buy and pay according to our area prices.

When contacting us, please let us know measurements and numbers (if any are marked as this affects prices). Also let us know your selling price if you have one. Dinnerware patterns wanted include:

- Restaurant Ware, Jade-ite or white
- Jade-ite Swirl
- Alice
- Mixing bowls
- Jade-ite novelty pieces
- Glasses
- Jade-ite Shell
- Jade-ite Charm
- Box sets (no snack sets, please)
- Jade-ite refrigerator jars
- Butter dishes
- Grease jars

Two of a Kind
115 E Main St.
Delphi, IN 46923
765-563-6479
veronica.edington@gte.net

I am seeking Jade-ite dishes to use in my home. I understand that Fire-King put out many pieces and I tend to like the plainer ones (that I believe are restaurant ware). But I have not seen many of the patterns available and would like to see them if you have them. I am not limiting the search for these dishes just to one company as I'm interested in color and character. And I'm sure that many of them will compliment each other. Please call or write with descriptions and possibly a photo. I am particularly interested in obtaining not only dishes but also utility pieces such as mixing bowls and refrigerator boxes. I will pay shipping on all purchases. Thank you!

Melissa Arbogast
35162 Dolphin St.
Princeton, MN 55371
612-389-0849

First Aid Kits

I am a long-time, West coast collector of **first aid kits and virtually anything related.** I buy single items and manuals to go into the kits as well. Most kits and items fall into the $5.00 to $10.00 range — however, really unique kits and ones made prior to 1940 may command a higher value ($20.00). I am **not** interested in American Red Cross first aid manuals because they are too common.

I also collect **Boy Scout memorabilia, especially books; lifeboat and life raft supplies; civil defense, emergency preparedness, and safety items; and early psychology books.**

Dallas Stout
P.O. Box 9546
Brea, CA 92822
DandDStout@aol.com

Fishing

We are collectors of **old fishing equipment and paraphernalia. All must be pre-1950** and in good to excellent condition. We are interested in single pieces or whole 'tackle boxes.' Feel free to send photos (will return).

Sam Kennedy
212 N 4th St.
Coeur d'Alene, ID 83814
208-769-7575

Fishing

	We Pay
Wood Spear Fishing Decoys	10.00-100.00
Old Gigs, w/handles or w/o handles	20.00+
Wood Lures, w/glass eyes, ea	3.00+
Wood Tackle Boxes	20.00-100.00+
Trout Creels	40.00-200.00
Bamboo Fly Rods	20.00-200.00
Fish Nets	2.00
About Anything Else Fishing Related	15.00-50.00

As an old-time collector, I will pay the following prices for **quality tackle in excellent condition**. My collection is mostly Heddon but I also buy most other manufacturers' tackle. Rare lure colors will add to the price. Sorry — no plastic or repaints wanted. Call weekday evenings.

Harold Ruth
332 R Ave.
Paton, IA 50217
515-968-4544 or 712-336-3335 or 712-336-5500

Heddon	**We Pay**
Black Sucker	1,000.00
Bottlenose Tadpolly	300.00
Musky Lucky 13	125.00
Sharkmouth Minnow	350.00
Spin Diver	350.00
730 or 740 Punkinseeds	100.00+
Punkinspin	30.00
8" Musky Vamp	250.00
6" Musky Vamp	175.00
700 Muskollunge Minnow	700.00
Bat Wing Ice Decoy	600.00
River Runt Spooks	4.00
Musky Crazy Crawlers	100.00
Yowser	125.00
5-Hook Minnows	100.00-500.00
4-15 or 4-18 Reels	1,000.00

Other Companies	**We Pay**
Winchester Spinners	30.00
Winchester 5-Hook Lures	400.00

Glass Minnow Traps	**100.00**
2-Piece Reel & Lure Boxes	**4.00-100.00**
1st Model Pflueger Supreme Reel	**150.00**
Later Model Pflueger Supreme Reel	**12.00**
Talbot Nevada Reel	**300.00**
Granger, Heddon, Winchester, South Bend Cross Built Split Bamboo Fly Rods	**100.00+**
Shakespeare Musky Minnow	**250.00**
Shakespeare Rhodes Minnow	**400.00**
South Bend Bass-Oreno	**5.00**
Moonlight Bullhead	**75.00**
Creek Chub Jigger	**90.00**

Wanted: **fishing tackle catalogs:** old and new; especially those from Creek Chub, Heddon, Pradco, Pflueger, Shakespeare, Hardy, Allcock, South Bend, Ogden Smith, Farlow, Abu, and D-A-M. I have paid from 50¢ to $700.00 each for catalogs and use them for research for old fishing tackle. I will also buy photocopies of tackle catalogs if I can't get originals and will pay copy costs plus a premium.

Reels wanted are Mepps Vamp and Baby Vamp fixed spool spinning reels and some Mitchell spinning reels having conical-shaped wooden or metal handle knobs if in excellent condition. I will pay $150.00 for these.

Lures wanted include the wooden Heddon Punkinseed in excellent condition; I will pay $100.00 for it. Please contact me if you have any old fishing tackle for sale.

Stu Lawson
4430 Gladys Ave.
Santa Cruz, CA 95062
831-476-6475 or fax 831-475-6449
FISHNSTUFF@aol.com

We buy **pre-1960s wooden and plastic lures, fishing catalogs, tackle displays, and related items** including cardboard and wooden boxes, sinkers, reels, etc. Items must be in good condition or repairable; no repaints. Price depends on age, condition, and needs. We pay a bonus for collections and full tackle boxes.

Engelwood Antiques
2020 Townshop Rd.
Fall Creek, WI 54742
715-877-3468

Fishing

Collector buying **old fishing and hunting items**, including but not limited to:

- Rods
- Lures
- Duck Calls
- Catalogs
- Wooden Tackle Boxes
- Wooden Decoys, waterfowl, shore birds, and owls
- Reels (especially Kentucky reels)
- Creels
- Game Calls
- Spearing Decoys
- Glass Minnow Traps

All manufacturers wanted; free estimates provided in exchange for the opportunity to purchase.

Bob Walstrom
2235 Nancy Pl.
Roseville, MN 55113
612-487-6687

Collector wanting to buy **old fishing and hunting items** that include such things as:

Ducks Unlimited Pins, 1937–1972 (also state pins)
Ducks Unlimited Duck-A-Nickle Can
Wisconsin Hunting, Fishing, and Trapping Buttons
Old Duck Hunting Photos
Old Gun Powder Cans
Field & Stream Honor Pins
Wisconsin Decoys
Mason Decoys
Duck, Goose, Crow, and Turkey Calls
Live Decoy Holders and Cages
Wisconsin Live Decoy Tags
Old Duck Hunting Books
Pre-1940 Hunting Magazines
2-Piece Shell Boxes
Old Hunting Calendars, Sporting Advertising Posters, Gun Powder Advertising
Hubley Cast Iron Paperweights, Bookends, and Doorstops (dogs and horses)

Dean Dashner
349 S Green Bay Rd.
Neenah, WI 54956
920-725-4350
dashners@athenet.net
http://www.athenet.net/~dashners

I would like to buy **older hunting and fishing items** — rods, reels, lures, creels, shotguns, bear traps, decoys, mounts, artwork, and advertising. I will consider anything interesting. Please call.

Frank Vernana
781-396-0479

Florence Ceramics

Florence Ceramics figurines must be in excellent condition. **I will pay full book price for rare figurines.** I also wish to purchase **ceramic display signs advertising Florence Ceramics items.**

June Marks
1469 10th St.
Greeley, CO 80631
790-351-8404

	We Pay
Blue Boy & Pinkie, pr	600.00
Madame Pompadour & Louis XV, pr	800.00
Lillian Russell	800.00
Catherine	300.00

We recently inherited some Florence figurines. We liked them so much, we decided to collect them. We are interested in **Florence, Royal Doulton, Lefton, quality German, Japanese, or any other manufacturer of well-made figurines.** I will pay shipping and insurance. Call or send a photo, description, and your asking price. All pieces must be in perfect condition.

Steve and Susie Arnhold
3085 F ½ Rd.
Grand Junction, CO 81504
970-434-8064

Flow Blue

I am purchasing **the Watteau Dalton pattern of Flow Blue.**

Melanie Boutiette
410 W Third St., Suite 200
Little Rock, AR 72201

Watteau Dalton Pattern	We Pay
Butter Pats	10.00-30.00
Cereal Bowls	25.00-30.00
Soup Bowls	40.00-60.00
Cups	30.00-60.00
Dinner Plates	30.00-60.00
Bread Plates	25.00-35.00
Salad Plates	25.00-35.00
Platters	75.00-450.00
Soup Tureen	200.00-600.00
Punch Bowl	200.00-600.00
All Other Pieces	Write

Folk Art

We are buyers of **older pre-1950 folk art.** Highest prices paid for highly visual and more unusual pieces. Feel free to send photos along with pricing — they will be returned.

Sam Kennedy
212 N 4th St.
Coeur d'Alene, ID 83814
208-769-7575

	We Pay
Whirly Gigs	100.00+
Weather Vane	35.00-500.00
Old Painted Signs	50.00-1,000.00+
Trade Symbols	100.00+

Mechanical Wooden Toys	**100.00-3,000.00**
Original Paintings	**100.00+**
Pictorial Hook Rugs	**100.00+**
Quilts	**50.00-500.00+**

Gambling

We are buyers of **old gambling paraphernalia — with a special interest in the days of the old West**. We buy almost anything that relates. Feel free to send photos (will return).

Sam Kennedy
212 N 4th St.
Coeur d'Alene, ID 83814
208-769-7575

	We Pay
Old Cards, pre-1930	**10.00+**
Dice, ivory, ea	**5.00+**
Poker Chips, w/names, ea	**25¢-1.00**
Poker Chips, ivory, ea	**10.00+**
Racks of Old Poker Chips	**20.00-100.00**
Roulette Tables	**500.00+**
Sleeve Cheaters	**10.00+**
Pocket Pistols & Knives	**20.00-150.00**
Chuck Luck Cages	**100.00+**
Gambling Wheels	**50.00-1,000.00**
Leather Dice Cups	**20.00-40.00**
Ivory Dice Cups	**200.00+**

I buy **gambling chips** (ivory, pearl, casino, or composition poker types, etc.), **small gambling equipment** (faro, keno, poker, etc.), **playing cards, gambling ephemera** (catalogs, books, movie lobby cards, cigar box labels, etc.), and **other old items which are gambling related or have gambling-related images** (match safes, lighters, watches, etc.). I can buy one item or an entire set or collection. References furnished on request. I reimburse for postage on items sent for inspection (call first).

All items (except for casino chips and catalogs should be from before World War II. In general, I do **not** want (1) gambling toys (e.g., plastic roulette wheel); (2) chips that are plain with no design (except mother-of-pearl chips);

(3) plastic chips (except Catalin) and chips with interlocking rims; (4) bridge-sized playing cards (i.e., the narrow, 2¼" wide decks); and (5) large, heavy items (coin-op machines and furniture-like gambling equipment).

It is a good idea to send pictures and photocopies. Please indicate color, quantity, and condition of chips. For playing cards, be sure to include a photocopy of the ace of spades and joker and indicate the completeness and condition of the cards and their box. Call first, if you like.

Robert Eisenstadt
P.O. Box 020767-F
Brooklyn, NY 11202-0767
718-625-3553 or fax 718-522-1087
chipe@ix.netcom.com

	We Pay
Chip, ivory, engraved w/nonconcentric design, 1½" dia, ea	**25.00+**
Chip or Marker, mother-of-pearl, engraved w/nonconcentric design, at least ⅛" thick, ea	**20.00**
Chip, Catalin, marbelized red, dark green and yellow, 1½" dia, set of 100	**30.00**
Chip, engraved or inlaid clay composition, per 100 quantity	**25.00+**
Chip, embossed clay composition, any except Jockey on Horse design, per 100 quantity	**15.00**

Games

I am interested in buying **hand-held games or 'pocket puzzles.'** These games are typically round and have moving parts or beads inside that are moved or shaken into place. I am very interested in games made in Germany or that are advertising related.

Old Kilbourn Antiques
Phil Helley
629 Indiana Ave.
Wisconsin Dells, WI 53965
608-254-8659

You may have just the games I am looking for! You may also find it is in your best interest to sell them directly to a collector. If you have games from the 1800s through WWII that have great covers, pieces, and historic interest, then you'll have my interest and may end up with a sale worth your while! I buy games throughout the year and am looking for great **American games and other games needed for my research interests.**

Listed are some examples of prices I'll pay (or have paid) for great American games. Prices paid depend on quality, rarity, theme, size, and condition. Please **no Rook, Pit Flinch, Touring, Bingo, or Lotto.**

Patrice McFarland
P.O. Box 400
Averill Park, NY 12018-0400
greatgames@webtv.net

	We Pay
Early Milton Bradley, 1860-1890s	**25.00-600.00**
Early Parker Bros, 1883-1920s	**25.00-1,500.00**
Early McLoughlin Bros or John McLoughlin, 1820s-1890s	**100.00-4,000.00**
R Bliss Mfg	**500.00-4,000.00**
1800s-1910s Baseball/Player Related	**200.00-4,000.00**
W & SB Ives, early 1800s	**200.00-4,000.00**
Game of Business by Magie (**not Big Business**)	**My Best Prices Paid!**
Landlord's Game, **any**	**My Best Prices Paid!**
Pre-1934 Handmade or Limited Manufacture Monopoly, Finance, Etc	**My Best Prices Paid!**
Deluxe or Library Edition Monopoly, pre-1950	**250.00-5,000.00**
Games Circa 1920s through 1940s	**25.00-600.00**
Game Company Catalogs	**25.00-600.00**

I need **old video game stuff from the 1970s and 1980s.** I love **Pac Man, Donkey Kong, and Tron stuff as well as the old PONG-type and Atari TV games.** I also want to buy **hand-held video games and toys related to older video games.**

Robb Sequin
P.O. Box 1126
Dennisport, MA 02639
508-760-2599
rsequin@capecod.net

	We Pay
Hand-Held Games, w/box	**10.00-75.00**

TV-Based Games, w/box	**15.00-50.00**
Vectrex, w/box	**100.00**

Gas Station Items

Gasoline station memorabilia or 'petroliana' is **any item relating to service stations or oil companies.** There are countless subcategories of petroliana with some collectors specializing in one type of item (pump-top glass advertising globes or road maps from a specific company). Of particular interest to me are the smaller product tins offered by filling stations. These include motor oil and other petroleum product cans, oil bottles, handy household oil and lighter fluit cans, tire tube patch repair kits, etc. Another interest is in items that were giveaways to thank a loyal customer or entice a new one. Giveaways (also called promotionals, promos, or go-withs) include gas pump shaped salt and pepper shakers, miniature oil can banks, license plate attachments, tire ashtrays, ice scrapers, and tons more items. Other industry-related petroliana I buy include signs, thermometers, uniforms, pins, badges, name tags, real photos, can display racks, expired credit cards, and more.

When offering an item(s) to sell, please include a photocopy or clear photograph (will be returned) along with your asking price and an accurate description of the item's condition.

Ed Natale
P.O. Box 222
Wyckoff, NJ 07481
201-848-8485

	We Pay
Badge, hat or uniform, cloissone	**50.00-100.00+**
Can, Oilzum, 5-qt	**50.00**
Can Rack, Flying A	**150.00**
License Plate Attachment	**up to 40.00**
Handy or Household Oil Tins, metal or plastic spout	**5.00-50.00**
Lighter Fluid Tins, metal spout	**5.00-30.00**
Motor Oil Bottles	**20.00-100.00**
Road Maps, w/station graphics, 1920s-1930s, ea	**20.00-40.00**
Road Maps, w/other graphics, pre-WWII, ea	**3.00-20.00**
Map Rack, Texaco	**100.00**
Tire Ashtrays, colored glass inserts, Depression era	**20.00-40.00**
Thermometer, pole shaped w/sign	**10.00-50.00**
Tire Tube Repair Patch Kit, cardboard or tin, ea	**5.00-30.00**
Salt & Pepper Shakers, Husky	**300.00**

Salt & Pepper Shakers, Red Crown **100.00**
Salt & Pepper Shakers, others wanted **20.00-100.00**
Sign, Edison Battery, tin **100.00**
Sign, Fisk Tire, porcelain **250.00**
Sign, Mobilgas Pump **50.00-125.00**
Sign, Sunoco Rest Room **150.00**
Any Motorcycle-Related Item .... **Call or Write**
Any Marine-Related Item .... **Call or Write**

Glassware Other Than Depression Glass

Back in the 1940s (before 1948), a family member purchased glassware from a factory in Flemington, New Jersey, as a gift to her mother. I have since inherited these pink dishes. However, one of the sherbet dishes is missing. I have seen pieces in the same pattern at area antique places, but not in pink, and no one has given a name for it. The **pattern has a daisy-type flower with eight petals and measures 1⅛" across.** The sherbet dish wanted is 3¾" tall and has a 3¼" diameter foot. I would be willing to pay $20.00 for this item. I would also be interested in purchasing other matching pink pieces if the price is reasonable.

Ilene L. Burdick
P.O. Box 7
Coudersport, PA 16915-0007
814-274-9798

Shell Pink was made by the Jeanette Glass Company. It is a creamy pink milk glass made from 1957 to 1959. The only thing that ties the patterns together is the color!

April and Larry Tvorak
P.O. Box 94
Warren Center, PA 18851
570-395-3775
april@epix.net

We Pay

Lazy Susan **120.00**
Cake Plate, flat **85.00**
Cookie Jar w/Lid **125.00**

Glassware Other Than Depression Glass

Butterfly Cigarette Box **75.00**
Grape Octagonal Dish **25.00**
Punch Bowl w/Base **100.00**
Punch Ladle, pink plastic **15.00**

I am looking for **Wheatware, Free Flow, Kemple reproductions of Hand-Crafted Treasures, Lace & Dewdrop pattern pieces, pearl crystal lady figures, and boy and girl bookends** (these came in three colors and three styles). Also wanted are **salesman/party literature and old pricing lists of products.** These were made from 1968 to 1976. Condition of items is of utmost importance and must be mint. Please send list of your items and your asking price.

Sharla Roberts
R.R. 2, Box 260
Solsberry, IN 47459

I am interested in buying one piece or an entire collection of **stretch glass or iridescent stretch glass.** Prices depend on color, shape, and size, and will range from $15.00 to $500.00. I am particularly interested in candlesticks, water sets, and the more unusual pieces.

Also wanted is the early American pattern glass in the **Hawaiian Lei pattern.** This was made by the Higbee glass company around 1900. I'm interested in purchasing unusual items such as tumblers, mugs, a cruet, a syrup, banana boat/stand, punch bowl and base, punch cups, etc.

Royal Doulton's Vanborough stemware is also wanted. I would like goblets, tumblers, water pitchers, and decanters. Prices for stems and tumblers are from $40.00 and up. Please send photos of your items along with their measurements and descriptions as well as your asking price.

Calvin L. Hackeman
8865 Olde Mill Run
Manassas, VA 22110-6132
703-368-6982

I am interested in **Cambridge patterns of Rosepoint, Elaine, Diane, and Wildflower.** These are etched patterns.

Katherine Hartman
7459 Shawnee Rd.
N Tonawanda, NY 14120-1367

I am interested in **Cherokee Rose crystal by Tiffin.** I need serving pieces and some stemware.

Bob Gramer
P.O. BOx 597
Linden, MI 48451-0597
810-735-7115
www.michu.com

We are buying and selling through mail order **Cambridge, Heisey, Fostoria, Tiffin, etc.** Especially wanted is **Tiffin's Fontaine, Twilight.**

Jay Adams
248 Lakeview Ave., Suite 208
Clifton, NJ 07011
973-365-5907 or fax 973-471-5325

I would like to buy **Tiffin glass.** Please call 1-419-447-9875 after 5:00 pm EST.

Wanted to buy: **early Fenton art glass** as off-hand art glass, carnival glass, dancing ladies, elephant flower bowl, and September Morn nymph figures. Also wanted is **early Imperial** as free-hand art glass and carnival.

Debbie Coe
Coes Mercantile #2
Lafayette Schoolhouse
748 Hwy. 99W
Lafayette, OR 97127
503-640-9122

We collect **Venetian glass shoes, other pieces, and beads.** Prices paid range between $15.00 to $75.00.

Bill and Linda Miclean
499 Theta Ct.
San Jose, CA 95123
408- 224-1445

Golf

I would like to buy **Bing Crosby National Pro-Am Golf Tournament items** from Rancho Santa Fe and Pebble Beach, California.

William Lyons
719-687-1227

Graniteware

I am always looking for **quality graniteware in all the swirl colors — especially red.** Also wanted are **unusual gray items.** Send photos.

Daryl
Box 2621
Cedar Rapids, IA 52406
319-365-3857

Greeting Cards

As a commercial graphic artist, I really appreciate the artwork on **old greeting cards of the 1900s through the 1940s** and even use them for inspiration in my own work. I started collecting them in the 1970s and now have thousands! I don't cut them up or use them in collage. They are preserved in their original state, just as they were when your grandmother received them! Remember the shoe box full in the closet? Now you know what to do with them! All holidays are wanted: Mother's Day, Birthday, Easter, Christmas, Halloween, April Fool's Day, Baby Shower, gift cards, etc. The cards should be in good condition (no mildew or tears; not brittle nor brown) and no cards after the early 1950s, unless they are unusual. Used cards are acceptable. Flat cards are also fine (the ones which are not folded or don't open, and which don't have postcard backs). **No postcard greetings, please.** I prefer loose cards rather than scrapbooks or albums, but would like to hear about anything you have. Please write or call first. Postage will always be reimbursed. As with any collectible, condition is the most important consideration when figuring out a price.

Linda Cervon
10074 Ashland St.
San Buenaventura, CA 93004
805-659-4405 or fax 805-659-4776

	We Pay
Loose Cards, w/attachments or pop-up feature, ea	**50¢-1.00**
All Other Loose Cards, ea	**15¢-25¢**
Cards Glued Into Albums, ea	**10¢**

Gum Memorabilia

This collector is looking for **anything and everything connected with chewing gum or bubble gum.** Premium merchandise, advertisements, counter machines, character bubble gum dispensers, display cases, Wrigley items, packages of gum, novelty wax packs (with gum), comics, or whatever Double Bubble collectibles you might find are wanted. Please write or call.

Chewing Gum Chronicles
11048 Fremont Ave. N
Seattle, WA 98133
206-361-2728

Halloween

I am buying Halloween jack-o'-lanterns and papier-mache candy containers such as witches, pumpkin people, cats, etc. Also wanted are Halloween postcards, invitations, party books, games, hard plastic toys, decorations (mint-condition only), nut cups — anything Halloween except masks and costumes. The price I pay depends on condition, size, rarity, and age. Send photo or sketch along with description of condition and your asking price. I buy Halloween all year around.

Jenny Tarrant
4 Gardenview Dr.
St. Peters, MO 63376

Hawaiian Souvenirs

Aloha from the Big Island of Hawaii's most unique antique shop. We are in the market for **any and all old Hawaiian souvenirs taken home by our tourists.** We will consider the tackiest 1950s kitsch up to the very finest precontact artifacts — royalty items, surfing memorabilia, etc.

All types of items are desired, including oil and air-brush paintings, documents, postcards, any old paper, coins, currency, et al. Hula-related items are hot; please look for nodders, pins, dolls, skirts, moving lamps — all. Aviation interests include Pan-Am Clipper, Hawaiian Air, Aloha, Trans-Pacific, etc. Surfing items are in constant demand, especially Duke items, trophies, medals, boards, books, and photos. We pay premium prices for old cruise ship or restaurant menus, souvenirs, prints, photos, luggage tags, and anything nautical.

As always, we buy all signed Mings jewelry, old ukuleles, books, souvenir spoons, wooden perfume bottles, prints, Santa Anita ware, postcards, Don Blanding or John Kelly anything, etc.

Please call us first for guaranteed satisfaction, postage paid by us, and an immediate reply to all inquiries.

Antiques-Art-And-?
P.O. Box 742
Kealakekua, HI 96750
808-323-2239

Head Vases

A head vase is a vase in the shape of a lady's head with a hole in the top for flowers or plants. They were made for florists. Some were made as heads of men, children, babies, and animals — but all had a hole in the top or side for flowers or plants. Primarily made in the 1950s, some were made as early as the 1940s and later in the 1960s. Even in the 1980s and '90s Barbie heads were made as well as a few others. Ceramic was the usual material used; although some were made of chalk. Head vase planters range from 2" tall to over 20"! Most will range in size from 4½" to 6½".

I will buy any head vase you have to sell. The price paid will depend on condition and height of head. I am especially interested in buying lady heads having jewelry and hats. Please send picture if available or detailed description giving a reference number from one of the collector books on head vases. It is very important that you send your phone number, too. I will buy one or thousands!

Other interests include **Depression glass, pottery, Art Deco items, and Beanie Babies.**

Jean Griswold
3953 Woodbridge Way
Tucker, GA 30084
707-908-1333

Hippie Collectibles

The Hippies were long-haired, irreverent, free-spirited, nonconformist young people during the 1960s and early 1970s. They created a counterculture which expressed itself in new forms of art, music, clothing, political behavior, and anti-establishment attitudes. They coalesced in the Haight-Ashbury area of San Francisco. There were 'Be-Ins,' protest marches, impromptu concerts, and community meetings. Books, posters, records, handbills, leaflets, underground newspapers, magazines, buttons, underground comics, and other items relating to the period are collectible.

Richard Synchef
22 Jefferson Ave.
San Rafael, CA 94903
915-507-9933

We Pay

Anti-Vietnam War Posters....................**30.00+**
Items Relating to 1968 Democratic National Convention in Chicago......**20.00+**
Underground Newspapers, especially from Haight-Ashbury or other main areas....................**10.00+**
Books Written by Timothy Leary, Abbie Hoffman, Jerry Rubin, Tom Hayden, Others....................**20.00+**
Handbills or Leaflets, published by Yippies, Black Panthers, SDS, White Panthers, or other political groups....................**10.00+**
Books, Records, Handbills or Buttons on Free Speech Movement, Berkeley CA, 1964....................**30.00+**
Posters Related to Political, Social, Environmental Rallies or Meetings.**25.00+**

Hockey Cards and Related Items

I am actively buying **hockey cards issued before 1980.** Cards made by Topps, O-Pee-Chee, Parkhurst, Bee-Hive, Hamilton Gum, Maple Crispette, tobacco issue and more are wanted that were made between 1900 and 1980. Also I'm purchasing **old hockey items such as coins, programs, books, pucks, sticks, uniforms, and guides.** Please send a description or call. I have 25 years' experience! If you have any questions, please call or write.

Bill Hedin
Box 1435
Framingham, MA 01701-1435
508-820-3019

Holly Hobbie

I buy, sell, and trade **anything to do with Holly Hobbie.** Items wanted include plates, dishes, figurines, dolls, jewelry, mugs, cups, kitchen and bath items, general household items, music boxes, bells, eggs, cookie jars, banks, holiday items, and the list goes on!

Wilma Schiebel
HCR 63 Box 116C
Yellville, AR 72687
870-436-5874

Homer Laughlin

I would like to buy a **square salad plate and a covered teapot in Homer Laughlin's lovely Springtime pattern.** Please send me a picture and your asking price. I will buy only pieces in mint condition. Also, I would like to help others complete their sets of various antique china patterns (any kind). Of course, I would expect a finder's fee; and my time is limited to weekends only. I will be going on a roadside sale in August. It will extend from Tennessee into Kentucky. Please write to me if you want me to search and perhaps buy for you.

Geanie Massengale
68 Cline Circle
Dunlap, TN 37327

Hummel Figurines

I am purchasing **Hummel figurines** the year around. I'm looking for the **odd and unusual** for my private collection and for resale. I am looking for rare eye-open versions of earlier Hummels, Crown, and Full Bee backstamps. Call for **free quote.**

Some wants are listed here but all offers are considered and welcome. Please feel free to call. If I am unavailable, please leave a message and I will get back ASAP; or, mail a list complete with trademark, condition, Hummel number, and asking price.

Bill Stenger Antiques
Gas Plant Antique Arcade
1246 Central Ave.
St. Petersburg, FL 33709
813-544-2431 (leave message)
billantq@gte.net

	We Pay
At the Fence, TMK 2	**1,200.00**
Helping Mother, TMK 2	**2,000.00+**
Merry Wanderer, **double step base only**, TMK 1 or 2	**300.00+**
Others Wanted Too!	**Call or Write**

I buy **old and rare or unusual Hummel figurines** made by the Goebel Company. I prefer Crown or Full Bee marks.

Beverly Nelson
1010 Lorna St.
Corona, CA 91720
909-737-0977
nelac@earthlink.net

Indian Artifacts

We are buyers of **all authentic Indian artifacts of the United States, Canada, and Alaska**. We are only interested in pieces that are pre-1950 and can pay the most for pieces pre-1900. Feel free to send photos for evaluation (will return).

Sam Kennedy
212 N 4th St.
Coeur d'Alene, ID 83814
208-769-7575

	We Pay
Arrowhead Collections	**25.00-1,000.00+**
Beaded Moccassins	**100.00-1,000.00**
Beaded Pipe Bags	**300.00-1,000.00+**
Bows & Arrows	**300.00+**
Indian Pipes or Stems or Both	**200.00-1,000.00**
Navajo Weavings	**100.00-2,000.00+**
Northeastern Baskets	**50.00-200.00**
Northwestern Cornhusk Bags	**200.00-1,000.00**
Northwestern Baskets	**50.00-1,000.00+**
Southwestern Baskets	**50.00-1,000.00+**
Old Photos	**Varies**
Original Oil Paintings of Indians	**100.00-5,000.00+**
Painted Pueblo Pottery, prehistoric & historic	**100.00-5,000.00**
Tacked Indian Guns	**200.00+**
War Clubs	**100.00-500.00+**

Ivory

I buy **estate ivory and broken or damaged ivory carvings.** Our business does ivory restoration and custom carving. Most of the ivory I purchase are pieces in any form from one-eighth pound to full tusks as well as damaged carvings that are past the repair stage. I am interested in all colors: white, tan, black, etc. Call and let me know what you have or send good clear photographs with your name, phone number, and the best time to contact.

Mystic
P.O. Box 2544
Everett, WA 98203
425-353-2087 (9 am to 5 pm, PST)

Japan Ceramics

I am buying **Japan ceramic or pottery items used to decorate the kitchen.** Items such as spice sets (these may have a wood rack or shelf); condiment jars with cute heads such as Holt Howard, Lefton, or Davar; vegetable-head people salt and pepper shakers (such as a turnip or carrot had on a dressed body); etc. Also wanted are **Lefton or Josef Original angels or girls.** Send photo or sketch with condition and prices.

Jenny Tarrant
4 Gardenview
St. Peters, MO 63376
JennyJol@aol.com

I collect **made-in-Japan lustreware in all colors and patterns.** I have several parts of condiment sets or shaker sets and would like to find the missing pieces. I have other items as hair receptacles that I would like to find lids or bottoms. I am particularly interested in stoppers for oil/vinegar jars, a toast holder, and wall pockets. I will pay reasonable prices and shipping.

D.L. Rogers
123 Fisk Terrace
Fremont, CA 94538
510-651-9521

Jewelry

We are serious buyers of **vintage costume jewelry** and have written several books on collectibles including *Vintage Purses at Their Best* and *Vintage Compacts and Beauty Accessories,* as well as having appeared on The Discovery Channel.

We are especially interested in jewelry collections and individual pieces. We buy all fine-quality jewelry and especially like signed pieces or those from 1940 and before. We are always looking for good Bakelite pieces including carved or geometric bracelets and figural pins. Generally, we can pay better prices for those in top condition.

Being collectors and dealers, we tend to purchase more than those who purchase exclusively for their collection. We especially like rare and unusual pieces. You may send photos or photocopies or e-mail us (with or without images).

Lynell Schwartz
The Curiosity Shop
P.O. Box 964
Cheshire, CT 06410
203-271-0643
purses@aol.com

	We Pay
Christmas Tree Pins	**25.00+**
Haskell	**75.00-300.00+**

Jelly Bellies .... **125.00-375.00+**
Colorcraft Castle Pin .... **300.00+**
Trifari Sterling .... **Market Price**
Boucher Enamel .... **200.00+**
Schiaparelli .... **75.00-300.00+**
Chanel .... **Market Price**
Bakelite Geometric Bracelets, dots, zig-zags, etc .... **250.00-400.00+**
Bakelite Figural Pins .... **200.00+**
Carved Bakelite .... **140.00+**

Vintage costume jewelry has been my passion for at least fifteen years now. I have a large personal collection, and I also buy items for resale. I am particularly interested in large, ornate, or unusual pieces, signed or unsigned. I mainly collect items from the 1970s and earlier, but will consider newer items if they are extraordinary! I collect all types of costume jewelry: rhinestones, faux pearls, plastics, glass, porcelain, cameos, gold-tone, silver-tone, sterling, gold-filled, etc. Items should be in very good condition, although I will sometimes purchase good quality items in need of minor repairs.

Among my favorite items to collect are **charms and charm bracelets.** These may be any type of metal, and I am especially fond of enameled charms or charms with moving parts. Charm bracelets with a large number of charms will generally command higher prices. I also buy **compacts and Virgin Mary or madonna figurines.** Call, write, or e-mail if you would like to sell your items. I will need a detailed description, a color copy, or a photo of your item along with your asking price.

Leslie Ray
1908 Pin Oak Dr.
Springdale, AR 72762
501-750-7171
nubiaone@aol.com

Wanted to buy: **older vintage costume jewelry and men's tie tacs.** Pieces don't have to be made of precious metals or stones; they just need to be nice vintage pieces. Items in the form of birds, flowers, leaves, insects, or the shape of crosses are favorites — but I will consider all pieces. Pictures are very helpful.

Michelle Carey
2512 Balmoral Blvd.
Kokomo, IN 46902-3155
765-455-2094
mgcarey@netusa1.net

I would like to buy **daisy pins** from the 1960s. These are brightly colored enameled metal flower that may be from 2" to 3" in diameter. You may send photo or photocopy of your item. Thank you.

Linda Cervon
10074 Ashland St.
San Buenaventura, CA 93004
805-659-4405 or fax 805-659-4776

I buy **jewelry of all kinds**: high-grade diamonds, gold (10K through 22K), tennis bracelets, gold bracelets, watches (vintage only), signed costume jewelry (such as Weiss, Miriam Haskell, Eisenberg, Chanel, Tiffany), etc. I am always looking for **emeralds, garnets, rubies, and colored stones** but these must be in excellent condition. Call for a quote.

Sterling silver items such as novelties, baby items, mesh and enameled purses, are hard to estimate a price. Call for quote or fax me a picture and I will respond back ASAP. Other wants include: **sterling flatware, hollowware, candelabras, match safes, salt cellars, and spoons.** I have twenty-two years experience and immediately pay cash.

The Silver Lady
Joyce Lucas
23011 Moulton Pky. #C1-205
Laguna Hills, CA 92653
949-855-1500 or fax 949-855-1010

We are always interested in **fine and unusual jewelry.** Items of special interest are Victorian pieces in gold or silver, Art Nouveau, Edwardian, Art Deco, diamond jewelry from any time period, Mexican silver (1930s through 1950s), and Scandinavian silver (especially George Jensen). All items must be in good condition. We also buy **scrap gold, platinum, loose diamonds, old jewelry catalogs from the 1800s through the 1930s, and anything relating to gold mining in the US from the 1850s to the 1880s. When in Colorado visit us at our store or anytime at our website: http://www.tias.com/stores/demark.**

Greg DeMark
1745 N Main St. #9
Longmont, CO 80501
303-682-5321
demark@concentric.net

I am buying **silver jewelry of all kinds that is pre-1970 from the USA, Mexico, and Europe.** Items wanted include: necklaces, pendants, pins, earrings, and bracelets. Also wanted are decorator and table items. All items must be marked sterling or .925 or better. Please, no damaged or repaired items. Please send a good description of the item, a photo (or use a copier), with your price. I am looking forward to seeing what you have to sell. We will respond quickly.

Richard Haigh
P.O. Box 29562
Richmond, VA 23242
804-741-5770 (until 9pm EST)

I buy **old gold jewelry in need of repair** and pay fair market price. If your item doesn't need repair, contact me as I would like to buy it to practice on. I also buy **stones of any kind, undamaged gold items, and gold teeth.**

Kayla Conway
4500 Napal Ct.
Bakersfield, CA 93307
805-833-0291

Josef Originals

We buy **Josef Originals made from 1945 to 1985.** Thi is the period when Muriel Joseph George designed all the figurines and animals. It is very important that each piece is examined for chips and breaks. Because of the way they were fired, the figurines can break and be glued back together so it is hard to tell if a piece is broken. We do not buy figures made by George Good or Applause who bought the company in 1985. We buy pieces with glossy finish that are marked on the bottom with Josef Original in ink or incised, and usually have an oval sticker that is black with gold or silver letters. We do not buy anything with damage or repairs. Other wants include **motion lamps and Hawaiiana.**

Jim and Kaye Whitaker
Eclectic Antiques
P.O. Box 475, Dept. WB
Lynnwood, WA 98046
206-774-6910

	We Pay
Birth Month, common jewel, Japan	**8.00-10.00**
Birth Month, non-jewel, Japan	**12.00-15.00**
Birth Month, jewel, California	**15.00-20.00**
Birth Month, non-jewel, California	**12.00-15.00**
Figurine, International	**15.00-18.00**
Figurine, Birthday Girl, angel w/number	**10.00-15.00**
Figurine, miscellaneous, 3½" to 4½", ea	**15.00-18.00**
Figurine, miscellaneous, 5½" to 6½", ea	**25.00-30.00**
Figurine, miscellaneous, 7½" to 8½", ea	**35.00-45.00**
Figurine, miscellaneous, 9" to 10½", ea	**45.00-55.00**
Figurine, animals other than mice, depending on size, ea	**5.00-10.00**
Figurine, mice	**4.00-5.00**

Kansas

For a short time from the late 1800s to around 1912, there were many glass and pottery plants in the area of southeast Kansas. Abundant natural gas (which began to run out by 1912) attracted two well-known fruit jar producers (Mason and Ball) to the Coffeyville area. Other glass plants (whose products are unknown today) were also located there as well as several window-glass plants. A few of the products known to have been produced in the area are listed below. Also listed are sample miniature bricks which were put out by as many as a dozen or so different brick and tile plants.

Here, as everywhere else in the early days of the United States, a popular way for a merchant to advertise was to sell or give away a ceramic or glass souvenir featuring a view of a local park, a building, or a special event to visitors and local customers as well. Most of these plates, vases, jugs, etc., were made in Germany and England, as were view postcards and other items. Some souvenirs carried the message 'souvenir of (name of town, state).' We buy these as well as similar items with street names, buildings, etc. found on them. We also want postcards, calendars, or any advertising material.

Listed below are glass, pottery, souvenir, advertising, and related items we buy. We will buy other items and even some damaged pieces if contacted for prices. Please note that my hometown, Dearing, may also be spelled Deering. Please write or call before shipping.

Billy and Jeane Jones
P.O. Box 82
Dearing, KS 67340
316-948-6389

	We Pay
Premium Glass Fruit Jar, Coffeyville, KS, pt, ea	25.00
Premium Glass Fruit Jar, Coffeyville, KS, qt	15.00
Premium Glass Fruit Jar, Coffeyville, KS, half-gal, ea	20.00
Premium Glass Fruit Jar, Coffeyville, KS, 1-gal, ea	35.00+
Premium (Plain) Fruit Jar, sizes as above, ea	10.00+
Premium 'Improved' Jar, ea	30.00
Premium Lid w/Coffeyville, ea	3.00
Premium Wire Clip, ea	5.00
Premium Magazine Ads, Etc, ea	3.00
Lace Edge Glass Plate, w/'Premium Jar,' Coffeyville, 7", ea	100.00
Lace Edge Glass Plate, w/'Ball Jar,' Coffeyville, 7", ea	120.00
Lace Edge Glass Plate, w/'Pioneer Glass,' Coffeyville, 7", ea	50.00
Ball, The Mason, or Premium Wooden Boxes, Coffeyville, ea	75.00
Coffeyville, Independence, Cherryvale, Buffalo, Etc, Miniature Bricks, ea	Write
Any Tin or Cardboard Advertising Sign, Etc, marked as above	Write
Ashtray, Dearing, marked Smelter, early 1900s, ea	25.00
Stoneware Jug, bottom incised 'Made in Coffeyville,' brown	Write
Stoneware Crock or Churn, bottom incised 'Made in Coffeyville,' brown	Write
Terraco O&H Coffeyville, KS; Pitcher, terra cotta, brown pottery	30.00
Coffeyville Pottery & Clay Co (ie, Coffeyville Stoneware Co.) Miniature Jug	40.00
Coffeyville Pottery & Clay Co (ie, Coffeyville Stoneware Co.) Crock, Churn or Jug, smaller than 3-gal, w/nice imprint, ea	30.00+
Coffeyville Pottery & Clay Co (ie, Coffeyville Stoneware Co.) Crock, Churn or Jug, larger than 3-gal, ea	25.00+
Any Stoneware w/Sponge Decor, Advertising, marked as above, etc, ea	Write
Magazine Ad, Etc, relative to above	2.00+
Magazine Ad, Rea-Patterson Milling Co	2.00+
Advertising Signs (including Rea-Patterson), tin, cardboard, paper	Write
Advertising Items, Page Milk, Sweetheart Flour, Dearing, Millers Cash Store, Etc, ea	Write
Advertising Thermometer, Sweet & Pure or Sweetheart Flour, EX (write for G or poor prices), ea	150.00+
Picture or Postcard, any company listed, ea	Write
Picture, Dearing, marked Smelter, ea	10.00
View Postcard, Dearing, early 1900s, real photo, ea	15.00+
View Postcard, Coffeyville, Chanute, Independence, ea	3.00
View Postcard, other southeast KS towns, ea	1.00+
Calendar, Dearing, early 1890-1930, ea	15.00
Calendar, Coffeyville, Chanute, or other southeast KS towns, ea	3.00+
Calendar Plate, Dearing or Deering, early 1900s, ea	30.00
Calendar Plate, Coffeyville, Independence, early 1900s, ea	20.00
Calendar Plate, Caney, Wayside, early 1900s, ea	12.00+
Calendar Plate, Parsons, Oswego, Altamont, early 1900s, ea	12.00+
Plate, towns as listed above, china, scenic view, early 1900s, ea	10.00+
Plate, Dearing or Deering, china, scenic view, early 1900s, ea	25.00
Plate, Dearing, marked White's Amusement Park, ea	30.00

Milk Bottle Cap, Carlton Hall Dairy, ca 1950s, ea .... **1.00+**
Trade Tokens, Dearing, KS; Millers Cash Store, Etc, ea **25.00**
Hotel to Depot Tokens, metal or paper, Dearing, Coffeyville, Etc, ea .... **Write**
Vase, Jug, Etc, Dearing, china, scenic view, ea **25.00**
Vase, Jug, Etc, other southwest KS cities, china, scenic view, ea............. **8.00+**
Spoon, Dearing, sterling, ea.. **20.00**
Spoon, other southeast KS towns, sterling .... **Write**
Souvenir Item, Dearing, Heisey Custard or other glass companies, ea...... **35.00**

Kay Finch Ceramics

We especially want animal and bird figures and prefer those in the pink clay with pastel decoration, though we would be interested in hearing about any you might have for sale. There are a few we're especially looking for, and we'll list them below along with the few people figures we like. This type of ceramic figurine was made in California from the 1940s until 1963. They have a distinctive appearance and unique characteristics that make them easy to spot. The pink pieces are very often decorated with bright pastels, but even the white figures and those done in more naturalistic tones will have her trademark curliques and realistic, detailed modeling. Some items will have applied bows, flowers, etc. Most pieces are signed.

This list is by no means complete. We have very few of the large pieces, but space does not allow us to itemize everything we need. So large or small, if it's not in our collection, we'll want it, too. The only items we're definitely not interested in are the 'peasant' couples and the metallic-glazed figures. As for the amount we will pay, as any Kay Finch collector knows, it's a seller's market.

Sharon Huxford
1202 Seventh St.
Covington, IN 47932
phone 765-793-2392 or fax 765-793-2249; 800-292-3703

We Pay

Bunny Carrots in white.. **Market value**
Penguin Family, lg only... **Market value**
Flying Owl (wings spread), 10½" .... **Market value**
Horses (have none)... **Market value**
Jocko Monkey (preferably in blue & rose)................................. **Market value**
Mr. Tom Cat.. **Market value**
Siamese Cat, 10" .... **Market value**
Any of the miniature kittens (have Muff & Puff)......................... **Market value**

Papa Duck	Market value
American Indian Family	Market value
Sitting Baby, 5½"	Market value
Pajama Girl, 5½"	Market value
Littlest Angel, 2½"	Market value
Band of Angels & Christmas Tree	Market value
Girl Angel, 2½"	Market value
Cocker Spaniel Vicki in pink	Market value
Any others; no owls (except the one mentioned above) or pigs	Call

Kentucky Derby Glasses

I buy Derby glasses made prior to 1974. Glasses must have bright colors and have no chips, cracks, flaws, or fading. I'll split postage and shipping costs. Prices for glasses dating before 1952 will be negotiable. Other wants include: **Van Briggle, McCoy with floral designs, Nippon, Coca-Cola, cigarette memorabilia, Evening in Paris items, older McDonald's® items, children's books in mint condition from before the 1950s, and books authored by Janice Holt Giles, Jesse Stuart, or Robert Penn Warren.**

Betty Hornback
707 Sunrise Ln.
Elizabethtown, KY 42701

Derby Year	We Pay
1953	45.00
1954	45.00
1955	40.00
1956	60.00
1957	45.00
1958, both styles, ea	70.00
1959	30.00
1960	30.00
1961	40.00
1962	20.00
1963	22.00
1964	Do Not Buy
1965	20.00
1966	20.00
1967	20.00
1968	15.00

1969	**17.00**
1970	**20.00**
1971	**15.00**
1972	**15.00**
1973	**15.00**
1974	**6.00**
Any Unofficial Derby Glass, ea	**5.00**

Kitchen Appliances, Collectibles, and Glassware

H.J.H. Publications, Antiques & Collectibles, has been active in publishing books on collectibles since 1987 and has purchased rare collectibles since 1971.

One area of interest is **kitchen appliances.** We are interested in porcelain and unusual toasters, sewing machines, and 1890s battery-operated fans.

Other wants include: telephones, telegraphs, coin-operated machines, typewriters, old light bulbs, radios, medical quack devices, tin Vienna art, safety razors, patent models, early political campaign items, early American flags, Statue of Liberty models, circus items, boxing items, and old West gambling equipment. Contact us about your item.

H.J.H. Publications
Antiques & Collectibles
6731 Ashley Ct.
Sarasota, FL 34241
MR PROPANE@aol.com

Toasters	**We Pay**
Unusual Models	**50.00-500.00**
Porcelain Models	**1,000.00+**

I am buying **old electric fans with brass guards and brass blades.** Early fans with footed bases or tripod bases, bipolar fans (exposed coils), fans with unusual oscillating mechanisms such as flaps, veins lollipops, gyrating fans, etc., are wanted. Antique ornate ceiling fans are purchased as well. These may be round ball motor ceiling fans or mechanical belt-driven types.

Roger Anthony
23214 Whispering Willow Dr.
Spring, TX 77373
281-353-4576

We are looking for **glass kitchenware**. We like the opaque colors such as Jade-ite, delphite, ivory, etc. We are always looking for canisters with **good** lettering, rolling pins, mixing bowls, measuring cups, and pitchers, etc.

April and Larry Tvorak
P.O. Box 94
Warren Center, PA 18851
570-395-3775
april@epix.net

	We Pay
Canister, Jeanette, Jade-ite, tall sugar or coffee w/screw-on lid	**70.00-100.00**
Canister, Jeanette, Jade-ite, short tea w/screw-on lid	**40.00-60.00**
Canister, oval, transparent green, sugar or flour w/screw-on lid	**20.00-30.00**
Canister, McKee, Jade-ite w/glass lid	**25.00-30.00**
Canister, delphite blue, depending on size	**100.00-150.00**
Canister, spice (cinnamon, nutmeg, etc.), sm, ea	**40.00+**
Measuring Cup, Jade-ite, 3-spout	**85.00**
Refrigerator Water Jug, Jade-ite	**80.00-90.00**
Refrigerator Water Jug, Jade-ite, tall	**150.00+**

I am interested in several items:

Depression glass in apple green: rolling pin with screw-on wooden handles, a canning funnel, a spoon rest, and a wall-hung glass razor blade sharpener/stropper.
Depression glass in pink: straw holder, clocks, round furniture casters, lamps (especially heart-shaped valentine vanity and bed lamps)
Depression glass in pink or apple green: sugar shakers, cocktail shakers, wall pocket hanging vases, shaving mugs, wall-hung toothbrush holders, rosette-style cabinet knobs/drawer pulls, bobeche or prisms and their holders that fit onto candlesticks, faceted and pointed handle salad forks and spoon sets, covered batter jugs, covered cigarette boxes (also wanted in Mayfair/Peacock Blue color), vanity items (perfumes, colognes, powder puff boxes, vanity jar sets, tumble-ups, etc.)
Cambridge or Imperial Co.: Decagon keyhole handled items or footed nudes

(cigarette boxes, comports, candlesticks, etc.)
Hocking Co.: ribbed beer or coffee mugs
Crystal Co.: small wooden washboard with green glass insert
Lancaster Co.: Open Lace and Jubilee Blanks with curled feet items
Sneath Co.: ribbed, rectangular spice or canister jars with metal lids
Busy Betty child's toy washing machine with glass tub, pentagon-shaped handled scoops, small or large size, individual items wanted or sets
Westmoreland Co.: desk blotter set (or individual items as blotter corners, pencil tray, letter holder, ink well, postage stamp box)

All glass must be in excellent condition with no etched patterns. Please send a list and/or photo of what you have for sale and your asking price. I buy and sell. I would also be interested in finding some kitchen appliances from the 1930s. All appliances must be in excellent shape, but don't have to be in working order. Please send a list. I buy and sell.

Sunkist Jr. mixer juicer (combo mixer with beater blades and juicer)
Armstrong Co.'s Perc-O-Toaster (combo coffeepot and toaster)
Universal Co.'s ornate heart-shaped toaster with ivory handles
Magic Maid Co. yellow mixer and/or its miscellaneous attachments
Sunbeam Co. yellow Mixmaster with wood handle or no handle, and/or the coffee grinder or can opener attachments.

Mary Faria
P.O. Box 32321
San Jose, CA 95152-2321
408-258-0413

I love **anything in blue or blue and white.** Mixing bowls, canister sets, graniteware, utensils, glass, pottery, appliances, linens, dish towels, dishes, advertising, etc. I also like the **sky blue of Hall or Universal Crockery as well as their navy blue.** I need **70" or larger round tablecloths.**

Deborah Golden
3182 Twin Pine Rd.
Grayling, IL 49738
517-348-2610

I would like a **Gem doughnut machine** that need not be in working condition, but must be complete. **Gem doughnut machine advertising items of all types** are wanted as well. I will pay in a range from $50.00 to $100.00 for items I need.

Other interests include **Iowa chauffeur badges, Beretta handgun paper**

items for the years 1915 through the early 1960s, and any old advertising from Waterloo, Iowa, manufacturing companies.

Orrin E. Miller
1920 Franklin St.
Waterloo, IA 50703-5022

Lace, Linens, and Needlework Items

Vintage linens and lace items have been my passion for a number of years. I have a large personal collection, and I also buy items for resale. Items should be in very good condition, although I will sometimes purchase good quality items in need of minor repairs. Call, write, or e-mail if you would like to sell your items. I will need a detailed description, a color copy or photo of your item, and your asking price.

D.J. Malone
P.O. Box 1041
Fayetteville, AR 72702
501-442-4124
JaAntiques@aol.com

Lamps, Lanterns, and Lighting Fixtures

We buy select old lamps. We collect **unusual early oil lamps and the later electric Deco-type figural lamps**. Quality, condition, and rarity are important to us. The oil lamps with glass bowl and metal figural stems are fairly common, and it is the **all-glass lamps with figural stems** that we seek. We have written the books and collector manual-price guides for Aladdin kerosene and Aladdin electric lamps so we can help you identify and value them. We will buy certain ones needed for our collection. The lamps must be complete and in excellent working condition to bring the best prices. Write for free information on our books and annual antique lamp show and sale. Please describe your lamp (kind of glass, color, frost, etc.); photographs are very helpful.

J.W. 'Bill' and Treva Courter
3935 Kelley Rd.
Kevil, KY 42053
phone or fax 502-488-2116

I am buying gas light fixtures and gas shades, old electric fixtures, and electric shades. Both types of lighting came in single-arm style, two-arm style (or three-arm style, etc.) and are similar if not identical in appearance. Electric fixtures have sockets where the gas fixtures have a place for a burner and a key to turn the gas on and off. If you have parts — loose arms, tubing, escutcheons, globe holders (fitters) — anything that slides over the black pipe to cover it up or attaches to it then I would be interested. Gas burners of any kind as well as partial fixtures with an arm or tubing missing are okay. Any of these things that date from 1918 or before. Don't worry if you only have a few little things.

David Fox
522 E Kentucky St.
Louisville, KY 40203
502-583-7809

Fixtures & Parts	We Pay
Single Arm	**10.00+**
Two Arm	**12.00+**
Three Arm	**25.00+**
Four Arm	**45.00+**
4" Gas Shade	**8.00+**
5" Gas Shade	**12.00+**
3¼" Gas Shade	**5.00+**
2⅝" Gas Shade	**10.00+**
2¼" Electric Shade	**3.00+**
3" Electric Shade	**3.00+**
Shade Holders (Fitters), 4", 5", 3¼", 2⅝", 2¼", 3", ea	**3.00+**
Books, Trade Pamphlets	**5.00+**

We would like to buy **pre-1945 lighting fixtures** including shades for ceilings or walls. Art Deco figurals or any early lamps are sought. Lamps and lighting fixtures may be from the turn of the century. Glass step-in type shades are especially desired. We are interested in the unusual. Quality and condition are very important as is rarity. Rewiring is not a problem; however, all lighting must be complete (no missing parts). Before you replace your old fixtures, call us as we may be able to buy your new items for you.

Engelwood Antiques
2020 Townshop Rd.
Fall Creek, WI 54742
715-877-3468

Lefton

I am interested in purchasing Lefton china manufactured in the 1940s through 1960s. Please send photo or description of piece (or pieces) together with information about the fired-on mark (or paper label) with identification number (or numbers). The item must be in mint condition with no chips, cracks, or repairs. I have a lot of interest in dinnerware. Please write for information about my books, *Collector's Encyclopedia of Lefton China Books I and II* and *Lefton China Price Guide*, published by Collector Books of Paducah, Kentucky. Contact me about information about National Society of Lefton Collectors, a quarterly newsletter and annual convention.

Lefton China Collectibles
Loretta DeLozier
1101 Polk St.
Bedford, IA 50833
712-523-2289 or fax 712-523-2289
leftonlady@aol.com

License Plate Attachments

I collect cast aluminum license plate attachments also known as crests, piggybacks, and add-ons. These attachments were made of heavy sand-cast aluminum. The purpose of these crests was largely promotional. They were sold for about fifty-nine cents in all tourist meccas. Florida must have been like heaven for the traveling salesman who wrote orders for these crests. It seems every city and beach in Florida had a crest boasting its name and slogan. Examples would be 'Miami Beach,' 'Land of Sunshine,' or 'World's Playground.' They all seemed to have adornments flanking both sides of the name — for instance, 'Florida' with a palm tree on one side and a sailfish on the other.

I have sufficient 'Miami,' 'Miami Beach,' and 'Florida.' I want attachments from other Florida cities, towns, and beaches, as well as cities and towns from other states. I am paying $25.00 to $50.00 depending on rarity and condition. I will also consider broken ones if repairable. Please contact me for prices.

Edward Foley
129 Meadow Valley Rd., Lot #11
Ephrata, PA 17522
717-738-4813

License Plates and License Plate Key Chains

My wife and I would like to purchase the three **Tennessee car license plates listed below:**

1951 (the year I was born)
1958 (the year my wife was born)
1976 (the year we were married)

We want the plates to be in good condition as we want to hang them on the wall of our living room. We are willing to pay upwards to $25.00 per plate.

Eddie R. Davis
P.O. Box 1479
Morristown, TN 37816
423-587-1324 (work) or 423-581-6229 (home)
fax 423-586-8662
yes@lcs.net

I am seeking **key chain license plates** that were sent to the general population in all states from 1941 through 1975. My interest, however, is only for key chains **from 1941 through 1960.** Prices vary depending on rarity, condition, etc. A guide to prices would be somewhere in the $3.00 to $30.00 range.

Date, condition, and rarity are all contributing factors, bearing in mind that Illinois, New York, Ohio, and Pennsylvania are examples of the most common states; Delaware, Idaho, Montana, and Wyoming fall into the rarer category. Most low population states are sought after more aggressively. The three types of tags I'm looking for can be identified on the back by the wording: (1) Idento-Tag, (2) Disabled American Veterans, and (3) Goodrich. Rusty and damaged cases are of mild concern, but acceptable if insert is not damaged. Sometimes the D.A.V. tags are found on the original mailers which are desirable also. But vintage and rarity will play a part in the price paid. I respond to all mail and pay all postage.

Ed Foley
129 Meadow Valley Rd., Lot #11
Ephrata, PA 17522
717-738-4813

License Plates and License Plate Key Chains

I am buying mini license plate key chain tags such as **D.A.V., B.F. Goodrich. I-Dent-O-Tags, etc.** Of special interest are tags from the '40s and '50s as well as those from southern and western states. Prices paid depend on type, year, state, and condition. Most are from $4.00 to $7.00 — much more for B.F. Goodrich or rare tags.

I'm also interested in **pickle castors** (especially with colored, decorated glass). Silver-plated bases must be marked and the glass must be in excellent condition. Prices paid are generally from $200.00 to $500.00. Descriptions must be specific.

Virginia L. Young
15463 McNeil Rd.
Sterling, NY 13156
315-947-5840 (evenings before 9pm)

Lladro

We buy — or find buyers for — **Spanish Lladro porcelain figures and objects.** Our special interest is in the Collector's Society Members only 'annual editions' starting with the clowns issued in 1985 and 1986 and continuing to the present. We pay top prices for the annual club pieces and for selected other pieces.

All Lladro is marked on the bottom with the word Lladro etched into the porcelain (older items) or the blue-ink name and trademark (newer pieces). Every Lladro piece is identified by a four-digit numerical item number. The Collector's Society pieces we seek all have item numbers in the 7600 series. The item number is found on the box; numbers on the bottom of the piece itself are meaningless. All the prime pieces we buy have a special 'double-circle' identification on the bottom with the year printed in the circle. The circle imprint is about the size of a US quarter.

To receive top prices, pieces must have no damage and include the original box where possible. For selected pieces we may consider the purchase of damaged or broken pieces. Repairs should not be attempted; a broken item in pieces is worth more than a badly-repaired piece.

All Lladro porcelain is manufactured in Valencia, Spain, and the name Lladro appears on the bottom. A lower quality line of products with the trademark 'NAO' is also made by the Lladro company, however we **do not buy any NAO items.**

Charlotte Sanchez
Sanchez Collectibles
1555 East Glendale Ave.
Phoenix, AZ 85020
602-395-9974 or fax 602-241-0702
sanchcol@primenet.com

We Pay

#7600 Little Pals (1985), $95 original retail **1,200.00**
#7602 Little Traveler (1986), $95 original retail **600.00**
#5233 Charlie Chaplin (Tramp), $245 original retail **470.00**
#5057 Clown With Violin, $200 original retail **800.00**
RL-404 Girl at the Mirror (Norman Rockwell by Lladro), $450 original retail **900.00**

Limoges

Wanted: vases, jardinieres, punch bowl sets, and decorative hand-painted items. No plates, cups, or saucers please. Seeking only mint-condition pieces. Top dollar paid. Buyer pays shipping and will overnight cashier's check to you. Send photo and your price.

Holly Browning
13281 Heather Ridge Loop
Ft. Myers, FL 33912

Wanted: Limoges hand-painted porcelain pieces. Vases, punch bowls, cocoa sets, tea sets, dishes, plates, cups, and saucers are all wanted. I will pay over book price for large, perfect pieces.

d'Limoges An'tea'ques
20 Post Office Ave.
Andover, MA 01810
508-420-8773

Motorcycles

Wanted and paying cash for any **motorcycle parts, toys, pieces, old photos, frames, wheels, motors, gas tanks, front ends, speedometers — anything — even if broken or rusted**. Makes include American-made Harley, Pope, Thor, Thiem, Evans, Crocker, Racycle, Ace, Indian, Excelsior, Henderson, Arrow, Pierce, Cleveland, Merkel, Flying Merkel, Miami, Minneapolis, Marsh-Metz, Metz, Schickel, Yale, Franklin, Nera-Car, and Miller.

Please call or write. Items wanted include:

Motorcycles

Old Photos	Photo Postcards
Posters	Watch Fobs
Pocket Watches	Signs (porcelain, tin, wood)
Rings	Ribbons
Awards	F.A.M. Pins
Other Pins (1904–1965)	Gypsy Tour Items
Cloth Banners	Buttons
Old Match Safes	Oil Cans
Paint Cans	Display Cases
Paperweights	Dealer Items
Tools (wrenches, etc.)	Crates, Boxes
Pens, Pencils	Dealer Items

Old Riding Clothes (jackets, pants, etc.)
All Motorcycle License Plates (1916–1965, any state tags)
All Complete Machines, Parts, Pieces, and Side Cars
All Items Relating to American-Made Motorcycles (Ace, Indian, Emblem, etc.)

Tom Wilhelm
P.O. Box 534
Salisbury, NC 28145
704-647-0806
704-630-3818 (pager)

	We Pay
Award	25.00-50.00
Banner, cloth	100.00+
Clothing, old	25.00-300.00+
Display Case	100.00-1,000.00
Hat	75.00-100.00
Helmet	35.00-85.00
Oil Can, early	50.00-75.00
Motorcycle Tag	20.00-150.00
Pen	20.00-50.00
Photo, original only	10.00-200.00
Poster	75.00-300.00
Sign, neon	200.00-500.00
Toy, motorcycle	50.00-500.00
Watch Fob, FAM	75.00-100.00

Motorcycle memorabilia has been around as long as there have been motorcycles — about one hundred years. All types of advertising were used by the manufacturers to push their products. I am mainly looking for pennants, pocket mirrors, match safes, ashtrays, key fobs, pins, badges, and other items.

I also seek items related to the machines themselves such as oil and paint cans, tools, manuals and other literature, dealer items, and signs of tin, porcelain, or paper.

I am especially interested in **motorcycle club and gang memorabilia.** This includes AMA Gypsy Tour (and earlier) awards such as pins, fobs, jewelry, patches, pennants, programs, belt buckles, etc. Also wanted or any photographs and news clippings about clubs, plaques, banners, trophies, awards, club jackets with insignia or patches, courtesy cards, and nearly anything else.

Please send photocopy or good photograph (will be returned) of your items along with your asking price and accurate description of condition. Thanks.

Ed Natale
P.O. Box 222
Wyckoff, NJ 07481
201-848-8485

I would like to buy **1960s through 1970s motorcycle license plates.** Also wanted are **1970s Kawasaki parts or related items and aluminum BMX bikes by Kawasaki. Call evenings.**

Jeff
414-886-0477 CST

Movie Memorabilia

I collect *Gone With the Wind* memorabilia. I am searching for the following items. I am **not** looking for posters, lobby cards, or dolls. Also wanted is a Whiting & Davis 'Clark Gable' mesh purse.

Barb Kieffer
P.O. Box 429381
Cincinnati, OH 45242

	We Pay
Button, *Gone With the Wind* book shape, leather	**up to 5000.00**
Bookends, cast iron Scarlett & Rhett, pr	**up to 150.00**
Magazine, *Gone With the Wind* cover, early 1940s	**up to 75.00-100.00**

Pin, leather ....**up to 100.00**
Powder Box, Pinaud ....**up to 150.00**
Purse, Clark Gable, by Whiting & Davis **350.00**
Scarf ....**up to 75.00**

I still enjoy **buying, selling, and authenticating autographs, photos, documents, music, lobby cards, and posters** of:

Gershwin	Harlow
Berlin	Dashiell Hammett
Kern	Raymond Chandler
Porter	Ian Fleming
Beatles	Ernest Hemingway
Ellington	Nijinsky
Waller	Pavlova
Hendrix	Babe Ruth
Joplin	Lou Gehrig
Garbo	Weissmuller
Marilyn	Robinson
Bogart	Many others

Please let me know what you have available for sale. Note: **no Nazi or politicians wanted.**

Sigmund Goode
P.O. Box 878
Capt. Cook, HI 96704
phone/fax 808-328-8119 (8am–6pm my time)

I buy any movie theater glass slides and also advertising glass slides. These measure 4" by 3¼". I also buy **any kind of movie memorabilia for 3-D movies.** These items are marked 3-D or 3-Dimension and may be such items as lobby cards, posters, press books, etc.

Chris Perry, Doctor 3-D
7470 Church St. #A
Yucca Valley, CA 92284
760-365-0475 or fax 760-365-0495

Music Boxes and Devices

I am a private collector interested in purchasing **all types of antique musical boxes, phonographs, radios, etc.** Items wanted include horn phonographs, disk and cylinder music boxes, Victrolas, automatons, etc.

Jim Allen
420 S 46th St.
Lincoln, NE 86510
402-483-5789

I am looking for **table model wind-up phonographs with or without horns as well as their parts.** I also collect **phonograph-related items** such as advertising, record dusters, needle tins, cabinet keys, needle cutters, etc.

Hart Wesemann
399 North Main
Bountiful, UT 84010
801-295-7227

H.J.H. Publications, Antiques & Collectibles, has been active in publishing books on collectibles since 1987 and has purchased rare collectibles since 1971.

Of special interest are **phonographs made by Edison, Columbia, and Victor** — just to name a few. **Other wants include:** unusual and porcelain toasters, telephones, telegraphs, coin-operated machines, typewriters, sewing machines, old light bulbs, 1890s battery-operated fans, radios, medical quack devices, tin Vienna art, safety razors, patent models, early political campaign items, early American flags, Statue of Liberty models, circus items, boxing items, and old West gambling equipment.

H.J.H. Publications
Antiques & Collectibles
6731 Ashley Ct.
Sarasota, FL 34241
MR PROPANE@aol.com

Phonographs	**We Pay**
Edison Spectacle Machine Class S	**25,000.00**
Edison Water Power	**25,000.00**

Edison Idelia	**10,000.00**
Columbia Bell Tainter, any model	**10,000.00**
Victor Model D	**2,500.00**
Victor Model B	**4,500.00**
Victor Model A	**3,500.00**

Music Memorabilia

I would like to buy **New Wave and Punk Rock items from 1975 through 1983**. I'm looking for records (picture discs, 45 rpm records with picture sleeves, EP records, bootlegs, and rare stuff), promotional novelties such as DEVO plastic hair, clothes, etc., and some posters.

I am desperately seeking the soundtrack to a movie called *Ladies and Gentlemen: The Fabulous Stains*. Also wanted is the original *Valley Girl* soundtrack and a *Bow Wow Wow* EP (with C30., C60., C90., Go!). I am interested in **anything pertaining to Lou Reed, Velvet Underground, Iggy Pop, and stuff from Andy Warhol's Factory days.** I have interest in many groups from this era so give me a call or write!

Barbara Brecker
76 Sicard St.
New Brunswick, NJ 08901
888-532-8697 or 732-246-1589
SalandRei@aol.com

	We Pay
Fabulous Stains Soundtrack	**30.00**
Other Records	**Call or Write**
Novelty Items	**Call or Write**

Nippon

Wanted are **all types of vases, urns, plaques, and unusual Nippon pieces.** Hand-painted scenes, coralene, and molded-in-relief pieces are most desirable. Pieces must be in excellent condition. No cracks, chips, or heavily-worn items wanted, please. High prices paid. Send photo for our review and we will return it along with your asking price. We pay all shipping charges and will overnight a cashiers check to you.

H. Browning
13281 Heather Ridge Loop
Ft. Myers, FL 33912

Noritake

I am buying **Deco Noritake**. I especially want figural lady pieces, lamps, powder puffs, and large figurals. I am the president of the Noritake Collector's Club and a member of the Nippon Collector's Club. I have a large group of friends and acquaintances who are also looking for specific pieces and will make contacts for you. I am only interested in pieces that are in excellent condition and that are clearly marked Noritake. I do not follow the price guides and will pay much more or less depending upon rarity and condition. I am **not interested in dinnerware.**

Timothy Trapani
145 Andover Pl.
West Hempstead, NY 11552
516-292-8355 (after 4 pm EST)

Noritake (Deco)	**We Pay**
Powder Puffs, Deco women	**150.00+**
Figural Lamps	**1,000.00+**
Gemini Bowls	**1,000.00**
Lady on a Chair Box	**1,500.00+**
Lady Figural Bowls & Dishes	**175.00+**
Indian Princess	**1,000.00+**
Deco Punch Bowls or Sets	**600.00+**
Sisters Bowl	**1,000.00+**

North Dakota Collectibles

We live in a small rural community in southwest North Dakota and are interested in buying **items originating in North Dakota, South Dakota, and Montana prior to the 1950s.** Wanted are souvenir items with town names (especially North Dakota towns of Bowman, Rhame, Marmarth, Scranton, Reeder, Amidon, Haley, and Griffin).

Items of most interest with these names are souvenir glassware items in red, green, blue, or white; advertising mirrors; and crocks. No alcohol or tobacco promotional items wanted please. We also buy **Dakota Territory memorabilia, small artifacts or cavalry items, books by North Dakota or regional authors, pottery by Messer (see Pottery in this book), and old salt and pepper collections.**

We pay from $10.00 to $100.00 for most items with no cracks or chips. Please send a photo or a detailed description. We will try to pay your asking price, or we will make you an offer.

Please see our listing under Pottery in this book for more wants. Thank you.

Stan and Carrie Soderstrom
15 First St. SW
Bowman, ND 58623
701-523-5717

Optical

I am buying **eyeglasses and other eye wear.** I prefer items from the **1700s through the 1920s** — one piece or a collection. I also look for **unique opera glasses.**

Kayla Conway
4500 Napal Ct.
Bakersfield, CA 93307

Outboard Boat Motors

I collect all **toy metal outboard boat motors**. These may be electric, tin windup, steam powered, or gas powered. Most of these motors were made in Japan from 1955 to 1970 by KO. I want nice, clean motors with no repaints or chipped paint. No plastic motors are wanted. I will pay 10% extra if you have the original box. Also wanted are **gas-powered race cars.**

Richard Gronowski
140 N Garfield Ave.
Traverse City, MI 49686-2802
616-491-2111

	We Pay
Evinrudes, 40 HP or 75 HP, ea	125.00
Gale Sovereign, 60 HP	200.00
Gale, 30 HP or 35 HP, ea	125.00
Johnsons, 40 HP or 75 HP, ea	125.00
Oliver, 35 HP	200.00
Mercury, black, 100 HP	200.00
Mercury, MK 55, MK 800, MK 78 or MK 75, ea	125.00
All Other Johnsons, Mercurys, Scotts, Evinrudes, Gales, ea	75.00
Sea-Fury	75.00
Sea-Fury Twin	150.00
Fuji or Orkin, ea	125.00
Tin Winups, ea	75.00
Generic's I.M.P, Langcraft, Yamaha, Super Tigre, Speed King, Sakai, New Evince, Le-Page, Swank, Aristocraft, Etc., ea	50.00

Padlocks

I am presently buying **padlocks** for my collection. Some of my main interests are as follows:

Round push key locks of all brass; most are four-lever, five-lever, six-lever, or eight-lever; some have a university, business, or express logo
1904 World's Fair lock with brass plates on both sides
Hardware company locks such as Belknap (Blue Grass); Bindey; Bingham; Hibbard, Spencer, Bartlett (OVB); John Pritzloff (Pritzloff); Norvell-Shapeleigh (Shapeleigh); Marshall-Wells (Zenith)
Locks marked Beaver, Badger, Big Five, Gopher, Marswells, Mars, Wells, Watchman, Gibralter, E.C. Simmons, Keen Kutter, Supplee Biddle, and Winchester Repeating Arms

I pay 90% of book price. For example, if a lock book price is $60.00, I'll pay $54.00. Please write and tell me about the items you have.

Wilmer Lee Barnoz
1137 Frank Ave.
Huron, SD 57350

Paper and Ephemera

Dear Friend — this is a list of mainly paper items that I always buy. If you have anything on this list please send me a brief description (title, condition, date, number) for my immediate offer. (If this is too much trouble merely pack everything up and mail for full payment, same day received!) I pay generously for everything I need and do repeat business with most sellers (since 1964). If required, bank and trade references are available, so deal in total confidence. If you have any questions, feel free to phone me. Thank you.

Comic Books: 1900–1960s (these have mainly 10¢ and 12¢ cover prices, Giants 25¢), but I will consider higher-condition 1970s (15¢ and 20¢ cover price primarily). Duplicates are okay. Lesser condition comics have little value but if pre-1960, send. If you are not sure about dates, or anything, don't worry about it; I'll appraise.

Big Little Books: 1933–1950. Those fat little books about 3" x 5" with titles like Flash Gordon, Dick Tracy, Tarzan, Buck Rogers, etc. Publishers were mostly Whitman and Saalfield although there were others. Note: any with missing pages or covers have no value.

Sunday Comic Pages and Complete Comic Sections: 1880–1960s. On complete sections, I'd like to know what strips, number of pages, condition, and date. Loose pages are harder to assess. Merely do the best you can, or quite simply: shoot the works to me and trust my generosity. (This has worked out very well.)

Walt Disney Books, Magazines, Comic Books, Etc.: 1928–1950s. All old Disney paper items are wanted. Publishers include David McKay, Whitman, Blue Ribbon, and others.

Pulp Magazines: 1930s–1940s. Those magazines printed on cheap paper with titles such as Doc Savage, The Shadow, Spider, G-8, air, horror, and spicy titles. (No others wanted.)

Song Magazines: 1920s–1960s. These were mainly words only with titles such as *Song Hits, Songs That Will Live Forever, 400 Songs, Hit Paraders*, etc. Anything with song lyrics (not music) is wanted. Lesser condition is acceptable on these.

Radio, TV, Cereal Premiums: 1930s–1950s. Items such as decoders, rings, pin-back buttons, badges, booklets; characters as Buck Rogers, Captain Midnight, Orphan Annie, Tom Mix; ads found in newspapers and other publications — all these and others wanted.

Cards (Gum, Candy, Sports): 1930s–1960s. Give company, date, condition or send.

Music (Popular, Jazz) Magazines and Books: 1920s to present.

Original Comic Book and Comic Strip Art

Books by L. Frank Baum, E.R. Burroughs; Pop-Up Books

Personality-Related Items: Including magazines, books, and toys relating to Marilyn Monroe, Elvis, James Dean, John Wayne, Shirley Temple, Superman, etc.

To speed delivery please indicate 'gift' on parcel and place a value of $20.00 or less on each parcel. Do not put invoice or letter in parcels. Please send via post office cheapest way (I'm in no hurry). Please pack well, with newspapers, as the mail can be rough.

A finder's fee will be paid to you if you put me in touch with a prospective seller. I do professional appraisals. For more information, please contact me.

I offer 100% satisfaction on all transactions. (I always have and always will.) I look forward to doing business with you. Incidently, Willowdale is a suburb of Toronto, which is 90 minutes from Buffalo, 3½ hours from Detroit; for those with a truck full of items to sell who want to bring them in personally, which is also okay with me.

Ken Mitchell
710 Conacher Dr.
Willowdale, Ontario
Canada M2M 3N6
416-222-5808

I buy **paper**. Almost anything before 1950 can have value. Before you throw away what may be a treasure, contact me or ship for my offer by check. I pay all return shipping costs if offer is not accepted. No high pressure. If I'm not interested in purchasing, I may be able to put you in touch with other dealers or auction houses.

I will always pay a minimum of 3 to 10 cents each for pre-1950 envelopes with stamps attached. 1,000s needed. Will pay much more for specific items. Don't toss out great Aunt Millie's correspondence or that accumulation of old letters. It could be your retirement. I will travel to see larger holdings. Prefer contents intact but not necessary.

Remember: anything paper, pre-1950s – calendars, schedules, comic books, business cards, stamps, magazines, checks, stock and bonds, affadavits, trading cards, deeds, newspapers, catalogs, autographs, brochures, postcards, labels, pictures, books, greeting cards, games, event tickets, and more – anything paper, pre-1950.

Wolf Berry, The Paper Wolf
3 Maple St.
Canisteo, NY 14823-1317
607-324-2000 (work)
607-324-2001 (fax)
607-698-4943 (home)
berrywein@webtv.net
APS #189125

Paper Money

We are major buyers of **all types and designs of large-size US currency issued between 1862 and 1923**. Of particular interest are the 'home town' national bank notes issued by the US government but bearing the name of the local national bank and signed by the bank cashier and president. A few examples are listed below. Please call or write on any notes not listed. Naturally, condition is very important. Prices listed are for clean, bright, undamaged specimens. Badly worn and damaged notes are worth less. Superb examples are worth much more.

Glenn G. Wright
P.O. Box 311
Campellsport, WI 53010
800-303-8248
Our 38th Year

US Large-Size Currency	We Pay
1862 $1 US Note	100.00+
1875 (or earlier) $1 National Bank Note	100.00+
1875 (or earlier) $2 National Bank Note	400.00+
1901 $10 US Note	250.00+
1896 $1 Silver Certificate	125.00+
1896 $2 Silver Certificate	225.00+
1896 $5 Silver Certificate	350.00+
1899 $5 Silver Certificate	225.00+
1923 $5 Silver Certificate	200.00+
1891 $100 Silver Certificate	2,000.00+
1890 $100 Treasury Note	10,000.00+
1886 $5 Silver Certificate	275.00+
1875 (or earlier) $10 National Bank Note	150.00+
1875 (or earlier) $20 National Bank Note	300.00+
1882 $5 National Bank Note	50.00+
1882 $10 National Bank Note	60.00+
1902 $5 National Bank Note (red Treasury seal)	50.00+
1882 $20 Gold Certificate	200.00+
1882 $50 Gold Certificate	450.00+
1882 $100 Gold Certificate	350.00+
1922 $10 Gold Certificate	35.00+
1922 $20 Gold Certificate	80.00+
1922 $50 Gold Certificate	250.00+
1922 $100 Gold Certificate	225.00+
1922 $500 Gold Certificate	2,500.00+

US Small-Size Currency	We Pay
1928B $2 US Note	**10.00+**
1928C $1 Silver Certificate	**25.00+**
1928E $1 Silver Certificate	**80.00+**
1933 $10 Silver Certificate	**1,200.00+**
1928 through 1934 $500 Federal Reserve Note	**550.00+**
1928 through 1934 $1,000 Federal Reserve Note	**1,060.00+**
1928 $500 Gold Certificate	**800.00+**
1928 $1,000 Gold Certificate	**1,500.00+**

Paperweights

Collector and author (*The Dictionary of Paperweight Signature Canes*, Paperweight Press, 1977) desires antique (pre-1900s) glass paperweights: French, American, English, and Bohemian. Millefiori, flowers, and fruit designs are preferred. Also desire modern, artist-signed paperweights such as Stankard, Ysart, and Kaziun as well as modern Baccarat, St. Louis, and Perthshire limited edition paperweights. **Pre-1966** *Paperweight Collector Association (PCA) Bulletins* **and other books desired**.

Private collector buying one paperweight or entire collections. On older paperweights, surface wear and minor chips to the base are not a problem. Please write or call first with description or photo together with your asking price.

Andrew H. Dohan
20 Chester County Commons
Malvern, PA 19355-1942
610-722-5800
Dohan@juno.com or ahdegd@aol.com

Passports

I am a hobby collector of **expired passports from the world over.** Historically, these have come in two basic forms: the folio document sheets were used until the mid-1920s, and then the booklet types came into use as we know them today. Passports have a long and interesting history and each one tells a story. I have established one of the first grading systems for this young hobby which so far is narrowly traded.

I collect passports for my interest in geography, travel, history, and heraldic coats of arms. I am also in constant contact with the Passport

Historical Research and Preservation Society in Belgium.

I pay a range of $5.00 to $25.00 **for passports, depending on country, type, condition, and age. ($10.00 is the average price.) More specifically, I collect** pre-1950 US and outdated foreign passports of any year. Cancellations are okay. I pay a premium for special edition/special-use passports. All that I buy must be outdated. I suggest you send a photocopy when writing.

David McDonald Yawn
Employee Communications
P.O. Box 727
Memphis, TN 38194-1712
901-922-1447
editorwriter@hotmail.com

Passports	**We Pay**
US Passports, 1946-1950, ea	**5.00**
US Passports, 1925-1945, ea	**$12.00**
US Passports, 1915-1925, ea	**15.00**
US Passports, before 1915, ea	**18.00-25.00**
Foreign Passports, after 1940, ea	**5.00-10.00**
Foreign Passports, before 1940, ea	**12.00-15.00**
Other Foreign Passports, small or now nonexistant countries, depending on date, ea	**12.00-15.00**

Pencil Sharpeners

I am looking for **pocket pencil sharpeners made of pot metal or Bakelite plastic**. I am especially seeking figural and comic character sharpeners. They can be marked US, Occupied Japan, Japan, German, or Bavaria. Paint and decals must be in good to mint condition.

Phil Helley
629 Indiana Ave.
Wisconsin Dells, WI 53965
608-254-8658

	We Pay
Airplane, Bakelite	**29.00**
Armored Car, metal on rubber wheels, w/whistle, Japan	**60.00**

Charlie McCarthy, Bakelite **36.00**
Cinderella, decal on Bakelite, round **27.00**
Donald Duck, Bakelite **40.00**
Dog, metal, German **40.00**
Drummer Musician, metal, German **30.00**
Indian Chief, metal, Occupied Japan **45.00**
Magnifying Glass w/3 Kittens, metal, German **55.00**
Mickey Mouse, Bakelite **50.00**
New York World's Fair, Bakelite **35.00**
Nude Boy w/Silver Cap, metal, German **40.00**
Popeye, decal on Bakelite, rectangular **32.00**
Scottie Dog, Bakelite **16.00**
Tank, Keep 'Em Rolling, Bakelite **30.00**

Old mechanical, cast-iron pencil sharpeners and pointers are wanted. **Turn-of-the-century models with complex mechanisms** often featuring chain drives, spinning blades, and fancy iron work bodies are sought. Some used sandpaper disks and drums. I do **not** want any which resemble in any way the type of pencil sharpener you may have on your desk. If it looks bizarre, I want it! For machines in mint condition I will pay $150.00 for a US Automatic, a front wheel Jupiter, or a Planetary. Others may be higher. I am particularly interested in Dixon, Angell, and Sibley models. See my web site: http://www.every-era.com

Roger Graham
Every Era Antiques
855 57th St.
Sacramento, CA 95819
916-456-1767

Pendelfin Rabbit Figurines

I am interested in purchasing quality **Pendelfin figurines and display pieces retired prior to 1975.** Quality and condition are extremely important. Please send description and asking price. I will respond to all inquiries.

George Sparacio
P.O. Box 791
Malaga, NJ 08328
609-694-4167 or fax 609-694-4536
mrvesta@compuserve.com

Pepsi-Cola

We buy **pre-1965 Pepsi-Cola advertising memorabilia** in excellent to mint condition. Areas of interest include calendars; tin, porcelain, cardboard, and paper signs; diecuts and window displays; festoons; light-up signs; playing cards; clocks; thermometers; trays; salesman samples and miniatures; trucks and toys; etc. Our experience includes over ten years of collecting soda-pop memorabilia, editors for several antique and advertising price guides, and writers of a monthly column dedicated to soft drink collectibles. As collectors we can offer top dollar for quality pieces and collections. Condition and rarity are important factors that must be taken into consideration when determining the value of an item. We are willing to travel to purchase items or pay for shipping and handling. Besides purchasing for our collection, we assist in determining the authenticity, age, and value of items at no charge. Please feel free to call us or write with your inquiries. A clear photograph is always helpful for a quick response.

Craig and Donna Stifter
P.O. Box 6514
Naperville, IL 60540
630-789-5780

	We Pay
1941 Calendar, complete pad	**200.00+**
1951 Calendar, cardboard w/tear-off day pad	**400.00+**
1940 Sign, cardboard, self-framed, 24x34"	**400.00+**
1951 Sign, cardboard w/easel back, When Folks Drop In, 19x21"	**75.00+**
1948 Cut-Out Display, Girl in Window, cardboard w/real curtains at window	**450.00+**
1945 Cut-Out Display, cardboard showing 4 fountain glasses, 12x18"	**250.00+**
1936 Sign, tin showing bottle, 11x49"	**300.00+**
1967 Sign, Say Pepsi Please, shows bottle & logo	**100.00+**
1950 Sign, More Bounce to the Ounce!, porcelain, 18x48"	**400.00+**
1950 Sign, Drink Pepsi-Cola Now!, celluloid, 9" dia	**100.00+**
1945 Sign, die-cut 3-dimensional tin crown, 31" dia	**175.00+**
1940 Glass Mirror Sign w/Thermometer, shows girl at bottom, 8x18"	**300.00+**

1954 Light-Up Sign, multipurpose shadow box design, 19x9" .... 350.00+
1942 Thermometer, Bigger & Better, shows bottle, 16" .... 175.00+
1939 Serving Tray, Bigger & better, Coast To Coast .... 300.00+
Toy Truck, friction powered, Japan, 9" long .... 125.00+
1945 Toy Hot Dog Wagon, plastic, 7x6" .... 125.00+
1955 Clock, Say Pepsi Please, neon light, 36" dia .... 600.00+
1961 Clock, Think Young — Say Pepsi Please!, double-bubble glass, 5" dia .... 500.00+
1940 Salesman Sample Cooler, 10x8" .... 1,000.00+
1940 Festoon, 7 pieces showing Pepsi & Pete .... 900.00+

Perfume Bottles

We purchase **perfume bottles of all types**: miniatures, Czechoslovakian crystal bottles, Baccarat, Lalique, DeVilbiss atomizers, and commercial perfume bottles. Commercial bottles are these that originally contained perfume when they were sold, such as Matchabelli Windsong in a small crown-shaped bottle. Commercial bottles should, if possible, have a label and the original box.

Monsen and Baer
Box 529
Vienna, VA 22183
703-938-2129 or 703-242-1357

Miniatures — **We Pay**

Czechoslovakian, crystal, 2" .... 25.00+
Dior, Schiaparelli, Guerlain or Coty .... 5.00+
Ceramic, metal crown top .... 40.00+

Atomizers — **We Pay**

DeVilbiss, 6" .... 100.00+
Volupte, 5" .... 75.00+

Lalique — **We Pay**

Most 1930s or Before .... 500.00+
D'Orsay, black glass, Ambre d'Orsay .... 500.00+
Molinard Calendal Nudes .... 500.00+
Roger & Gallet Le Jade, green glass .... 1,500.00+

Perfume Bottles

Commercial	We Pay
Vigny Le Golliwogg	100.00+
Hattie Carnegie, bust of woman	100.00+
Ciro Chevalier, knight, black glass, in box	150.00+
Schiaparelli, Zut, woman's torso, in box	600.00+
Schiaparelli, Success, Fou, green leaf, in box	800.00+
Lucretia, Vanderbilt, blue glass, in box	750.00+

Baccarat	We Pay
Elizabeth Arden, It's You, hand	800.00+
Houbigant, Buddha, in box	200.00+
Ybry, green square	200.00+
Ybry, purple or orange square	500.00+
Christian Dior, Diorissimo, in box	2,000.00+
Christian Dior, dog	5,000.00+

Perfumes by Bourjois Perfume Company are wanted. I buy unusual presentations or rare single bottles of any fragrance produced by the Bourjois Company. I also buy **paper items such as catalogs, display stands, and any other promotional material from the company.** I am also buying **their compacts, lipsticks, and other cosmetic items.** The Bourjois Company produced the famous blue bottles of Evening in Paris. They also produced about one hundred other fragrances.

Beverly Nelson
1010 Lorna St.
Corona, CA 91720
909-737-0977
nelac@earthlink.net

Pez Dispensers

I collect **Pez dispensers from before 1985.** I am looking for **any Pez-related items** as well. **No Pez with feet (tabs at the bottom) except wolves from 1984 Sarajevo Olympics wanted.** Also I'm interested in broken Pez and Pez parts as well such as look-alikes such as Yummies, Totems, TV Pals, Fruit-Heads, and Ziffers. I am paying great prices! Call, e-mail, or write!

David Gross
76 Sicard St.
New Brunswick, NJ 08901
888-532-8697 or 732-246-1589
SalandRei@aol.com

Phonographs and Music Devices

I am a private collector interested in purchasing **all types of antique musical boxes, phonographs, radios, etc.** Items wanted include horn phonographs, disk and cylinder music boxes, Victrolas, automatons, etc.

Jim Allen
420 S 46th St.
Lincoln, NE 86510
402-483-5789

I am looking for **table model wind-up phonographs with or without horns as well as their parts.** I also collect **phonograph-related items** such as advertising, record dusters, needle tins, cabinet keys, needle cutters, etc.

Hart Wesemann
399 North Main
Bountiful, UT 84010
801-295-7227

H.J.H. Publications, Antiques & Collectibles, has been active in publishing books on collectibles since 1987 and has purchased rare collectibles since 1971.

Of special interest are **phonographs by Edison, Columbia, and Victor** — just to name a few. **Other wants include:** unusual and porcelain toasters, telephones, telegraphs, coin-operated machines, typewriters, sewing machines, old light bulbs, 1890s battery-operated fans, radios, medical quack devices, tin Vienna art, safety razors, patent models, early political campaign items, early American flags, Statue of Liberty models, circus items, boxing items, and old West gambling equipment.

H.J.H. Publications
Antiques & Collectibles
6731 Ashley Ct.
Sarasota, FL 34241
MR PROPANE@aol.com

Phonographs	**We Pay**
Edison Spectacle Machine Class S	**25,000.00**
Edison Water Power	**25,000.00**
Edison Idelia	**10,000.00**
Columbia Bell Tainter, any model	**10,000.00**
Victor Model D	**2,500.00**
Victor Model B	**4,500.00**
Victor Model A	**3,500.00**

Photographica

We are looking to purchase **all types of photographic equipment and photo-related items.** We are in the market for cameras, lenses, tripods, toys, figurines, photos, and books. Any item that relates to photography is wanted. Prices will vary due to condition and working order of the items. Send make, model, condition, and a brief description of your item; a photograph is helpful and will be returned. Send SASE to receive a quicker response.

HM Collectibles
3457 Julington Ck. Rd.
Jacksonville, FL 32223
hforsythe@ilnk.com

I am buying **original Civil War images and ephemera through the 1880s** in the following formats: CDV's (carte de viste), tintypes (in or out of cases), ambrotypes, daguerrotypes, and the hard (gutta percha) cases. Also wanted are **original Civil War papers, dug artifacts, guns, accoutrements, and autographs of notable Civil War generals** from the North and South. The price I pay depends on condition of the item, content of the image, and if the image is identified, etc. The better the condition, and especially if it is identified to a soldier, the more I pay. I am also interested in trades and carry a large selection of images for purchase. I will do appraisals on same and also do research on names from the Civil War period.

Shades of Blue & Gray
Dan Furtak
3543 S Ferguson
Springfield, MO 65807
417-887-0009
dugspring@worldnet.att.net
http://home.att.net/~dugspring/

Images	We Pay
CDV's	**5.00-5,000.00**
Ambrotypes	**5.00- 5,000.00**
Daguerrotypes	**5.00-5,000.00**
Signed Documents of Notable Civil War Figures	**10.00-10,000.00**

I buy **all kinds of stereocards** but my favorite subjects are World's Fairs, Hollywood, movie theaters, Art Deco, and anything relating to movies. I buy many kinds of boxed sets. I will pay $400 for the ten stereoview set for *The Phantom of the Opera* with Lon Chaney.

Chris Perry, Doctor 3-D
7470 Church St. #A
Yucca Valley, CA 92284
760-365-0475 or fax 760-365-0495

Pie Birds

I am an advanced pie bird collector searching for **old pie birds** (see listing below, these are just a few of the ones I seek). I will consider any pie birds (in bird shapes only please) that you have to offer and will answer all letters. If you would like to information about the pie bird club, Pie Birds Unlimited, the biennial convention, or 'Four & Twenty Blackbirds' (a pictorial identification and value guide) please let me hear from you.

Linda Fields
158 Bagsby Hill Ln.
Dover, TN 37058
615-232-5099 (after 6 pm)
Fpiebird@compu.net

Pie Birds	We Pay
Brown Body Cleminson Rooster	75.00
Camark Cobbler Bird, any color	100.00+
Donald Duck, w/Walt Disney over arch	500.00
Miniature Crow, TG Green, 2¼"	50.00
Morton Rooster, pink & blue, lg	75.00
Puff Chested Canary	50.00
Rooster, marked Italy	50.00
White-Bodied, Black-Headed Bird, w/wide mouth	35.00
White Rooster, w/bright Mexican colors	50.00
Yellow Headed Broad-back Crow	25.00

Political

Political buttons of all kinds, new and old, are collectible, but the most desirable are the celluloid-coated pin-back buttons (cellos) produced for presidential campaigns between 1896 and 1920. Many of these are attractively and colorfully designed, which enhances their value. Most buttons since 1920 have been produced by lithography directly on metal discs (lithos).

Collectors generally favor presidential buttons — especially picture pins from 1960 or earlier. Jugates, which feature presidential and vice-presidential candidates' pictures, are especially desirable; for example, James Cox-Franklin D. Roosevelt jugates from the 1920 campaign sell for up to $50,000.00! There are, however, numerous other specialties within the hobby, including state and local, third party, and 'cause' items. Political items made before 1896, including medallions, ribbons, and small photographs in inscribed frames or cases, are also very collectible, and some command high prices.

Value depends on scarcity, historical significance, design, collector demand, and condition — buttons with cracks, gouges, deep scratches, and/or rust-colored stains (foxing) lose most or all of their value. Reproductions exist, and many are marked as such, but some expertise is often needed to distinguish real from fake.

I will purchase **quality items in any of the categories listed below** if they are in collectible condition. Send me a photocopy of whatever you have. If you wish, state your price; if not, I will make an offer. I will respond to all correspondence whether or not I purchase your items (include a reply postcard or stamped envelope). If I do not want to buy, I will give an informal appraisal. The price ranges below are for *picture pins only* in excellent condition.

Michael Engel
29 Groveland St.
Easthampton, MA 01027
413-527-8733
IWWlives@aol.com

Presidentials, 1896–1960	**We Pay**
McKinley, Bryan, T Roosevelt, Taft, Wilson, sm picture buttons	**5.00+**
McKinley, Bryan, T Roosevelt, Taft, Wilson, lg picture buttons/jugates	**15.00+**
Parker, Hughes, sm picture buttons	**5.00-20.00+**
Parker, Hughes, lg picture buttons/jugates	**25.00-500.00+**
Harding, Coolidge, sm picture buttons	**5.00-20.00+**
Harding, Coolidge, lg picture buttons/jugates	**100.00-500.00+**
Cox, picture buttons	**50.00-100.00+**
Davis, picture buttons	**100.00+**
Hoover, Smith, picture buttons	**5.00-20.00+**
Hoover, Smith, jugates	**100.00+**
FDR, Landon, Willkie, picture buttons	**5.00-20.00+**
FDR, Landon, Willkie, jugates	**10.00-50.00+**
Truman, picture buttons	**10.00+**
Truman, jugates	**100.00+**
Stevenson, Eisenhower, JFK	**2.00-10.00+**

Other Categories	**We Pay**
Pre-1896 Items	**25.00+**
Third Party Candidates, pre-1960	**10.00+**
State & Local, pre-1920	**2.00-10.00**
Woman's Suffrage	**25.00+**
Civil Rights/Vietnam	**2.00-10.00**
Eugene V Debs	**75.00+**

Political

I am a collector and dealer in **political campaign collectibles of all types but in particular political campaign buttons/pins from all eras**. I will buy single pieces or entire collections. Please send photocopy of the item or (if too large to photocopy) a word description and the price you want for the item. Top prices are paid for all types of political campaign items: buttons/pins, posters, 3-D items (dolls, banks, etc.), presidential seal items, brochures, and anything that was used in political campaigns — especially for President but local offices are also of interest.

Ronald E. Wade
2100 Lafayette Dr.
Longview, TX 75601
903-236-9615

	We Pay
Button, Kennedy-Doolan, words only	**35.00**
Button, Nixon for Governor, w/red, white & black photo	**65.00**
Button, Not for Sale, Nixon for President, photo White House	**100.00+**
Button, Ford — Its a Better Idea on Republican elephant, 1976, red, white & blue	**100.00**
Button, Texans for Ford w/Texas outline, red, white & blue	**25.00**
Button, Draft Bush US Senate, Texas, 1964, blue & yellow, 1½"	**150.00**
Button/Pin, any Eugene V Debs for President, good condition	**100.00**
Land-On Washington, photo Alf Landon, red, white & blue	**750.00+**
Button, Time for a Change, I Like Ike, shows baby	**100.00**
Button, outline of Texas w/Ike (Eisenhower), 3"	**250.00**
Button/3-D Item from 1928 Houston Democratic National Convention	**100.00+**
Poster, George Bush for Congress, Houston, 1966	**100.00**
Poster, Lyndon B Johnson for Congress, Texas, 1937	**500.00**

Postcards

We purchase **postcards of all ages and types, good-plus condition only.** Complete collections, accumulations, single cards, old store stock, inventories — all are acceptable. Foreign, chromes, real photos, topicals, greetings, state views are purchased as well as top-of-the-line signed artists, poster art, Art Nouveau, Santa, and especially Halloween. Call us!

Chris Russell & The Halloween Queen Antiques
Pamela E. Apkarian-Russell, The Halloween Queen
P.O. Box 499
Winchester, N.H. 03470
603-239-8875

	We Pay
Art Nouveau Cards by Alphonse Mucha	**25.00-100.00**
Cards Depicting the Armenian Holocaust	**20.00+**
Italina Artist-Signed Cards	**5.00+**
Linen Cards of Black People	**1.00+**
Silk-Suited Santa Cards	**15.00**
Winch Publishing Halloween Cards	**35.00**
Real Photo Cards of Main, USA, Streets (depending on town)	**2.00-10.00**
Real Photo Cards of Black People	**5.00+**
Real Photo Cards of Movie Actresses or Actors (Shirley Temple, Marilyn Monroe, Josephine Baker, Louis Armstrong, etc.)	**5.00-40.00**
Views of Tourist Sights (mountains, lakes, monuments or cathedrals), per thousand	**5.00**
Views of Lg Cities (London, Paris, New York, Boston, etc.), per thousand	**5.00**

I would like to have **old postcards or real photos of railroad depots located in Ohio.** Views wanted include those from Leonardsburg, Eden Lewis Center, White Sulphur, Berlin Station, Tank Town in Delaware County along with New Dover in Union County. I will pay $25.00 and up for postcards I don't have in my collection. Please send photocopy and describe.

R. Edmonds
#98 Renner St.
Delaware, OH 43015

Wanted: **postcards (1910–1920), letters, and ephemera about Ella Wheeler Wilcox,** 'laugh and the world laughs with you, cry....' Please contact us about your items.

John and Charlotte Hanson
1318 Camden Lane
Ventura, CA 93001
805-643-2869

Help me find **old Hawaiian cards** to ad to my collection! Photocopy your cards; it is a good way to show your items. Send information about condition and postmark (if used). I will pay $1.00 to $2.00 each for unused Hawaiian postcard.

Helianthus
P.O. Box 262
River Falls, WI 54022

Wanted to buy are **large holdings of small towns in New Jersey, Pennsylvania, upstate New York, and Brooklyn.** I want real photo postcards for resale.

Elly Opps
7426 Amboy Rd.
Staten Island, NY 10307

Wanted: **Prairie Du Chien, Wisconsin, postcards from before 1950**. I pay about $1.00 each. Also wanted are **Old Sleepy Eye postcards.** Tell me about your items.

Checks Antiques
Janice Check
115 S Dousman St.
Prairie Du Chien, Wi 53821
608-326-6014

Posters

Vintage posters featuring travel, products, sports, and transportation are bought. I am especially interested in **early 20th-century American posters** with artists such as Ragan, Penfield, Muchley, Reed, and others. I will also buy **poster books, catalogs, and other ephemera associated with posters and poster production.** European, Russian, and Asian posters are also wanted. Entire collections purchased. Describe image, main text line, size, artist, and condition to receive my offer. I will pay $1,000.00 for certain posters by Leslie Ragan. Many posters are worth as much as $5,000.00. Visit my web site at http://www.every-era.com.

Roger Graham, Every Era Antiques
855 57th St.
Sacramento, CA 95819
916-456-1767

Pottery

I am interested in several **different lines of pottery and dinnerware.** Please contact me with information about your items. If you call, evenings only please. Pottery wanted includes:

- Homer Laughlin, children's ware
- Red Wing, Raymor Modern Artware
- Vernon Kilns, art pottery and dinnerware
- Eva Zeisel, Bay Ridge Specialty, Hyalyn, Riverside China, and children's ware
- Brayton Laguna
- Salem China, Free Form shape
- Russel Wright, metal, glass, pottery, and wood
- Gladding-McBean/Catalina
- Catalina Island

Ray Vlach, Jr.
5364 N Magnet Ave.
Chicago, IL 60630-1216
312-225-5692 (evenings only)

We are buying **pottery and china from the following list for resale**. Please send pictures and description of items, including any marks and your asking price. All pieces **must be in mint condition** — free of all nicks, chips, cracks, bruises, glaze crazing, or any other damage.

- Blue Willow
- Fiesta
- Friar Tuck Monks by Goebel
- Hull
- LuRay
- Memory Lane by Royal China
- Currier & Ives by Royal China
- Franciscan
- Hall
- Liberty Blue by Staffordshire
- McCoy
- Roseville

The Glass Packrat
Pat and Bill Ogden
3050 Colorado Ave.
Grand Junction, CO 81504

Pottery

We live in a small rural town in southwest North Dakota and are interested in buying pottery made in North Dakota before 1965. Items may be marked **Dickota, Messer, Rosemeade, WPA (Ceramics Project, Works Project Administration), or UND (University of North Dakota, School of Mines)** and have paper stickers, incised, or ink-stamped marks. Not all pieces may be marked or still have their stickers, but if you know your piece originated in North Dakota, contact us. We are also interested in **matte glaze earth-tone art pottery whether marked or not, 1940s and older; stoneware and yellow ware, Roseville, Watt, Shawnee, McCoy, Van Briggle — we will consider others.**

Pieces may be salt and peppers, wall pockets, vases, flowerpots, bookends, jugs, or other items. A photo, drawing, or description of your item or collection is helpful. We prefer that you price your item(s), but we will make offers on approval.

Stan and Carrie Soderstrom
15 First St. SW
Rt. 2, Box 300
Bowman, ND 58623
701-523-5717

	We Pay
Most Items, ea	**25.00-200.00**

I am a collector of **Roseville** that is interested in buying one or all pieces in perfect condition. Please send a detailed description including mold number and photos (if possible) and your asking price. All letters will be answered that include SASE. I am also interested in **Camark, Hull, McCoy, and Shawnee pottery.** Other interests include **Christmas and Halloween decorations made prior to 1960; old, ornate souvenir and demitasse sterling spoons; wall pockets; ladies mesh, enameled handbags and old compacts; and old carnival and Depression glass.** Please send description, photos, and price desired.

Marilyn Seiler
16934 Cactus Blossom Dr.
Pflugerville, TX 78660

I am buying **extremely damaged pieces of Roseville pottery.** I am **not** interested in pieces with small chips, small cracks, or light crazing. I need badly damaged pieces. For example, pieces with missing handles, pots that are in several pieces or pieces which are shattered. Generally speaking, the pieces will be damaged beyond repair or be considered too expensive to repair.

Andrew E. Thomas
4681 N 84th Way
Scottsdale, AZ 85251-1864
602-947-5693 or fax 602-994-4382

Royal Bayreuth figurals are wanted: Santa Claus, rabbit, mouse, kangaroo, platypus, snake, clowns, devil and cards, people, flower pitchers, bowls, and candlesticks.

Dorothy Earle
15 Burning Tree Dr.
Newburgh, NY 12550
914-562-8139 or 954-946-3284

Member of a pack-rat family wishes to start a collection of **Royal Doulton Middle Earth characters.** Please send SASE with a list of any pieces you may have. With SASE, all pictures will be returned. I can also be reached by e-mail at paxton71@gte.net. Thanks and God bless.

Harold M. Paxton, III
5800 58th St. N
Kenneth City, FL 33709
727-544-8974
paxton71@gte.net

Wanted by a Florida dealer: **all Royal Doulton dog figurines and Middle Earth series figurines.** I do wish to hear from you if you have **Elegant Ladies and/or Handsome Gentlemen** too. If you have a large collection, please mail list with HN numbers from the bottom of the pieces along with color descriptions. Please call for free quote. Buying quality figurines seven days a week! Thanks and have a wonderful day.

Bill Stenger, Collector/Appraiser
Gas Plant Antique Arcade
1246 Central Ave.
St. Petersburg, FL 33709
727-544-2431
Billantq@get.net

Prayer Ladies

Prayer Ladies are china figurines made by Enesco. They have reddish brown hair, a high-necked dress of pink, blue, or white with blue trim and a prayer on their apron. We **do not** buy napkin holders, salt and pepper shakers, or toothpick holders. We do buy other Enesco lines such as **Snappy the Snail and Kitchen Independence**. Please include large SASE with all correspondence. Prices listed are for pink ladies only.

April and Larry Tvorak
P.O. Box 94
Warren Center, PA 18851
570-395-3775
april@epix.net

Kitchen Prayer Ladies, Pink	We Pay
Cookie Jar	125.00
Clothes Sprinkler	150.00
Bank	85.00
Crumb Sweeper	100.00
Planter	30.00
Bell	35.00

Premiums

I am interested in purchasing early items offered through **radio programs from the late 1920s to the 1950s. I am very interested in Superman, Green Hornet, Buck Rogers, Radio Orphan Annie, Tom Mix, and Space Patrol**. Major interests are giveaway ring premiums. Samples of prices paid are listed below. Please also see my listings in this book under **Cracker Jack and Pencil Sharpeners**.

Old Kilbourn Antiques
Phil Helley
629 Indiana Ave.
Wisconsin Dells, WI 53965
608-254-8659

Radio Premiums **We Pay**

Babe Ruth Watch Fob **50.00**
Buck Rogers Solar Scout Knife **200.00**
Buck Rogers Solar Scout Uniform **250.00**
Capt Marvel Decoder, paper **150.00**
Capt Marvel Statuette **500.00**
Capt Video Saucer Ring **150.00**
Green Hornet Secret Compartment Seal Ring **300.00**
Jack Armstrong Lieutenant Whistle Badge **170.00**
Operator #5 Skull Ring **500.00**
Sgt. Preston Camp Stove & Tent **450.00**
Space Patrol Cosmic Smoke Gun **150.00**
Space Patrol Ring, plastic **200.00**
Spider Ring **750.00**
Superman Secret Compartment Ring **600.00**

I am buying **plastic cereal premiums and paper Funny Face items**. I'm also interested in **any character-related cereal boxes from the 1950s to 1970s**.

Jim Rash
135 Alder Ave.
Egg Harbor Twp., NJ 08234-9302
609-485-7644

I buy **cereal premiums from the '50s through the '70s**. Character items such as Quisp, Quake, and Yogi Bear are especially valued. Condition is important. Items must be complete and, if mechanical, in working order. Near-mint to mint condition items are preferred. Listed here are only samples of my wants. Please also see my listing under **Cereal Boxes** in the back of this book.

Scott Bruce
10 Notre Dame Ave.
Cambridge, MA 02140
617-492-5004
e-mail: scott@flake.com

Cereal Premiums **We Pay**

Cornelius C. Sugarcoat Walking Toy, 1958 .... **150.00-200.00**
Beverly Hillbillies' Elly May Doll, 1964 .... **50.00-75.00**

Gary Lewis' *Doin' the Flake* Record, 1964 .... **25.00-30.00**
Trix Rabbit Mug, Placemat & Bowl, 1964 .... **35.00-50.00**
Lovable Truly, inflatable, 1964 .... **75.00-100.00**
Tony the Tiger Cookie Jar (head), 1965 .... **50.00-75.00**
Quisp Propeller Beanie, 1966 .... **300.00-400.00**
Quake Cavern Helmet, 1966 .... **300.00-400.00**
Dr. Dolittle Medical Bag, 1967 .... **35.00-50.00**
Apple Jack Mug & Bowl, 1967 .... **35.00-50.00**
Yellow Submarine Rub-On Sheets, 1969 .... **25.00-30.00**
Quisp Bank, ceramic, 1971 .... **600.00-750.00**
Monster Cereal Squeeze Toys, 1980 .... **35.00-50.00**

Prints

I am a collector of old, original **prints of children.** I buy Bessie Pease Gutmann (my favorite), Meta Morris Grimball, Eda Soest Doench, Charlotte Becker, Zula Kenyon, Maude Fandgel, Frances Tipton Hunter, Jessie Wilcox Smith, Ida Waugh, and others. I am also interested in old calendars, magazine covers, advertising, sheet music, postcards, books, and any other printed material with pictures of children. Please send photo and asking price.

Other interests include **cat collectibles, children's books, lace and linens, needlework items, Victorian collectibles, and Virginia Rose dinnerware by Homer Laughlin China Co.**

Eunice Gentry
1126 Prairie Ave.
Cleburne, TX 76031
817-556-3746 or fax 817-556-9929

Yard-long prints are lithographs. The ones we collect show **lovely ladies dressed in fashions of the early 1900s to the late 1920s**. Although called yard longs, few actually were exactly a yard long, and some have been trimmed to fit into smaller frames. Various yard longs range in width from 6" to 11" with lengths of around 27" to 37". Some have the artist's name on the front, and most have advertising and a small calendar on the back. A few of the companies whose advertising appears on the reverse of yard longs are Pompeian Beauty Products, Diamond Crystal Salt, Pabst Extract, Walk-Over Shoes, and Selz Shoes.

We collect only prints that are in excellent condition (meaning no highly visible creases, tears, or water stains). The colors must be bright and crisp, not noticeably faded. We prefer untrimmed, original-length prints with the original frame and glass.

The following are examples of specific yard longs we would like to find for our collection. There are many others not listed that we would also like to have.

Also wanted are **German die-cut and embossed calendar tops showing pretty ladies, and Art Deco picture frames** made of glass with reverse-painted geometric designs and metal corners that range in size up to 12x14". (An illustrated flyer is available on request.) See also Boxes, Compacts, and Purses in this book.

Mike and Sherry Miller
303 Holiday Dr.
Tuscola, IL 61953
217-253-4991
miller@tuscola.net
http://www.tuscola.net/~miller/

Yard-Long Prints	**We Pay**
1913 Pabst, signed Stuart Travis	**100.00-150.00**
1914 Pabst, signed Alfred Everitt Orr	**110.00-165.00**
1918 Selz, unsigned	**175.00-200.00**
1925 Selz, unsigned	**175.00-200.00**
1929 Pompeian, signed Bradshaw Krandall	**100.00-135.00**

Purses

We collect **metal mesh purses painted with multicolored designs**. Most were made by the Whiting & Davis Co. (W & D) or the Mandalian Manufacturing Co. in the 1920s and early 1930s.

We are **not** interested in all-painted mesh bags. We do not want purses that could be described as average or plain. We're looking for bags with striking designs, unusual features, or ornate frames. Purses with excessively worn, faded, or damaged paint are not candidates for our collection. Minor wear and a few separated links are acceptable, and the more unusual the purse the more forgiving we tend to be.

One style of mesh purse with an unusual feature that we particularly look for is the vanity bag. **Mesh vanity bags** combine a purse and a compact and were made in a variety of different styles. Some have the compact made into the corner or center of the purse frame. Other purses, including many made by R & G, have a round frame with a mesh bag attached below and the compact mounted on top. One Whiting & Davis model, the 'swinging compact' mesh vanity bag, has a compact attached to the purse frame by a metal bar allowing the compact to swing out from the purse.

Below are just a few examples of bags we're trying to find. There are many other bags with similar features we'd like also to add to our collection. Request our illustrated want list or view our want list and examples of painted mesh purses on our website.

Sherry and Mike Miller
303 Holiday Dr.
Tuscola, IL 61953
217-253-4991
miller@tuscola.net
http://www.tuscola.net/~miller/

Painted Metal Mesh Purses	We Pay
Child's Size (2x3" to 3x4"), geometric design on mesh	**50.00-75.00**
Child's Size (2x3" to 3x4"), figural design on mesh	**75.00-125.00**
Purse w/Art Deco 'Moderne' Geometric Design (5x7")	**100.00-150.00**
Purse w/Ornate or Unusual Frame (5x8")	**125.00-175.00**
Purse w/Betty Boop or Mickey Mouse	**450.00+**
Mandalian Purse, painted swans or deer	**150.00-200.00**
Mandalian Purse, elaborate floral design & painted frame (5x10")	**175.00-225.00**
R & G Vanity Bag, w/cloisonne lid & octagonal top	**300.00-350.00**
W & D Purse, snow-covered log cabin scene	**150.00-200.00**
W & D Purse, painted dragon (5x7")	**300.00-350.00**
W & D Corner Compact Vanity Bag	**550.00+**
W & D Swinging Compact Bag	**550.00+**

We are serious buyers of **vintage purses and purse frames** and have written several books on the subject including *Vintage Purses at Their Best* and *Vintage Compacts and Beauty Accessories,* as well as having appeared on The Discovery Channel. We are especially interested in purse collections and old store stock frames. We buy **all fine quality purses including, beaded glass, enameled mesh, petit-point, and tapestry purses; and jeweled purse frames, celluloid frames, and all fancy frames are wanted.** Generally, we pay better prices for those in top condition.

Being collectors and dealers, we usually purchase more than those who purchase exclusively for their collection. We especially like rare and unusual purses. We also buy **purses in poor condition, tiny beads, purse frames, carry chains, pendant drops, and purse parts.** You may send photos, photocopies, or e-mail images.

Lynell Schwartz
The Curiosity Shop
P.O. Box 964
Cheshire, CT 06410
203-271-0643
PURSES@aol.com

	We Pay
Mesh Bag, w/celebrity face	**500.00-1,000.00+**
Mesh Bag, w/fancy frame	**150.00+**
Mesh Bag, w/Disney character	**150.00+**
Mesh Bag, w/compact, jewels	**200.00+**
Beaded Bag, w/scenes or figures	**500.00+**
Beaded Bag, w/florals	**200.00+**
Dance Purse or Trinity Plate	**125.00+**
Fancy Purse Frame	**35.00+**
Carry Chain, Beads, Pendant Drops, Etc	**Market Price**
Postcards, depicting people holding purses	**Market Price**

I am a collector and interested in purchasing **old, enameled mesh handbags.** I prefer examples in good to very good condition. I particularly would like enameled scenes with nice frames. Please send SASE with photos and price you are asking. I am also interested in **ladies' Victorian-style vanity boxes, dresser sets, compacts, photo albums, antique jewelry, celluloid and porcelain boxes, and lithographed prints from the Victorian era. Please see other items wanted under Pottery in this book.**

Marilyn Seiler
16934 Cactus Blossom Dr.
Pflugerville, TX 78660

Radios

I collect **Catalin and mirrored radios as well as novelty radios** such as Charlie McCarthy, Coca-Cola, Pepsi, and Hopalong Cassidy. I am looking for **radio-shaped items such as banks or products in the name** such as Radio Beer,

Radio Perfume, etc. Also wanted are **clocks, barometers, desk sets, etc., made of Catalin.**

Richard O. Gates
P.O. Box 187
Chesterfield, VA 23832
804-748-0382 (day) or 804-794-5146 (night or weekends)

Wanted to buy: **crystal radio sets of the 1950s or earlier, a ceramic bug with a crystal radio inside, and also a National SW54 shortwave radio from the 1950s in original condition.** Please contact me and give details about your item.

Larry Flinchpaugh
Consign It Stores, Inc.
6 H St.
Bakersfield, CA 93304
805-325-2401 or fax 805-325-4209
flinchpaugh@juno.com

We Pay

Philmore Crystal Radio **25.00-100.00**
Ceramic Bug With Crystal Radio Inside, ca 1940 .... **50.00-100.00**
National SW54 Shortwave Receiver Radio, ca 1950s, original condition, no modifications **50.00-100.00**

Railroadiana

The term railroadiana is meant to cover all collecting facets of the golden age of railroading. Depending upon the collector's interest, items such as lanterns, tools, locks and keys, dining car wares (china, glass, silver, linen), advertising, timetables, signs, watches, and other items are eagerly sought.

Our particular area of interest is **authentic patterns of dining car china**. We prefer those pieces which have a top or side logo (design or mark) and/or a designated railroad's name on the underside of the piece. In addition, we seek to buy railroad station restaurant wares and even those pieces used by electric railways, ferry boats, and steamship lines. The following listing represents only a sampling of railroadiana items we seek to buy. We respond to all offerings. Other interests include **Shelley and Buffalo Pottery**.

Fred and Lila Shrader
2025 Hwy. 199 (Hiouchi)
Crescent City, CA 95531
707-458-3525

Railroad China	**We Pay**
Alaska RR, various patterns, pieces & shapes	**100.00+**
Butter Pats, any railroad	**35.00+**
Creamers, any railroad, any size	**45.00+**
Egg Cups, any railroad, any size	**45.00+**
Cup & Saucer, various sizes, sets	**50.00+**
Sant Fe RR, any pattern	**20.00-50.00+**
Southern Pacific RR, Prairie Mountain Wildflower, anything	**45.00+**
Teapots, Coffeepots, Chocolate Pots, any size	**100.00+**
Union Pacific RR, any pattern	**20.00-50.00+**
Any Railroad China	**Please Call or Write**

The Little Falls Railroad and Doll Museum Ltd. is constantly looking for **dolls and railroad memorabilia** to enhance and expand the museum. We are looking for any railroad-related items, especially those that operated in Wisconsin and Eastern Minnesota. We are seeking paper goods, equipment, and old trains of any kind. We negotiate prices as a set price is usually impractical. We will trade some items, and as with dolls, we are able to give recognition for donations on a tax ecxept basis.

We can be reached by phone, fax, or mail. All contacts will be answered.

The Little Falls Railroad and Doll Museum Ltd.
P.O. Box 177
Cataract, WI 54620-0177
phone or fax 608-272-3266
http://www.wi.centuryinter.net/Raildoll/

Railroad tie date nails are wanted — either a single nail or entire sets. Nails must be identified as coming from a specific line or railway. Prices vary according to rarity.

Tom Meyer
722 Wildwood Dr.
New Smyrna Beach, FL 32168-1834
800-382-4799
tntmaltesegth@webtv.net

Razor Blade Banks

Razor blade banks that are interesting ceramic, wood, or tin shapes and forms are sought. Especially wanted is the **Twinplex lithographed tin bank in the shape of a house and marked 'Home of Aged Banks.'** I will pay from $25.00 to $125.00 depending on condition.

Deborah Gillham
47 Midline Ct.
Gaithersburg, MD 20878
301-977-5727
dgillham@erols.com

Razors

Serious collector interested only in **fancy handled straight razors**. Ornate sterling silver and aluminum handled examples are wanted. Carved mother-of-pearl, and celluloid examples with raised figural handles — especially those with color — are wanted. I'm also interested in seven day razor sets in their original boxes. The razors must be in excellent condition. The better the condition, the higher my offer. Send clear photograph or photocopy. **Do not send any razors**. I will pay $100.00 or more for a fancy handle straight razor that I need for my collection.

Russ Palmieri
27 Pepper Rd.
Towaco, NJ 07082
973-334-5829

Records

I am buying **old 78-rpm (and some 45-rpm) children's records.** They can be any label, any year. It is most important that they have their original sleeves, album covers, jackets, etc. The exceptions would be picture discs. Most children's records without the original covers have little interest, since most collectors want these items mainly for the artwork.

When sending me information on what you have, simply indicate the record label and record or album number(s). I will contact you if I need further information. Also, describe the condition of the cover. I am not as concerned with the record condition unless it is missing, cracked, chipped, or otherwise unplayable. Occasionally I can use records without the sleeve (I may have an empty sleeve; or I may need the information on the loose record for research purposes).

Since there is no price guide for old kiddie records, I can not list how much I will pay except as on an individual basis. I can say that most records go for $1.00 to $10.00 with a small percentage going higher, and in some cases for several hundreds of dollars. Recordings of famous characters from TV, comics, movies, etc., naturally more desirable — basically because there is a crossover collectors' market for them.

Peter B. Muldavin
173 W 78th St.
New York, NY 10024
212-362-9606
kiddie78s@aol.com
http://www.members.aol.com/kiddie78s/

TV cartoon-related records from before 1960 are wanted such as TV Adventures of King Kong, Hanna-Barbera's Shazam!, Howdy Doody, etc. Also wanted are **'weird' music with album covers of majorettes, spacemen, monsters, rocketships, calendar girl cover art,** etc. I pay $3.00 to $5.00 for most common records but will pay $20.00 and up for a good condition, early Howdy Doody EP. I like Ray Scott and pay $3.50 for 78s I don't have but especially want his *Soothing Sounds for Baby* set. Ray Scott is just an example, what do you have?

Other wants include **buying and selling flour sacks, Higgins glass (signed), and Whitman Publishing Company books with dust jackets.**

Ross Hartsough
R.R. 2, Box 382
Honesdale, PA 18431
717-253-1433

	We Pay
Most Common Records	**3.00-5.00**
Early Howdy Doody EP, good condition	**20.00+**
Ray Scott 78 RPM	**3.50**
Ray Scott, Soothing Sounds for Baby Set	**50.00**

Over 8,400 LP records wanted! Records from the **1950s through the 1990s — jazz, soul, disco, funk, Black gospel, instrumentals, soundtracks, etc.** Any quantity wanted in excellent to never-played condition. We buy to sell and sell to buy! Send $30.00 for list of records wanted.

First Place Records
Dept. W
P.O. Box 3477
Texarkana, AR 75504
870-773-1597

I am a serious collector interested in **all Vogue picture records produced by Sav-Way Industries of Detroit in 1946 through 1947.** I will buy any Vogue but am especially interested in the following records needed to complete my collection:

R711	R713	R715	R784
S100 (12")	CG546 (12")	DCR (12")	

John Coates
324 Woodland Dr.
Stevens Point, WI 54481
715-341-6113
jcoates@coredcs.com

Wanted: **78-rpm records with scarce and unusual labels**. Following are some scarce labels and special series — **all of which are wanted**, regardless of musical content or lack thereof. All are pre-1940, and should not be confused with more modern labels having the same or similar names. For illustrations of these (and many other) labels, see my booklet, *Shellac Shack's Want List of 78 rpm Records*, and/or my book, *American Premium Record Guide*. Prices are minimums for the least desirable issues on each label; better issues will be bought at higher prices (sometimes multiples of quoted prices). Labels should be free of significant damage (writing, stickers, needle scratches, stains, tears, etc.), and the playing surface should be in nice, playable condition (some of the following will be bought at reduced prices, even if playing surface is impaired, if label is nice).

Also buying many other records on other labels and other eras: popular, dance bands, jazz, blues, hillbilly, celebrities, rock 'n roll, rockabilly, rhythm and blues, etc. No classical wanted unless on scarce labels. List must include label, record number, artist/band, and song titles. I will buy single records, collections, hoards, store stocks, and will travel if quality/quantity warrant.

Please note that that some of these labels may be confused with more modern, similarly named labels, reissues/repressings that reuse original names, logos, etc.

L.R. Docks
P.O. Box 691035
San Antonio, TX 78269
210-492-6021 or fax 210-492-6489

78-RPM Records w/Scarce, Unusual Labels	We Pay
Ajax (Canada)	4.00
Aurora (Canada)	5.00
Autograph (Marsh Laboratories, Chicago)	4.00
Belvedere (Hochschild, Kohn & Co)	4.00
Berliner (7", single-sided, embossed label)	8.00
Black Patti (Chicago Record Co)	50.00
Blu-Disc (#T-1001 through #T-1009)	35.00
Buddy (six cities/companies mentioned on label)	20.00
Carnival (John Wanamaker, New York)	10.00
Chappelle & Stinette	10.00
Chautauqua (Washington, DC)	10.00
Clover (Nutmeg Record Co)	3.00
Connorized	2.00
Dandy	4.00
Davega	2.00
Davis & Schwegler	5.00
Domestic (Philadelphia)	3.00
Edison (Needle Cut Electric)	6.00
Edison (Long-Playing 24-Minute)	10.00
Edison (Long-Playing 40-Minute, 12")	15.00
Edison (sample record, 12")	20.00
Electradisk	2.00
Everybodys	3.00
Flexo (small, flexible disc, by Pacific Coast Record Corp, San Francisco, or Hollywood Film Enterprises)	6.00
Golden (Los Angeles, not the children's record of circa 1950)	5.00
Gramophone (7", single-sided, embossed label)	8.00

Herschel Gold Seal (Northwestern Phonograph Supply)	5.00
Herwin (St Louis)	5.00
Hollywood Record (California)	5.00
Homestead (Chicago Mail Order)	4.00
Improved (7", single-sides, by Eldridge R Johnson)	8.00
Marathon (7", by Nutmeg Record Corp)	6.00
Meritt (Kansas City)	25.00
Moxie	10.00
Mozart (St Louis)	3.00
National (Iowa City, Iowa)	2.00
New Flexo (small, flexible disc)	5.00
Nordskog (with motto: The Golden-Voiced Records)	6.00
Odeon (American 'ONY' Series; not foreign/ethnic issues)	4.00
Paramount (12000 and 13000 Series)	2.00
Parlophone (American 'PNY' Series only)	3.00
Par-O-Ket (7", embossed, not paper, label)	4.00
Pennington (Bamberger & Co, New Jersey)	4.00
Personal Record (By Columbia, '-P' Series)	2.00
Phonograph Recording Company (San Francisco)	5.00
QRS (Cover Recording Co, New York)	5.00
RCA Victor Program Transcription	4.00
RCA Victor Picture Records (early 1930s)	15.00
Rialto (Railto Music House, Chicago)	10.00
Stark	5.00
Sunrise (Grey Gull affiliated, ca 1930)	3.00
Sunrise (RCA Victor product, ca 193)	20.00
Sunset (Made in California USA)	3.00
Sunshine (St Petersburg, Florida)	5.00
Sunshine (Los Angeles, Calif.)	10.00
Superior (Gennett affiliated, ca 1930-31)	4.00
Timely Tunes (RCA Victor product)	5.00
Tremont (American Record Mfg)	2.00
Up-To-Date (ca 1925)	25.00
Victor 23000-23041, inclusive	3.00
Victor 23250-23432, inclusive	5.00
Victor 23500-23859, inclusive	2.00
V-38500-V-38631, inclusive	5.00
Victor Pict-Ur-Music	3.00
Yerkes	4.00

John Marinacci
301 Murray Ave.
Bridgeville, PA 15017
412-221-4946 or 412-221-6763

Rhinos

Wanted: **anything and everything that depicts a rhino.** The scope of things includes figurines, clothing, pictures, toys, books, videos, movies, facts, stories, advertisements — anything that may be out there. These items are being used for a collection to help raise awareness and funds for the plight of the five endangered rhino species. The group responsible for this collection is called H.O.R.N.S. (Helping Out Rhinos Now Survive). We are also looking for other rhino collectors to swap information and duplicate items. If you know of any stores or dealers that have any items that may be of interest, drop us a note or give them information to contact us.

Helping Out Rhinos Now Survive (H.O.R.N.S.)
Attention: Don 'Rhino' Lobmeyer Jr.
P.O. Box 47696
Wichita, KS 67201-7696
312-264-0695
rhino@feist.com

	We Pay
Lenox Rhino	**50.00**
Funrise 2-in-1 Rhino Toy	**200.00**
Rhino Stein	**10.00**
Rhino Shaving Mug	**500.00-1,000.00**
Rhino Solid Perfume	**100.00**
Rhino Postcards	**5.00-10.00**
Stamps & First Day Covers	**1.00-25.00**
Books, Videos, Games	**up to 25.00**
Salt & Pepper Shakers	**up to 25.00**
Fast-food Items	**up to 20.00**
Cookie Jar	**up to 50.00**

Round Oak Stoves

I am buying **Round Oak Stoves' advertising and selected stoves.** The Round Oak Stove factory was located in Dowagiac, Michigan. They mainly advertised with an Indian (Doe-Wah-Jack). Advertising items must be in very good-plus condition. Chips, tears, water stains, etc., will subtract from price. Stove prices are for complete models in very good condition.

Items **not** of interest are sad irons and solid finials as these are reproductions. Also, I'm **not** interested in porcelain stove brochures or catalogs. There are many items not listed that are of interest — let me know what you have! If possible, please send photos of large items or photocopys of smalls (postcards, trade cards, catalogs, etc.) along with accurate descriptions of condition.

Greg Marquart
P.O. Box 8615
Benton Harbor, MI 49023
616-926-7080

Round Oak Advertising	We Pay
Litho, devil by stove	450.00+
Litho, Dutch boy or standing Indian	450.00+
Calendar, depending on year	up to 300.00
Cardboard Standup	up to 750.00
Plate, depending on color	up to 225.00
Sign, tin	up to 350.00
Sign, glass corner	Call
Pocket Mirror	up to 75.00
Mug	up to 75.00
Trade Card	up to 15.00
Postcard	up to 20.00

Round Oak Stoves	We Pay
All 12" Models	500.00+
All 14" Models	up to 500.00
Parts for 12" or 14" Models	What Do You Have?
Kate Lee, 16" or 18"	2,000.00+

Finials	We Pay
Standing Indian (less without feathers)	125.00+
Others	up to 75.00

Wanted to buy: **anything made by the Round Oak Stove Company except the stoves themselves** (for the simple reason that they are too big to ship). I do love the sales literature, signs, calendars, ashtrays, owners' manuals, and some of the chrome trim parts. I am especially interested in the stove tops or finials as they were called. They are usually in the shape of a full-body Indian or may have just the Indian's face. The Indian, Doe-Wah-Jack, was their trademark and sometimes his name will be on a finial. I will pay up to $125.00 for one of these finials. If you have any of the items mentioned, please send SASE for reply or call after 7 pm CST.

I am also interested in **anything related to US-made water-pumping windmills.** See also my listing under Windmills in this book.

Dennis L. Schulte
708 Allamakee St.
Waukon, IA 52172-1240

Russel Wright

I collect a variety of items designed by **Russel Wright from the 1930s through the 1950s.** He worked in many different materials from aluminum to wood. His items can have a slick machine quality or follow naturalistic forms. Some of the Russel Wright designs I collect are:

American Modern: coffeepots, stack sets, tumblers, stoppered carafes, and children's pottery sets in original boxes
Bauer: most pieces
Highlight dinnerware by Paden City Pottery and Glass Company: pottery items in the Pepper glaze and Snow Glass pieces
Casual dinnerware by Iroquois China: original shaped coffee and A.D. pots in Charcoal glaze
Lamps: made of ceramic or wood
Metal ware: items made of chrome, chrome and aluminum, chrome and glass, and steel items as andirons, animal forms, bowls, salad servers, vases, etc.
Oceana: all items and other wood pieces
Pinch/Highlight Stainless Steel by Hull: ice teaspoons and serving pieces all glass, laquerware, and pottery
Linens: bandannas, bold plaids, and abstracts
Advertising and company brochure items

Please describe, state condition, price, and enclose SASE for a written response. Photographs are helpful for some items and will be returned. I may be interested in other items not listed also. Phone calls are welcome, but please don't call looking for free appraisals. Thank you.

Ray Vlach, Jr.
5364 N Magnet Ave.
Chicago, IL 60630-1216
312-225-5692 (evenings only)

Salesman's Samples and Miniatures

I am a collector of **salesman's samples and promotional items for various manufacturers of pre-1970s furnaces, boilers, water heaters, and air conditioning equipment.** Examples include Lennox, Holland, Mueller, G.E., etc.

Larry Wessling
2805 Kingsridge
Blue Springs, MO 64015

Salt and Pepper Shakers

I buy **novelty salt and pepper shakers**. I buy from one set to an entire collection. I have been known to buy eight to ten thousand set collections. No collection is too large for me to handle. Price I am willing to pay per set depends on what is in the collection and the condition. Please contact me for details. I buy through the mail. Photos or videos are required. If the collection is large enough, I will drive to buy it.

The Salt and Pepper Man
Larry Carey
P.O. Box 329
Mechanicsburg, PA 17055
717-766-0868
snpman@itech.net

	We Pay
Advertising	**20.00+**
Black Americana	**20.00+**
Black Americana Condiment Sets	**200.00+**
Plastic Gas Pumps, no Esso wanted	**25.00+**
Comic Characters	**45.00+**
Nodders w/Figural Bases	**75.00+**
Miniatures	**20.00+**
Storybook Sets	**30.00+**
Condiments (salt, pepper & mustard) w/figural bases, particularly sets made in Germany & marked on the bottom	**150.00+**
Poinsetta Studios, Calif	**25.00+**
Goebel (Hummel), from Germany	**25.00+**

Fruit & Vegetables w/Faces .... **20.00+**
Shawnee Pottery .... **20.00+**
Rosemeade Pottery .... **25.00+**
Messer Pottery, North Dakota .... **50.00+**
People, Animals, Huggies or Go-With Sets **1.00-20.00**

Plastic figural gasoline pump salt and pepper shaker sets that stand approximately 2½" tall are just one example of the many specialty versions of novelty salt shaker collectibles. Produced for and distributed free by service stations from the early 1950s through the 1970s, these miniature replicas of actual gas pumps were made for almost every brand of gasoline during that era. Brands representing those with the most service stations are the most common and are least desirable, such as Esso, Texaco, and Phillips 66.

I'm seeking to buy sets representing the gasoline brands listed below. Many may still be in their original boxes; others will be unpackaged. Write with your find, and I'll respond immediately to your inquiry. Also see my listing under Thermometers in this book. **Prices paid range from $25.00 to $150.00 a pair for these brand names:**

Aetna
APCO
Amlico
Ashland
B/A
Bay
Boron
CALSO
Carter
Clark
Cliff Brice
Comet
Crystal Flash
Derby
Dixie
Fleet-Wing
FS (Farm Service)
Frontier
Getty
Hancock
Hudson
Hi-Speed
Imperial
Jet
Keystone
Kayo
Leonard
Lion
MFA
Martin
Pan-Am
Paraland
Rocket
Site
Speedway 79
SOC
Tenneco
UTOCO
Vickers
Zephyr

Peter Capell
1838 W Grace St.
Chicago, IL 60613-2724
773-871-8735

Scales

We buy **all types of coin-operated scales in any condition. Also incomplete scales and parts** are wanted. We specialize in Watling scales. Scales wanted for use in homes, movie theaters, stores, and restaurants. We want to buy or sell, rent, and lease scales; we have parts and repairs available. Send a photo of scale along with serial and model numbers. We also buy all other types of scales. Prices are for complete working scales.

Bill and Jan Berning
135 W Main St.
Genoa, IL 60135
815-784-3134 or 815-895-6328

	We Pay
Pace Scales	**50.00-300.00+**
Rockola	**40.00-200.00+**
Lollipop Scales	**300.00-2,000.00+**
Public Scales	**50.00-300.00**
Pioneer	**300.00-500.00**
Watling Fortune Scales, sm	**100.00-300.00+**
Advertising Scales	**100.00-2,000.00+**
Ticket Scales	**40.00+**
Electronic Scales	**25.00-500.00+**
Hamilton Scales	**100.00-10,000.00+**

Scandinavian Modern

Wanted are items in Scandinavian Modern from the 1950s through the 1960s. We are buying Krenit bowls. These are metal with a black exterior and a colored enamel interior and came in all sizes and shapes. Scandinavian ceramics wanted include those made by Rorstrand, Gustausberg, Palshus, and other makers. Anything by Oanusk, wooden bowls, cutting boards, metal pitchers, etc., is wanted. We like to buy clean, modern, decorative and useful things from Scandinavia. **No furniture** items are wanted. Call or write with picture.

Cityslickers Collectibles
Richard and Anni Frey
61 Marine St.
Bronx, NY 10464
718-885-0898

Scientific and Technical-Related Antiques

I am buying:

Surveying instruments: pre-1910 compasses, transits, levels, etc.
Microscopes: pre-1900, large, elaborate or simple forms, etc.
Astronomy-related items: planetariums, globes, telescopes, navigational instruments, etc.
Medical instruments and curiosities: cased surgical sets, anatomical models, phlegmy and phrenological items, quack medical devices, etc.
Precision and scientific instruments: associated with physics demonstration, telegraphy, mining and assaying, exploration, pre-1900 motors, etc.
Calculating and computing devices: decorative and unusual forms only
Typewriters: decorative and/or unusual forms only
Photographica: daguerreotypes, cased and unusual photographs, unusual cameras
All related items: trade catalogs, early books and photographic images.

Write or call:

Dale R. Beeks
P.O. Box 117
Mt. Vernon, IA 52314
319-895-0506 or 800-880-5178

Sewing Collectibles

I am a collector of **all types of sewing items. No cloth** items are wanted but items made of silver, Bakelite, or gold are sought. Items wanted include things such as stanhopes, sewing birds, sewing cases, pin disks and cubes, scissors, and small boxes. Please include your phone number and asking price when contacting me.

Kayla Conway
4500 Napal Ct.
Bakersfield, CA 93307
805-833-0291

	We Pay
Needle Cases	**25.00+**
Thimble, gold	**50.00+**
Sewing Birds	**50.00+**
Sewing Chatalaine	**25.00+**
Tatting Shuttles, any	**10.00+**

Wanted: **tatting shuttles** of sterling, enamel, Mauchline Ware (or Scottish transfer ware), Tunbridge ware, advertising, wood, or any unusual celluloid shuttle. **Needlework tools and/or sewing boxes complete with needlework tools** are wanted as well. I prefer items to be from the 1800s to 1940s and in good to excellent condition. I will pay top dollar according to the item, its condition and age.

Judy McGraw
92 Horse Apple Ln.
Denison, TX 75020
903-463-7158

I want to find **pig tape measures.** These usually have the name of a town, city, park, business, or tourist area stamped on their back or side. They were probably souvenirs or giveaways. The tape measure pull is either under the tail or in the mouth. The pigs are made of plastic or celluloid and came in various colors. Usually they were made in Japan and some wear hats. Being about 2½" long and 1½" high, they will say 'This little piggy comes from...' or have small designs instead. I will pay up to $25.00 for a good quality piece that has legible lettering and a working tape. Please contact by writing and I will call back or write. Thanks.

Diane Carver
22068 2275 East St.
Princeton, IL 61356

Collector interested in buying **war-related notions** — needle packets, pin cushions, etc.; and **thimbles** of fancy sterling, enamel, ivory, brass with words, or aluminum with advertising (these may or may not have cases). I'm also buying **cloth tape measures in plain casings or with scenes and faces. Tape measures with figural cases** of metal, celluloid, ceramic, ivory, or wood are also wanted. Send a photocopy if possible and your asking price. Thank you.

Bernie Biske
47529 Cheryl Ct.
Shelby Twp., MI 48315-4707

Shelley China

We wish to buy **Shelley China (or the earlier Wileman pieces)** to accommodate our Shelley China replacement service. We particularly wish to buy the Dainty shape (6-flute), Ludlow shape (14-flute), Oleander shape, and more 'modern' shapes of Eve, Mode, Vogue, Regent, and the graceful Queen Anne shape. Individual pieces, luncheon sets, dessert sets, full dinner sets, as well as figurines, vases, and Shelley advertising ware. We respond to all offers.

Fred and Lila Shrader
2025 Hwy. 199 (Hiouchi)
Crescent City, CA 95531
707-458-352511

	We Pay
Bowl, Vegetable; oval or round, open	75.00+
Bowl, Vegetable; oval or round, w/lid, per set	150.00+
Butter Pats	40.00+
Cake Plate, flat or pedestal, ea	75.00+
Children's Ware: Attwell, Hilda Cowham (cup & saucer set, egg cup, plate, etc.) ea	45.00+
Coffeepot, Teapot, Chocolate Pot, various sizes, ea	150.00+
Cup & Saucer Sets, various sizes, per set	35.00+
Egg Cups	40.00+
Napkin Rings	40.00+
Place Card Holders	40.00+
Plates, various sizes, ea	20.00-50.00+
Shakers (individual or sets)	40.00+
Toast Racks, ea	40.00+
Anything Not Listed	Please Call or Write

Shoe-Button Covers

I am always buying shoe-button covers. Somewhat similar in appearance to today's blouse-button covers, shoe-button covers were very popular from 1900 until 1925. They were created to brighten up the drab, usually dark-colored buttons that were part of most women's shoes manufactured during the era. The buttons were necessary to secure the straps which gripped the ankles.

I have earned an excellent country-wide reputation for fair and prompt offers. That is why people send me their shoe-button covers and I mail them a check or an offer (whichever the seller prefers). And, unless you are sending covers containing gold, silver, or precious stones, there is probably no need to incur the high cost of insurance.

The prices which I pay are dependent on the condition, style, and rarity of the shoe-button covers. While sets are preferred, I also purchase 'singles.' The availability of the original box can enhance the value by up to 20%. The following chart illustrates the prices which I typically pay.

Eugene R. Klompus
P.O. Box 346
Prospect Hts., IL 60070

	We Pay
Set of 4, silver w/hand-etched design, unbranded, ca 1915	**15.00**
Set of 3, French manufacture, ca 1900	**20.00**
Set of 4, French manufacture, poor condition, ca 1895	**35.00**
Set of 2 (incomplete set), Frere brand, ca 1905	**4.00**
Single Cover, silver, etched scroll, ca 1920	**5.00**

Silhouettes

Silhouettes on glass are wanted that were made from the 1920s through the 1950s. I am not interested in the newer ones. These are **convex or flat glass with painted-on silhouettes**. The silhouettes made on convex glass were of black, red, rose, blue, white, or yellow colors. Any color, shape, or size is wanted. Related items such as ashtrays, books with silhouette illustrations, china, lamps, jewelry or boxes, trays, wastebaskets, etc., are sought as well. I am also looking for **old catalogs, salesmen's samples, or anyone with information about Fisher** (they made pictures and trays with wildflower backgrounds). Other wants include **butterfly wing pictures and jewelry**. Prices will depend on condition and rarity. I will accept collect calls, but photographs or photocopies are very helpful.

Shirley Mace
P.O. Box 1602
Mesilla Park, NM 88047-1602
505-524-6717 or 505-523-0940
Shmace@nmsu.edu

Silver and Silverplate

I am buying **popular patterns of silver-plated flatware, hollowware, etc.** I prefer pieces in excellent condition without monograms. Prices must be reasonable; I will pay for shipping and insurance. Below is a sample of some wanted pieces.

Sterling is also bought, sold, and traded. I'm especially seeking Versailles 1988 by Gorham and also Sir Christopher, but all patterns will be considered.

Other interests are collecting, buying, selling, and trading: **Shawnee pottery, Regal china (no Jim Beam), Old McDonalds Farm (Regal), Watt pottery, Roseville pottery, pre-1930s Weller pottery, Rookwood pottery, Coors pottery, and most other American art pottery.** Please call for a fair quote.

Rick Spencer
801-973-0805

	We Pay
Alhambra, 1907, Anchor Rogers	**2.00-75.00**
Berkshire, 1897, 1847 Rogers	**2.00-150.00**
Berwick, 1904, Wm Rogers	**2.00-150.00**
Bride's Bouquet, 1908, Alvin	**1.00-100.00**
Century, 1923, Holmes & Edwards	**50¢-60.00**
Charter Oak, 1906, 1847 Rogers	**2.00-200.00**
Columbia, 1893, 1847 Rogers	**1.00-150.00**
Eternally Yours, 1941, 1847 Rogers	**50¢-75.00**
First Love, 1937, 1847 Rogers	**50¢-75.00**
Floral, 1903, Wm Rogers	**2.00-150.00**
Glenrose, 1908, Wm Rogers	**2.00-150.00**
Grenoble, 1906, Wm Rogers	**2.00-200.00**
La Vique, 1908, 1881 Rogers	**1.00-200.00**
Modern Art, 1904, Reed & Barton	**75¢-125.00**
Moselle, 1906, American	**3.50-600.00**
Old Colony, 1911, 1847 Rogers	**75¢-125.00**
Holly, 1906, EHH Smith	**63.00-250.00**
Thistle, 1905, EHH Smith	**1.00-125.00**
Vintage, 1904, 1847 Rogers	**1.00-200.00**

MidweSterling is the biggest buyer of **used silverware (knives, forks, spoons, ladles, etc.) and hollowware (trays, pitchers, tea sets, goblets, trophies, etc.)** nationwide. There are five types of metallic silverware and hollowware: sterling, silverplate, stainless, pewter, and Dirilyte. Generally, if it is

sterling it will be marked 'sterling' or '925' or '925/100.' The marks '800' or '900' or 'coin' mean it is respectively 80% or 90% or 90% pure silver. Sterling is 92.5% pure silver. Rarely is sterling not marked sterling or '925.'

Generally, if it is **silverplate** it has a metal color of sterling but not the marks of sterling. Some common marks on silverplate are any word with 'plate,' 'Wm Rogers,' '1847 Rogers Bros,' 'Holmes & Edwards,' or 'EPNS.' **Stainless** will have the look of stainless and be marked 'stainless,' '18/8' or only with the manufacturer's name. Virtually no value are restaurant stainless, premium/promotion stainless, and stainless sold through low-end retail stores. **Pewter** is generally marked 'pewter' and **Dirilyte** (gold colored) is marked 'dirilyte.'

A combination of the following determines value: pattern, maker, condition, rarity, size, style, version of piece; and of course, supply and demand. Dented knife handles, pitted knife blades, monograms, and excessive wear all detract from silverware value. Dents, missing pieces, broken parts, and monograms all detract from hollowware value.

MidweSterling also offers a repair service including knife reblading and garbage disposal damage repair. We perform a careful apprasial for maximum value to buy your merchandise. Pictures of hollowware and photocopies of flatware front and back with trademarks are necessary if you do not know the pattern name. Listed here is a general model of values — most patterns will fall into this range. Fancier and/or heavier and/or older hollowware is worth the most. Weighted or cement filled sterling hollowware is usually worth very little. Note also that stainless, silverplate, pewter, or Dirilyte hollowware is only valuable if very elaborate.

MidweSterling
4311 NE Vivion Blvd, Dept WTB
Kansas City, MO 64119-2890
816-454-1990 (Closed Wednesday, Sunday)
fax 816-454-1605

Most Patterns	**We Pay**
Sterling Hollowware, not weighted, per pc	**5.00-10,000.00**
Sterling Flatware, per pc	**5.00-50.00**
Sterling Souvenir Spoons, fancy, old, per pc	**10.00-200.00**
Stainless, Silverplate, Pewter, or Dirilyte Flatware, per pc	**5¢-5.00**

Sterling silver flatware and hollowware are bought at best prices. Condition is everything and items **must** say sterling or .925; if it doesn't, it isn't sterling. I do **not** buy plated items and am not interested in anything EPNS, coin silver, or .800 E.P.C. nickel silver.

On sterling flatware, if you do not know the pattern name and manufacturing company, lay two or three pieces on a copy machine and take a picture. Then fax it to me and I will identify it for you and quote you a price. When I call, I will need to know what is in the sets (how many knives, forks, serving pieces, etc.). The more information you can give, the better.

Prices paid depending on pattern are from $6.00 up to $55.00 per item or piece. I also buy **sterling souvenir spoons, perfume bottles, sterling jewelry, and baby items as rattles and toys.** It's best to call for a price quote. I have been in business for over twenty-two years and would like to hear from you — especially if you have an unusual item.

The Silver Lady
23011 Moulton Pky. C1-204
Laguna Hills, CA 92653
949-855-1500 or fax 949-855-1010

	We Pay
Sterling Flatware, per item	**6.00-55.00**
Sterling Silver Salt Spoons	**5.00+**
Sterling Match Safes	**25.00+**
Sterling Salt Cellars	**10.00+**
Sterling Charms	**10.00+**
Sterling Figurines	**10.00+**
Sterling Vases	**10.00+**
Sterling Candlesticks	**up to 500.00**

Rogers Bros. 1906 Grenoble serving pieces and place pieces are wanted. No dinner forks or teaspoons, please. I am also interested in **unusual eye cups.**

Deborah Golden
3182 Twin Pine Rd.
Grayling, IL 49738
517-348-3610

Skookum American Indian Dolls

Serious collector interested in buying top quality Skookum dolls. The dolls must be in original excellent condition (without replacement parts). The older dolls have leather shoes, newer dolls have plastic shoes. The faces are papier-mache, not plastic. Original boxes are a plus but not a necessity. Send clear photocopy or photograph or call for an immediate response.

Jo Ann Palmieri
27 Pepper Rd.
Towaco, NJ 07082
973-334-5829

Snowdomes

I am an advanced snowdome collector (I wrote the first book, *Snowdomes* and founded the newsletter and collector's club, *Snow Biz*). I want unusual items and am willing to pay for them. I collect **plastic snowdomes** from small, obscure tourist attractions, sites, towns; and advertisements or promotional domes for any type of product including (but not limited to) TV and radio stations, newspapers, hotels, restaurants, food products, political campaigns, etc. Here are a few specific ones I happen to know about, but my wants are certainly not limited to this list. **I don't care if they have water, as long as the plaques are very legible.**

Nancy McMichael
P.O. Box 53310
Washington, DC 20009
202-234-7484

	We Pay
Albany, New York State Capitol, plastic	**2000.00**
Angel, figural, all plastic, 5"	**50.00-75.00**
Black Cat, figural, all plastic, 5"	**50.00-75.00**
The Bounty at Tahiti, plastic	**15.00**
The Bounty at Cape Horn, plastic	**15.00**
Boy Scout Jamboree, older plastic dome not new glass	**25.00**
Chrysler Building, plastic	**25.00**
Chrysler Building, glass, older	**75.00**
City Island, New York, plastic	**25.00**
Coney Island, plastic	**25.00**
Dogpatch USA, w/Daisy Mae & Lil Abner, TV shaped brown plastic	**15.00**
Elf, figural, all plastic, 5"	**50.00-75.00**
Dwarf, figural, all plastic, 5"	**50.00-75.00**
Flagship Hotel, advertising, plastic	**15.00**

Grim Reaper, figural, all plastic, 5" 50.00-75.00
Greek God, figural, all plastic, 5" 50.00-75.00
Howdy Doody, figural, all plastic, holds water ball in lap 100.00
Indian Chief, figural, all plastic, 5" 50.00-75.00
Kentucky Horse Farm, Louisville, Kentucky, plastic 25.00
Letchworth State Park, plastic 25.00
Lighthouse, figural, all plastic, 5" 50.00-75.00
Los Angeles Civic Center, plastic 20.00
Madison Square Garden, plastic 25.00
Monticello, NY, plastic 20.00
Owl, figural, all plastic, 5" 50.00-75.00
Palisades Park, N.J., plastic 25.00
Pine Creek Railroad, Allaire, N.J. 30.00
Playland, Rye, NY (might say Rye Playland) 40.00
Sarasota, Florida (or any tourist attraction in Sarasota) 15.00
South Fallsburg, NY, plastic 25.00
The Shell Factory, Ft. Myer, Florida 25.00
Tar Heels (from University of North Carolina); older plastic dome 20.00

Soda Fountain Collectibles

We collect **early soda fountain material but especially paper items** which provide so much information about this wonderful business. Our interests range from trade catalogs, trade magazines, photos of early soda fountain interiors, straw dispensers, syrup dispensers, pottery root beer mugs, soda glasses marked with the product name, glass malted milk dispensers, mechanical shake makers, etc. We also own three of the marble soda fountains made in the 1870s and '80s. Someday a book about soda fountain history will result from all of this. Please note that condition is very important.

Some specific items of interest include:

Photographs, interiors of old soda fountains before 1910
Soda Fountain Magazine, all issues dated before 1930
Other trade magazines (*Western Druggist, Soda Dispenser, Candy & Ice Cream, Confectioners Journal,* etc.) dating before 1920
Trade Catalogs by Tufts, Green, Bigelow, Morse, Gee, Dows, Puffer, Pick, Lippencott, Onyx, Zwietusch, Liquid Carbonic, Low Art Tile, etc.
Magazine covers before 1930 having soda fountain or ice cream themes
Opalescent swirl straw jar with an original matching glass lid
Heisey glass straw jar with open sides
Root beer pitchers in blue and gray pottery
Root beer mugs: Miners, Liquid Carbonic, and Papoose
Syrup bottles with glass labels

Harold and Joyce Screen
2804 Munster Rd.
Baltimore, MD 21234
410-661-6765 (after 6pm EST)
hscreen@home.com

Souvenir China

Wanted: rolled edge 10" souvenir/historical plates from Staffordshire, England, and imported by **Rowland and Marsellus, Royal, and A.C. Bosselman,** as well any other souvenirs with scenes of cities or towns that have any of these importers' marks. We buy all unusual Rowland and Marsellus souvenir china. Their back-stamp mark may be written in full or be shown as R&M in a diamond. (R&M was a New York importer from Staffordshire, England.) Blue transfers on white are of cities, towns, or personalities and were produced from 1900 through 1930. **Also wanted are German white porcelain divided dishes that usually have a large gold or orange and red lobster handle**. Please write or call. All calls and letters answered.

David Ringering
Key Ring Antiques
4063 Durbin Ave. SE
Salem, OR 97301

	We Pay
Rolled-Edge Plate	**50.00+**
Coupe Plate, 10"	**45.00+**
Fruit & Flower Bordered Plate, 9½"	**35.00+**
Souvenir Plate, 9"	**25.00+**
Tumbler	**40.00+**
Cup & Saucer	**50.00+**
Vase	**150.00+**
Pitcher	**150.00+**
Miscellaneous Piece	**90% of book value**
Divided Lobster Dish, German	**50.00+**
Souvenir Tumbler, German, metal w/North American scene	**10.00+**

Sporting Collectibles

I buy **sports tickets, sports books, programs, and other publications such as guides and annuals. Also wanted are pennants and other forms of memorabilia. Baseball, football, basketball, hockey, boxing — all sports — all items wanted.**

Bob Adelson
13610 N Scottsdale #10
Scottsdale, AZ 85254
602-596-1913

Stamps

I am buying quantities of US cancelled stamps. They can be on or off paper. Please send an inquiry first if you have large quantities. Always include SASE for my response. I usually respond quickly unless I'm on a trip. I pay promptly. Please write first before you send.

Fred Susukida
4224 Waialae Ave.
Ste. 5-236
Honolulu, HI 96816

	We Pay
US Cancelled Stamps (common variety, on paper okay), per thousand	**1.50**
Foreign Stamps (on paper okay), per thousand	**1.00**

Stangl Pottery

We especially want the following patterns of Stangl dinnerware:

- Blueberry
- Colonial #1388
- Country Life
- Fruit
- Garden Flower
- Chicory
- Country Gardens
- Cranberry
- Fruit and Flowers
- Garland

Grape
Jeweled Christmas Tree
Magnolia
Newport
Rooster
Blue and Yellow Tulip
Town and Country spatterware
Holly
Lyric
Mediterranean
Ranger
Thistle
Wild Rose

We don't want brown stains, chips, or cracks but minor flaws are acceptable. We'll buy **any piece of Kiddieware,** even 'as is' — especially Wizard of Oz and Flying Saucer. **Stangl artware** especially Terra Rose green and blue, Sunburst/Rainbow, Tropical ware, early Pennsylvania Tulip, other matte or gloss artwares, and lamps are wanted as well.

Perfect-condition Stangl birds, animals, animal planters, and piggy banks only but rare birds (those with values over $500.00) may have some damage. We also buy **specialty items** such as flowerpots, flower ashtrays, political mugs and pitchers, cigarette boxes, and any advertising or promotional items from this pottery company.

Bob and Nancy Perzel
Popkorn Antiques
P.O. Box 1057
Flemington, NJ 08822
908-782-9631

Swanky Swigs

Swanky Swigs are small decorated glass containers (juice glasses) with small flowers, sailboats, animals, dots, stars, or checkers and they come in different sizes — anywhere from 3 1/16" to 4¾". Kraft cheese spreads came in these containers and they date from the 1930s to the present. In most cases, I only need one each of the Swanky Swigs listed here.

Joyce Jackson
900 Jenkins Rd.
Aledo, TX 76008
817-441-8864

	We Pay
Antique #1, 4¾", black, blue, brown, green or orange	**20.00+**
Antique #2, 4⅝", orange, blue or black	**25.00+**

Band Pattern #5, 3⅛", red & black .... **20.00+**
Bustling Betsy, 4¾", green or orange .... **20.00+**
Checkerboard, 4⅝", white & green or white & blue .... **25.00+**
Checkers, 3⅛" .... **Call or Write**
Circles & Dots, 4¾", black or green .... **20.00+**
Cornflower #2, 4 3⁄16", dark blue, light blue or red .... **20.00+**
Ethnic Series, 4⅝", Scottish, burgundy .... **25.00+**
Ethnic Series, 4⅝", India, yellow .... **35.00+**
Fleur-de-Lis, 3⅛", black & red .... **Call or Write**
Kiddie Kup, 4¾", orange or black .... **20.00+**
Lattice & Vine, 3½", blue & white or red & white .... **35.00+**
Provincial Crests, 4⅝", Canada, burgundy & red .... **30.00+**
Star #1, 4¾", black or green .... **30.00+**
Special Issues, 3½", red tulip #1 (Del Monte) .... **60.00+**
Sportsman Series, 4⅝", Hockey, deep red **25.00**
Tulip #1, 3½", yellow .... **20.00+**
Tulip #1, 4⅝", black or yellow .... **20.00+**
Tulip #3, 4¾", dark blue or light blue .... **20.00+**
Any Glass Marked 'Greetings From Kraft' .... **Call or Write**

Swarovski

We buy — or find buyers for — **Swarovski 'Silver Crystal' figurines and objects.** Our special interest is the **Collector's Society Members Only 'Annual Club Editions'** starting from 1987 Lovebirds and continuing to the present. We pay top prices for the annual pieces and selected other pieces including most of the candle holders.

Swarovski Crystal is 33% lead and very easily nicked or scratched (lead is very soft). Serious collectors handle these pieces only with white cotton gloves to avoid damage.

To receive top prices, pieces must be free of any minor scratches or nicks; however, we will sometimes purchase damaged items or even badly broken pieces. We are also **often buying empty boxes and certificates for annual club pieces only.**

All Swarovski Crystal items were manufactured in Austria and each piece has either (the older) stylized block S trademark or the (newer) swan trademark etched into the glass, most often on the bottom of the item. Most boxes are cardboard cylinders (usually gray but sometimes other colors) with plastic caps on top and bottom and foam inserts to hold the piece inside. Regular boxes have also been used on some pieces, too. Some examples are listed below. We also pay a minimum of $50.00 for empty boxes or certificates for any of these except Dumbo.

Charlotte Sanchez
Sanchez Collectibles
1555 E Glendale Ave.
Phoenix, AZ 85020
602-395-9974 or fax 602-241-0702
sanchcol@primenet.com

	We Pay
1987 Lovebirds, $150 original retail	**3,200.00**
1988 Woodpecker, $165 original retail	**1,000.00**
1989 Turtledoves, $195 original retail	**700.00**
1993 Disney Dumbo, $195 original retail	**340.00**
1993 Elephant, $325 original retail	**1,000.00**

Swizzle Sticks

I am a long-time collector of **swizzle sticks.** I'm looking for examples from different states, countries, and business establishments. I prefer that they have some ornamentation on top or stems such as whistles, full-body animals, people, or objects that hang from the top. No plain sticks with a ball on the end are wanted unless they are made of glass. Prices for either collectible will depend on age, condition, and collectible value. You may give an asking price if you like. I will reply to all who contact me. Thank you.

Trisha Price
4815 W Clearwater #90
Kennewick, WA 99336
509-783-0920
Trisha@owt.com

Syrocowood

We collect pressed wood items made by Syrocowood and other companies such as Ornawood and Durawood. We are especially interested in brush holders, thermometers, and Scottie-related items. We are looking for items in excellent condition.

Carole Kaifer
P.O. Box 232
Bethania, NC 27010
910-924-9672

	We Pay
Brush Holders	10.00-25.00
Thermometers	5.00-20.00

Thermometers

I collect a specialized type of **advertising thermometer in plastic, shaped like old gasoline station pole signs.** Almost 7" tall, these thermometers, embedded under the gasoline sign in the support column, often had the dealer/distributor's name and location stamped on the base and often had a small paper calendar attached to the base. These were given away by the gasoline stations as a premium/gift item in the late 1950s through the mid-1960s. I am seeking regional and local gasoline brand thermometers such as those listed below. No national or more common brand thermometers such as Esso, Texaco, Mobil, etc., are wanted. Let me hear from you if you have one; I'll respond immediately. **Prices paid range from $15.00 to $35.00 each.**

APCO
Ashland
Barnsdall
Bay
CALSO
Clark
Deep Rock
Derby
Enco
Fleet-Wing
Frontier
FS (Farm Service)
Hudson
Husky
Keystone
Martin
M-F-A
Pan-Am
Humble
Shamrock
Signal
SOC
Speed-Wing
Spur
Sunoco
Tenneco
Total
United
76 (Union 76) UTOCO
Vickers
White Rose
Zenith
Zephyr

Peter Capell
1838 W Grace St.
Chicago, IL 60613-2724
773-871-8735

Tiffany

I have a small collection of **Tiffany silver.** I would be interested in any boxes, spoons, jewelry, etc., for my collection.

Other interests include: **pocket watches, Reddy Killowat, Royal Doulton, Beswick, match safes, old autographed books, eye cups, law enforcement badges, sterling silver, sewing items, stanhopes, Clarice Cliff, and purses.**

	We Pay
Tiffany Blue Bags	**4.00+**
Old Stock	**Call or Write**
Baby Items	**25.00+**
Sewing Items	**25.00+**
Razors	**25.00+**

	We Pay
Boxes	**10.00-50.00+**
Jewelry	**10.00-1,000.00+**
Spoons	**1.00-100.00+**
Other Smalls	**1.00-50.00+**

Please send photos and your asking price. Call or send your price list.

Kayla Conway
4500 Napal Ct.
Bakersfield, CA 93307
805-833-0291

Tire Ashtrays

I'm interested in buying most **tire ashtrays.** I'm aware of about 800 different ones now, and a listing here couldn't do justice to what's available. Please send a complete description of tire lettering and condition. Also, please note any defects such as burn marks on the tire or incomplete (or missing) painted advertising imprints/stickers on the ashtray insert. Contact me prior to shipping and provide a complete description in your first letter as well as your asking price. I also have tire ashtrays available for sale, as well as *The Tire Ashtray Collector's Guide*©. This guide details over 600 varieties and is available from me. I'll reply to all inquiries which include SASE.

Jeff McVey
1810 W State St. #427
Boise, ID 83702-3955
208-342-8447

Tools

My main interest is **old tools, specifically old screwdrivers.** I have special interest in ones made by blacksmiths or others that were handmade in a shop or garage. Other interests are **oil cans and tire gauges,** especially the dial type about the size of a silver dollar — both foreign and US-made types. These may have a reference to cars as Studabaker, Cadillac, Ford, etc. Anything unusual is desired.

Canes are my latest collecting passion — especially those made of wood like diamond willow or other interesting woods. Price range would be between $5.00 and $50.00 depending on condition.

Bill and Linda Miclean
499 Theta Ct.
San Jose, CA 95123
408-224-1445

Wanted: **tools of wood (and some of metal), working machinery, accessories, parts, and literature (catalogs, manuals, etc.)** I want older Delta, Craftsman, Walker-Turner, Duro, Yates/Maerican, Fay/Egan, etc. Especially wanted are older Oliver items and big wood lathe items.

Jeff McVey
1810 W State St. #427
Boise, ID 83702-3955
208-342-8447

Toys

I am known for my fair dealings and for paying top prices for **windups, robots, space toys, toys made by TPS, Japanese/German/English motorcycles, Japanese tin cars, clowns, character toys, celluloid, Disney, boats, airplanes, and battery-operated toys**. Of special interest are **pre-1950s holiday items, especially Halloween and Christmas**. On a number of occasions I have paid over $2,000.00 for a single toy. What do you have?

Mark Bergin
P.O. Box 3073
Peterborough, NH 03458-3073
603-924-2079 or fax 603-924-2022

	We Pay
Character Toys (any character, any type)	**up to 15,000.00**
Christmas Items (candy containers, Santa figures, old ornaments, figural bulbs, blocks, games, feather trees, figures of any Christmas character, etc)	**up to 1,500.00**
Halloween Items (candy containers, diecuts, jack-o'-lanterns, crepe paper goods, figures, etc), vintage only	**up to 1,500.00**
Robots or Space Toys, tin, Japanese, circa 1950s, w/original box	**up to $24,000.00**
Motorcycles, tin, German or Japanese	**up to 5,000.00**
Cars, tin, Japanese	**200.00-8,000.00**
Windup Toys, all types wanted	**up to 7,500.00**

I am buying **antique mechanical toys**. I primarily collect tin wind-up toys but am also interested in friction and battery-operated toys. **Toys made from 1900 to 1965** in good to mint-in-box condition are preferred. Listed below are some of the manufacturers that I am seeking. Please contact me if you have these or others available for sale. Thank you.

Scott T. Smiles
848 SE Atlantic Dr.
Lantana, FL 33462-4702
561-582-4947
ssmiles664@aol.com

	We Pay
Arnold	**75.00+**
Chein	**50.00+**
Lehmann	**100.00+**
Made in Germany	**50.00+**
Made in Japan	**50.00+**
Martin	**100.00+**
Marx	**50.00+**
Occupied Japan	**50.00+**
Strauss	**100.00+**
TPS	**75.00+**
Unique Art	**75.00+**
US Zone Germany	**50.00+**
Wolverine	**50.00+**

Never having grown up, I'm still interested in **toys — primarily tin wind-up toys and pre- and post-war Germany, Japan, and US; Japanese battery-operated toys; vintage board games; and Disney Toys.** I'm interested in many other things, too — **Halloween collectibles, Black memorabilia, Coney Island memorabilia, vintage cookware, Ruppert-Knickerbocker beer memorabilia, vintage costume jewelry, paper ephemera, advertising trade cards, vintage valentines,** and much more! So let me hear about what you have.

Judith Katz-Schwartz
P.O. Box 6572
New York, NY 10128-0006
212-876-3512
http://antiques.miningco.com

	We Pay
Early German, American or Japanese Windups	**50.00-1,200.00**
Post-War Japanese Battery-Operated Toys	**50.00-600.00**
Vintage Board Games, 1800s to 1970s	**20.00-600.00**
Disney Toys, pre-1960s	**250.00-1,400.00**

Toys

As a collector of **Baby Boomer-era items (1948 through 1972)**, I am interested in an endless number of items and toys produced as promotions for TV shows. I am looking for **children's lunch boxes and thermoses, Beatles and Elvis items, rock 'n roll memorabilia, super hero and other character dolls or items, robots and space toys, cap guns and sets, original boxes (even if empty), and much more.**

Any items relating to the following are wanted: Howdy Doody, Green Hornet, Beany and Cecil, Batman, Beatles, Brady Bunch, Jetsons, American Bandstand, Dark Shadows, Davy Crockett, Universal Movie Monsters, robots and space toys, Paladin, Munsters, Addams Family, Bonanza, Flintstones, Lost in Space, Space Patrol, Supercar, Star Trek, Star Wars series, Underdog, Rifleman, and many others. Price depends on the item. Any toys, character, advertising, or TV show-related items will be considered for purchase or trade.

Below is a listing of some of the items I am searching for and prices I am willing to pay for excellent condition items. I would pay a lesser amount for lesser-condition items. Mint-in-box items would be worth more to me. Please send photos if possible when sending an inquiry and a LSASE for a reply. I would like the opportunity to purchase your items. Thank you.

Terri's Toys and Nostalgia
Terri Mardis-Ivers
206 E Grand
Ponca City, OK 74601
405-762-8697 or 405-762-5174 (evenings)
fax 405-765-2657
toylady@poncacity.net

General Categories of Interest	We Pay
Miniature Boat Motors, metal, battery-operated, realistic forms w/Johnson, Evinrude, etc., printed on side	70.00+
Vehicles, versions of real cars, boats, etc., 8" or larger	30.00+
Promotional Model Vehicles, prior to 1980	20.00+
Other Vehicles	Call or Write
Cap Guns, through the 1960s	15.00+
Gun & Holster Sets, through the 1960s	up to 200.00
Dolls (Munsters, Beatles, Elvis, Addams Family, I Dream of Jeannie, Star Trek, Lone Ranger, Hopalong Cassidy & so many more!)	10.00-150.00
Cowboy Character items (except made of paper) for Lone Ranger, Gene Autry, Bonanza, Rifleman, Roy Rogers, Tom Mix & TV Show Westerns	Call or Write

Hopalong Cassidy	We Pay
Clothes Hamper	200.00
Chaps	40.00
Skirts	30.00

Guns	40.00
Holsters	70.00
Bicycle	500.00
Tricycle	500.00
Clocks, Dolls, Lamps, Bedspreads, Vinyl Flooring, Saddle, Figurines, Potato Chip Tin Can, Wallet & Other Items	25.00+

Elvis Presley Enterprises Items	We Pay
Scarves	35.00
Jewelry	100.00
Overnight Case	100.00
Doll, 1956	300.00
Guitar, 1956	250.00
Autograph book	200.00
Wallet	200.00
Handbag	200.00
Shoes	200.00
Record Player	200.00
Scrapbook	75.00
Pillow	20.00
Many Other Items Wanted	Call or Write

Beatles Items, circa 1960s to '70s	We Pay
Kaboodle Kit	200.00
Brunch Bag	200.00
Record Player	350.00
Guitar	150.00
Shoes	50.00
Thermos	60.00
Hat	20.00
Drums	200.00
Lamp	70.00
Drinking Glass	25.00
Alarm Clock	100.00
Many More Items Wanted	Call or Write

KISS & Monkees Items	We Pay
Guitar, Drums, Trading Cards, Radios, Toy Cars, Hand Puppets, Dolls, View-Master Reels, Lunch Boxes, Thermoses, Jewelry	30.00
Colorforms	20.00
Sleeping Bag	45.00
Tour Jacket	50.00
Record Player	50.00
KISS Waste Basket	30.00
KISS Make-Up Kit	20.00

I buy **Matchbox cars made from 1953 through 1969**. I will pay top dollar for most Matchbox cars with original boxes and accessories as listed in the price guide of the book, *Matchbox Toys 1947–1996* by Dana Johnson and published by Collector Books or *Lesney's Matchbox Toys, Regular Wheels, 1947 through 1969* by Charlie Mack and printed by Schiffer Publishing Ltd. I am also interested in buying old Hot Wheels, Johnny Lightning, Aurora slot cars, Husky, Corgi, Corgi Juniors, and Dinky. A color photo could be helpful. Please contact:

Richard Okula
P.O. Box 6393
Wolcott, CT 06716
203-879-6883

	We Pay
#1 Road Roller, metal rollers	**50.00**
#2 Dump Truck, metal wheels	**50.00**
#3 Cement Mixer	**50.00**
#4 Tractor	**65.00**
#4 Motorcycle 'Triumph'	**60.00**
#5 London Bus, metal or gray wheels	**50.00**
#6 6-Wheel Dump Truck, yellow or orange & gray	**50.00**
#7 Ford Anglia, gray wheels	**30.00**
#7 Milk Wagon	**75.00**
#8 Caterpiller Tractor, w/driver	**40.00-65.00**
#9 Fire Truck	**25.00-50.00**
#10 Sugar Truck	**40.00**
#10 Trailer Truck	**60.00**
#11 Tanker, green 200, yellow 75 or red	**50.00**
#12 Jeep, w/man	**50.00**
#12 Jeep, no man	**25.00**
#13 Tow Truck, tan	**60.00**
#13 Tow Truck, red	**50.00**
#14 Ambulance	**20.00-55.00**
#15 Prime Mover Truck Tractor	**50.00**
#16 Trailer	**40.00**
#17 Austin Taxi	**50.00**
#17 Van, blue or maroon	**200.00**
#17 Van, green	**60.00**
#18 Caterpillar Bulldozer, w/man	**50.00**
#19 MG Sports Car	**75.00**
#19 Auston Racer	**50.00**
#20 Stake Truck, metal or gray wheels	**50.00**
#21 Long Distance Coach	**50.00**
#22 Vauxhall Sedan	**50.00-200.00**
#22 Pontiac	**20.00**
#23 2-Wheel Camper	**50.00**

#23 4-Wheel Camper 10.00
#24 Excavator, metal wheels 50.00
#25 Dunlap Van 50.00
#25 Dunlap Van 50.00
#25 VW Beetle 60.00
#26 4-Wheel Cement Mixer 50.00
#26 6-Wheel Cement Mixer, blue barrell 500.00
#27 Cadillac 70.00
#27 Low Loader 85.00
#28 Compressor Truck, metal or gray wheels 50.00
#29 Milk Truck 50.00
#30 Silver 6-Wheel Crane 50.00
#31 Ford Wagon 50.00
#32 Jaguar XK 140, metal or gray wheels 65.00
#33 Ford Zodiac, green 50.00
#33 Ford Zodiac, gold & orange 125.00
#34 VW Van, green or turquoise 50.00
#35 Horse Truck 50.00
#36 Austin A50 .... 50.00
#36 Lambretta Motorcycle & Sidecar 125.00
#37 Coca-Cola Truck 65.00
#38 Refuse Truck .... 35.00+
#38 Vauxhall Wagon 30.00
#38 Honda Motorcycle & Trailer 20.00
#39 Ford Zodiac Convertible 60.00
#39 Pontiac Convertible, yellow 40.00
#39 Pontiac Convertible, purple 125.00
#40 Dump Truck 50.00
#41 D-Type Jaguar 65.00
#41 Ford GT, white 20.00
#41 Ford GT, yellow 200.00
#42 News Van 50.00
#42 Studebaker Wagon 20.00
#43 Hillman Minx 50.00
#43 Pail Loader 30.00
#44 Rolls Royce, blue 50.00
#44 Rolls Royce, gold 25.00
#45 Vauxhall Victor 50.00
#46 Morris Minor 1000 .... 50.00
#46 Moving Van, green 25.00
#45 Moving Van, blue 75.00
#47 Brook Bond Tea Van 50.00
#47 Ice Cream Truck 30.00
#48 Boat, metal boat 50.00
#48 Boat, plastic boat 30.00
#49 Half Track 40.00
#50 Commer Pick-Up 50.00
#50 Tractor 20.00

#50 Ford Kennel Truck........20.00
#50 Tractor........20.00
#51 Cement Truck........50.00
#52 Maseati Racer........50.00
#53 Aston Martin........50.00
#54 Personel Carrier........25.00
#54 Ambulance........15.00
#55 Army Amphibian........50.00
#55 Police Car, blue Fairlane........60.00
#55 Police Car, white Galaxie or Mercury........40.00
#56 Trolley Bus........50.00
#56 Fiat 1500, red........50.00
#57 Wolseley 1500........50.00
#57 Chevrolet Impala........50.00
#57 Fire Truck........15.00
#58 Airport Bus........70.00
#58 Pail Loader........30.00
#59 Ford Thames Van Singer........60.00
#59 Fairlane Fire Chief........60.00
#59 Galaxie Fire Chief........15.00
#60 Morris Pick-Up........20.00
#61 Army Scout Car........20.00
#62 Army Truck........40.00
#62 TV Van or Radio Rentals........45.00
#62 Cougar........20.00
#63 Army Ambulance........40.00
#63 Airport Fire Truck........20.00
#64 Army Tow Truck........40.00
#65 Jaguar, blue........50.00
#65 Jaguar, red........30.00
#66 Citroen DS19........50.00
#66 Harley Davidson Motorcycle & Sidecar........175.00
#67 Army Truck........35.00
#67 Volkswagon........20.00
#68 Army Radio Truck........35.00
#69 Nestles Van........55.00
#69 Hatra Tractor Shovel, yellow........15.00
#69 Hatra Tractor Shovel, orange........30.00
#70 Thames Van........25.00
#71 Army Water Truck........50.00
#71 Jeep Pick-Up........20.00
#71 Ford Wrecker........20.00
#72 Tractor........25.00
#73 Airforce Refueler........65.00
#73 Ferrari Racer........35.00
#73 Ford Wagon........15.00
#74 Refreshment Trailer........50.00
#75 Ford Thunderbird........100.00

I buy **toys of the 1950s, 1960s, and 1970s — Hot Wheels, Tonka Trucks, Matchbox, Corgi, Johnny Lightning, car models, dealer promotionals, lunch boxes, Mego dolls, GI Joe, and more.** Call or write today for top dollar for your old toys.

Todd Torgerson
19164 Evening Star Way
Farmington, MN 55024-7027
651-463-9491

	We Pay
Hot Wheels, 1960s through 1980s	**7.00-1,000.00**
Tonka Trucks, 1950s through 1970s	**20.00-150.00**
Dealer Promotionals, 1950s through 1970s	**20.00-100.00**
Model Kits, 1950s through 1970s	**8.00-50.00**
Matchbox, 1950s through 1970s	**7.00-75.00**
Slot Cars, 1950s through 1970s	**8.00-100.00**

I want to buy **older, used Hot Wheels and related items.** Boxfulls are okay. Please call Jeff evenings.

Jeff
414-886-0477 CST

As a child I spent a lot of my time playing cowboys and Indians and soldier. Now as an adult I am trying to reclaim some of those fun times that I spent as a child. So I am collecting the toy guns I played with as a boy. I am buying character **toy guns, holsters, and machine guns from the '50s and '60s.** As an advanced collector, condition is important. But I will consider guns that are not in excellent or mint condition. Here are some examples of what I am buying.

Paladin, Have Gun Will Travel, guns
Paladin, Have Gun Will Travel, holsters
The Rebel, Johnny Yuma, gun & holster
The Rebel, Johnny Yuma, scatter shot gun
Hopalong Cassidy, guns
Gene Autry, guns
Mattel Shoot 'N Shell
Tommyburst, machine gun

Ron Wright
P.O. Box 69
Burbank, OH 44214
330-624-3741

Wanted by collector: I seek **cap guns that have revolving cylinders from the 1950s and cast iron types** — the earlier the better. In **BB guns** I look for anything and everything except those with plastic parts or stocks. I will pay well for quality guns according to rarity; condition is also very important. Send photo and description and price to:

Terry Burger
2323 Lincoln St.
Beatrice, NE 68310
402-228-2797

My wife and I specialize in toy **cap guns, BB guns, and cowboy gun and holster sets** featuring Hopalong Cassidy, Roy Rogers, Gene Autry, Matt Dillon, Wyatt Earp, etc. I will pay a fair price for good stuff. **I have paid as much as $500.00 to $600.00 for BB guns and $600.00 to $700.00 for cap guns**.

We also buy steel and tin toy trucks, old knives, and antiques.

Paul D. Patchin
3425 Co. Rd. E-F
Swanton, OH 43558
419-826-8661

I collect all **toy metal outboard boat motors**. These may be electric, tin windup, steam powered, or gas powered. Most of these motors were made in Japan from 1955 to 1970 by KO. I want nice, clean motors with no repaints or chipped paint. No plastic motors are wanted. I will pay 10% extra if you have the original box. Also wanted are **gas-powered race cars.**

Richard Gronowski
140 N Garfield Ave.
Traverse City, MI 49686-2802
616-491-2111

	We Pay
Evinrudes, 40 HP or 75 HP, ea	**125.00**
Gale Sovereign, 60 HP	**200.00**
Gale, 30 HP or 35 HP, ea	**125.00**
Johnsons, 40 HP or 75 HP, ea	**125.00**
Oliver, 35 HP	**200.00**
Mercury, black, 100 HP	**200.00**
Mercury, MK 55, MK 800, MK 78 or MK 75, ea	**125.00**
All Other Johnsons, Mercurys, Scotts, Evinrudes, Gales, ea	**75.00**
Sea-Fury	**75.00**
Sea-Fury Twin	**150.00**
Fuji or Orkin, ea	**125.00**
Tin Winups, ea	**75.00**
Generic's I.M.P, Langcraft, Yamaha, Super Tigre, Speed King, Sakai, New Evince, Le-Page, Swank, Aristocraft, Etc., ea	**50.00**

We are interested in buying **old toys of any kind:** tin, cast iron, wooden, diecast, rubber, etc. Pressed steel, pedal cars, large or small — we buy them all!

We are also interested in **gas station items** such as signs, oil cans, old tools, giveaway items, and globes. Please send a picture and asking price.

Mid City Arts & Antiques
409 N Hampton
DeSoto, TX 75115-4917
Attention: Merle J. Vondrasek
972-223-6720

I would like to buy **Barney Google and Spark Plug** from the comic strip. Barney is a wooden man and his horse, Spark Plug, is felt and cloth. They were made in the 1920s. Price depends on condition.

Barb Farber
Rt. 1, Box 44
Reeder, ND 58649
701-563-4418

Toy soldiers and miniature figures have been commercially produced since the 1880s in Europe and the United States. They have been made in a wide range of materials including lead, iron, aluminum, composition, bisque, rubber, and plastic.

In addition to soldiers, companies produced farm figures, zoo animals, railroad and civilian figures, circus sets, cannons, tanks, trucks, forts, castles, and a wide range of other topics.

Condition is very important. Broken figures have no value. Those with badly worn paint also have very little value. Complete sets in their original boxes are the most desirable. I buy single figures or entire collections.

Dave Francis
148 King St.
Wadsworth, OH 44281
330-335-3717 or fax 330-335-3617
fphadv@bright.net

	We Pay
Individual Soldiers, ea	**2.00-100.00**
Complete Sets	**50.00-1,000.00+**
Farm or Zoo Animals, ea	**1.00-35.00**
Cannons, Tanks or Trucks, ea	**25.00-500.00**

I remember the good old days and have a fondness for trains. **Lionel HO trains, engines, cars, accessories are bought and sold.** Items may or may not have their original boxes. Let me hear about your items.

Grant Wehrfritz
4393 Old State Rte. 17
Livingston Manor, NY 12758

Looking for **transformers!** These robots that turned into vehicles were made by Hasbro from 1980 through 1989. I'm not interested in any made in the 1990s. I'm also looking for **Shogun Warriors, Voltron items, any Japanese-type robot, and character toys.** Boxed or loose figures, parts, empty boxes, instructions, etc. — all this wanted. Call, e-mail, or write for offer!

Barbara Brecker
76 Sicard St.
New Brunswick, NJ 08901
888-532-8697 or 732-246-1589
SalandRei@aol.com

I am a private collector of **cast iron zeppelin pull toys** and want to buy these for my private collection. Price will depend on type and condition. Please contact me with details about your zeppelin pull toy.

Robert G. Kassner
145 Teepee Trial
Southold, NY 11971

I'm a Christian collector as well as 'picker' (I buy for different people who are collectors or resell items) with interests in **baby boomer collectibles of the 1940s through 1980s.** Many wants are listed below; I'm also interested in **clocks, watches, cookie jars, lamps, lighters, phones, and radios.**

Do not send anything without our agreeing on price. I only buy old items in undamaged condition. SASE is a must. Please send photo and price. Please don't send anything without prior approval. I have been a collector/picker since 1971.

R. Gray
2047 Jeffcott St.
Ft. Myers, FL 33901
941-332-0153
bargainlady@webtv.net

	We Pay
Albee-Avon Mrs. Albee Figures	**up to 25.00**
Airplane Models, metal	**up to 25.00**
Animal Dolls	**up to 25.00**
Annalee Figures	**up to 50.00**
Breyer Horses & Animals	**up to 25.00**
California Raisins	**25¢ to 20.00**
Candy Containers, glass	**up to 25.00+**
China, featuring Disney, Garfield, Holly Hobbie, etc	**up to 25.00**
China, w/Aunt Jemima or Little Red Riding Hood	**up to 50.00**
China or Ceramic Items, featuring Care Bears, Garfield, Disney, etc.	**up to 20.00**
China, w/Western motif or railroad logo	**up to 25.00**
Figurines, marked HH, Florence, Occupied Japan, Goebel, Royal Doulton, Beswick, Josef, Lefton, Van Briggle, Amaco, Gonder, Kreiss, HR, Schmid, etc	**up to 25.00**
Figurines, flamingos or Scottie dogs	**up to 25.00**
Florida Souvenirs, old	**up to 25.00**
Flower Frogs	**up to 25.00**

Head Vases ....up to 25.00
Novelty Figural Items (phones, lights, radios, wind-up watches, clocks, lighters, advertising figures, etc ....up to 50.00
Nudes...up to 25.00+
Pixie Covered Jars, Bottles, Etc ....up to 25.00
Purses, plastic or Lucite...up to 20.00
Stuffed Animals, mohair..up to 50.00
Steiff Animals...up to 50.00
Taxidermy Items..Write
Toby Mugs ....up to 50.00
TV Lights or Revolving Lamps...up to 50.00
Unusual or Gaudy Items, old ....Call or Write
World's Fair Items, dated through 1964 ....25.00

I am looking for **Fisher-Price pull toys and playsets from 1932 to 1986**. I am especially interested in The Castle, Hospital, and Sesame Steet playsets or pieces. The paper litho on the toys must be intact with little to no edge wear. I am also looking for any wooden people in very good condition. I would also like to invite anyone interested in joining our Fisher-Price Collector's Club with a current membership of 250 strong nationwide and still growing. Below are just a few of the prices I am willing to pay for your Fisher-Price toys. Please call or write to me for more information on any of these areas.

Brad Cassity
1350 Stanwix
Toledo, OH 43614
419-385-9910

We Pay

Any Castle, Hospital, or Sesame Street People or Pieces, ea 1.50
Wooden People, like-new condition, ea 1.00
Castle, Hospital or Sesame Street House, w/no pieces 10.00
Pull Toy, 1970-1980, ea 10.00-20.00
Pull Toy, 1960-1970, ea 20.00-30.00
Pull Toy, 1950-1960, ea 30.00-125.00
Pull Toy, 1931-1950, ea 30.00-600.00
Fisher-Price Catalogs, ea 5.00-25.00

Trade Catalogs

Catalogs, manuals, publications (e.g., Deltagram), How-To books, etc., **by wood-working and metal-working machinery manufacturers** as Delta, Craftsman, Oliver, etc. are wanted. I'm also interested in **tire ashtrays.** See also my listing for tire ashtrays in this book.

Jeff McVey
1810 W State St. #427
Boise, ID 83702-3955
208-342-8447

Trading Cards

The Book Baron is always buying **old trading cards — sport and nonsport.** Especially of interest are Mickey Mantle baseball cards. For example, we will pay $200.00 for a Mickey Mantle 1960 Topps card in mint condition or up to $75.00 for any Michael Jordan Starting Line-Up action figure (mint on card). The Book Baron also buys **collectible toys** (Hot Wheels, Barbies, action figures, etc.), **records, and memorabilia.** We also buy **movies, video games and systems, books, compact disks, and cassettes.** The Book Baron is open Monday through Saturday, 9am to 9pm. Holiday hours are 11am to 5pm for Memorial Day, Fourth of July, Labor Day, Christmas Eve, and New Years Eve. We are closed on Thanksgiving and Christmas.

The Book Baron
Evelyn Hardy
3128 S Main
Joplin, MO 64804
417-782-2778 or fax 417-782-0024
BOOKBARN@prodigy.net

Tramp Art and Trench Art

We are buyers of **tramp art, most anything made from notched cigar boxes, and trench art, most anything made from brass cartridge shells.** Feel free to send photos (will return).

Sam Kennedy
212 N 4th St.
Coeur d'Alene, ID 83814
208-769-7575

	We Pay
Layered Box, 12x6x4"	50.00-150.00
Nine-Layered Notched Frame, 2x2"	50.00-150.00
Notched Dresser	200.00-1,000.00
Bowls of Cigar Sticker Labels	20.00+
WWI Shells, w/dates & names	25.00-75.00
Shells, w/pictures	25.00-75.00
Shell Airplanes	75.00-150.00
Shell Lamps	50.00-125.00
Shell Ashtrays	20.00+

Traps

A friend gave me an old live trap for mice that was made out of wire. In researching this trap, I found it is called a French Marty. Over 4,400 patents have been granted for mouse traps in the last 150 years. Traps were made of wood, wire, tin, metal, glass, and other materials that would drown, electrocute, behead, spear, mash — and a number of other ways to either dispatch or imprison mice. Some dropped mice into water, some lead them into rooms from which they couldn't get out. One was a mirror in which the mouse saw his reflection and fell through a trap door trying to get to the other mouse. Another was built like a miniature tricycle and when the mouse got into the front wheel (which was a treadmill), he would move the vehicle around the room to the amusement of the homeowners. I am interested in buying any of these or other **old, odd, and unusual traps of any kind — from mouse to bear.**

I am decorating my den with **old hunting, fishing, trapping, and guide items of any kind.** Please keep me in mind if you or anyone you know has any item you think I may be interested in. Send for a list of items I want.

Bob Bowering
P.O. Box 420
E Wilton, ME 04234

TV Guides

I would like to buy ***TV Guide*** magazines dating from 1948 through 1998 as well as **newspaper TV supplement magazines.**

Jeff Kadet
P.O. Box 20
Macomb, IL 61455
309-833-1809
jkadet@macomb.com

Twin Winton

The Twin Winton name was conceived by twins, Don and Ross Winton. In 1936 (when these 17-year-old twins started a small business making hand-decorated ceramic animal figures and sold them locally in Pasadena, California), Twin Winton became a successful pottery. Don continued to be the only designer for Twin Winton until the pottery closed in 1977. Besides designing for Twin Winton, Don has designed for other companies such as Disney, Brush-McCoy, Ronald Regan Foundation, and many others.

Twin Winton made their famed cookie jar collector series, salt and pepper shakers, and many other pieces. They also developed their distinctive wood-stain finish. As the author of *The Lost Treasures of Don Winton* published by Collector Books, I am interested in researching the company through finding original company correspondence, sales literature and brochures, original pieces, and especially any pre-1963 catalogs. Please let me hear from you regarding Twin Winton.

Mike Ellis
266 Rose Ln.
Costa Mesa, CA 92627
714-646-7112 or fax 714-645-4697

Typewriter Ribbon Tins

I would like to buy typewriter ribbon containers, both tin and cardboard, for my extensive collection. Ribbon tins were made from the 1890s well into the 1970s. Generally, the more graphically appealing a tin is, the more it is worth; however, plain but rare ribbon tins may also have value. The best way to find out what you have is to send a photocopy, a photo, or even a hand drawing of your item — or you may telephone me. I will answer all inquiries promptly. Please describe condition and enclose SASE. I also buy other typewriter-related collectibles which illustrate secretaries, typewriters, or tins such as blotters, secretarial erasing shields, carbon paper boxes, signs, rulers, tape measures, display cabinets, etc.

Hoby Van Deusen
28 The Green
Watertown, CT 06795
860-945-3456

Vernon Kilns

I collect **Vernon Kilns art pottery and dinnerware** manufactured in California between 1930 and the late 1950s. As a company, they produced a wide variety of items with distinctive styling. Some of the Vernon Kilns designers and patterns I collect are:

Jane F. Bennison — bowls, candlesticks, planters, vases, etc.
Harry Bird — dinnerware with birds, fish, and scenic patterns
Don Blanding — dinnerware marked Aquarium, Coral Reef, and Honolulu; children's pieces or sets
Walt Disney — dinnerware, figurines, hand-decorated bowls and vases
May & Vieve Hamilton — sculptural pottery, bowls, vases, and dinnerware
Rockwell Kent — dinnerware marked Moby Dick, Our America, and Salamina
Janice Pettee — art pottery figurines
Gale Turnbull — various dinnerware patterns
Advertising and company brochure items

Please describe, state condition, price, and enclose SASE for written response. Photographs are helpful and will be returned. I may be interested in other items not listed also. Phone calls are welcome; but please don't call looking for a free appraisal. Thank you.

Other wants include **Brayton Laguna, Catalina Island, and Russel Wright designs in glass, pottery, and wood.**

Ray Vlach, Jr.
5364 N Magnet Ave.
Chicago, IL 60630-1216
312-225-5692 (evenings only)

View-Master and Other 3-D Photographica

View-Master, the invention of William Gruber, was first introduced to the public at the 1939–1940 New York World's Fair and at the same time at the Golden Gate Exposition in California. Since then thousands of different reels and packets have been produced on subjects as diverse as life itself. Sawyers View-Master even made two different stereo cameras for the general public, enabling people to make their own personal reels, and then offered a stereo projector to project the pictures they took on a silver screen in full color 3-D.

View-Master has been owned by five different companies: the original Sawyers Company, G.A.F. (in October 1966), View-Master International (in 1981), Ideal Toy Company, and Tyco Toy Company (the present owners).

Unfortunately, after G.A.F. sold View-Master in 1981, neither View-Master International, Ideal, nor Tyco Toy Company have had any intention of making the products anything but toy items, selling mostly cartoons. This, of course, has made the early noncartoon single reels and three-reel packets desirable items.

The earliest single reels from 1939 to 1945 were not white in color but were originally dark blue with a gold sticker in the center and came in attractive gold-colored envelopes. Then they were made in a blue and tan combination. These early reels are more desirable, as the print runs were low.

From 1946 to 1957 most white single reels are very common, as they were produced in the millions. There are exceptions, however, such as commercial reels promoting a product or obscure scenic attractions, as these would have had smaller print runs. In 1952 a European division of View-Master was established in Belgium. Most reels and items made in Belgium are more valuable to a collector, since they are harder to find in this country.

In 1955 View-Master came up with the novel idea of selling packets of three reels in one colorful envelope with a picture or photo on the front. Many times a story booklet was included. These became very popular and single reels were slowly discontinued. Most three-reel packets are desirable, whether Sawyers or G.A.F., as long as they are in nice condition. Nearly all viewers are common and have little value, except the very early ones, such as Model A and Model B. These viewers had to be opened to insert the reels. The blue and brown versions of the Model B are rare. Another desirable viewer is the Model D, which is the only focusing viewer that View-Master Made.

Condition is very important to the value of all View-Master items, as it is with most collectibles. I buy most all desirable and scarce View-Master material in very good to mint condition.

Walter Sigg
P.O. Box 208
Swartswood, NJ 07877

View-Master and Other 3-D Photographica

View-Master	We Pay
Camera, Mark II, w/case	**100.00**
Camera, Personal Stereo, w/case	**100.00**
Close-Up Lens, for Personal Camera	**100.00**
Film Cutter, for cameras	**100.00**
Packet, scenic, 3-reel set	**1.00-25.00**
Packet, TV or movie, 3-reel set	**2.00-50.00**
Packet, Addams Family or Munsters, 3-reel set, ea	**50.00**
Packet, Belgium made, 3-reel set	**4.00-35.00**
Packet, miscellaneous subject, 3-reel set	**3.00-50.00**
Projector, Stereo-Matic 500	**200.00**
Reel, gold center, gold-colored package	**10.00**
Reel, blue	**2.50-10.00**
Reel, Sawyers, white, early	**25¢-5.00**
Reel, commercial, brand-name product (Coca-Cola, auto makers, etc)	**5.00-50.00**
Reel, 3-D movie preview (House of Wax, Kiss Me Kate, etc)	**50.00**
Reel, Belgium made	**1.00-10.00**
Viewer, Model B, blue or brown, ea	**100.00**
Viewer, Model D, focusing type	**30.00**
Any Advertising Literature, Dealer Displays, Etc (items not meant to be sold to the public)	**Write**
Original Factory Items	**Write**

I buy **many kinds of 3-dimensional items.** In the area of **3-D movie memorabilia**, any poster, press book, lobby card, still, or banner with 3-D or 3-Dimensional on it is desired. I also buy glass slides that were used in movie theaters. The slides measure 4x3¼". I buy slides from all eras, but prefer pre-1940 slides.

I want memorabilia on all short films in 3-D and am looking for memorabilia on the following movie titles. There must be '3-D' on the graphics:

Audio Scopiks, 1936
Dangerous Mission, 1954
Friese-Green Stereoscopic Films, 1893
Gorilla at Large, 1954
Heartbound, 1935
Jim the Penman, 1915
L'Arrivee Du Train, 1903
Lumiere Stereoscopic Films, 1935
M.A.R.S., 1922
New Audioscopiks, 1938
Niagara Falls, 1915
Pathe News, 1929
Plastigrams, 1922
Radio-Mania, 1922
Catwomen on the Moon, 1954
Faust, 1922
Gog, 1954
Grand Canyon, 1923
Jesse James Vs. the Daltons, 1954
Jivaro
Louisana Territoy, 1953
Lunacy, 1925
Movies of the Future, 1922
New York City, 1922
Ouch!, 1929
Plasticons, 1922
The Power of Love, 1922
Reve d'Opium (I Dream of Opium), 1921

The Runaway Taxi, 1925
The Ship of Souls, 1925
Teleview, 1921
Zigfield Frolic, 1929
Rural America, 1915
Southwest Passage
Washington, D.C., 1923
Zowie, 1925

Any 3-D magazines are wanted. These magazines are viewed with 3-D glasses or some kind of 3-D viewer. The photos look fuzzy and out of focus when seen without a viewing aid. I prefer pre-1960 3-D magazines, but will buy issues from any decade.

I buy **any kind of stereoscopic 3-D image** such as View-Master, True-Vue filmstrips, 3-D slides, lenticulars, stereocards, Novelviews, Stori-Views, etc. I also buy **any 3-D camera equipment** such as stereo projectors, stereoviewers, stereo cameras, and stereo slides. I pay $10.00 for View-Master advertising reels and $25.00 for True-Vue advertising filmstrips. Zeroxes of the stereoviews would be a great help. My favorite subjects are Hollywood, World's Fairs, movie stars, movie theaters, magic and magicians — anything movie related.

I prefer pre-1960 **3-D comic books** but will buy ones from all eras.

Chris Perry, Doctor 3-D
7470 Church St. #A
Yucca Valley, CA 92284
619-365-0475 or fax 619-365-0495

Wacky Package Stickers

I collect **Topp's Wacky package stickers and related items**. These were stickers that spoofed food and household items and were made from 1969 through 1976. I am only interested in pre-1977 Wacky stuff unless noted. I am looking for stickers that are die-cut and punch out instead of peel off; 1977 copyright stickers, vending machine stickers from 1982 (all have black backgrounds), two Wackies on one sheet, cloth stickers, first and second series stickers with a camel pictured on the back, and third series stickers with a white backing. Specific stickers include Band-Ache, Choke Wagon, Bum Chex, Grime Dog Food (must say Heavy Chunks), Split and Spill (must have Spic and Span on box lid), Pupsi Cola, Run Tony, Mutt's Paul Maul, Lavirus, and all 16th series stickers. Other wants include:

Art, original only
Beach towels
Clothing
Halloween giveaway Wackies
Banks
Can labels
Drinking glasses
Wacky ads (look like billboards)

Iron-ons
Necklaces
Plastered Peanuts, etc.
Wacky Wall Plaks
Jaymar jigsaw puzzles
POGS
Pillows
Wrappers, display boxes, store ads and displays
Cereal boxes (Cookie Crisp, Dinky Donuts, Laffel-Os) with giant Wackies on the backs
Inflatable pool toys (beach ball, inner tube, raft)
Posters of Toadal, Weakies, Cheapios, etc.
Mail-away wall posters, pins, and key chains
Patches of Glutton, Paul Maul, Sicken of the Sea, Botch Tape, Mrs. Klean,
Tattoos or charms of O-Pee-Chee (pre-1976 Canadian Wackies)

Call or write with anything you have! I'm a huge collector of this stuff and will pay a great price!

David Gross
76 Sicard St.
New Brunswick, N.J. 08901
908-246-1589
SalandRei@aol.com

	We Pay
Ratz Crackers Diecut (#4 or #32)	**300.00+**
Cracked Animals Diecut (#38)	**300.00+**
Good & Empty Wacky Ad (#25)	**300.00+**
Cereal Boxes, intact, ea	**100.00**
Miscellaneous Items (pins, clothing, beach towels, etc)	**Call or Write**
Original Art	**200.00**
Poster, Weakies, Cheapios or Toadal	**50.00+**
Wall Poster	**50.00**
Wall Placks, ea	**10.00**
All Types of Stickers	**Call or Write**
All Display Boxes, Wrappers and Advertising	**Call or Write**

Watch Fobs

I buy all **authentic advertising watch fobs**. Also wanted are stickpins, pinback buttons, mirrors, and **other small advertising items as well as radio premiums, political items, and hunting memorabilia** — especially relating to gunpowder.

David Beck
P.O. Box 435
Mediapolis, IA 52637
319-394-3943

	We Pay
John Deere, blue oval	150.00+
Farm Tractors	10.00-300.00+
Gun Powder	100.00+
Shoes	20.00-50.00+
State Farm	60.00+

Watches

They say: The 'first' watch made was in the year 1500. The minute hand did not appear until 1687. Watches with movable figures date back to 1790. There are 195,000 watches sold per day.

We say: Dig out those watches and turn them into money. Watches need not be working or in good shape. Our policy is to return your watch that day if you don't like our offer. In all these years, we are proud to say that we haven't returned one watch! Examples of prices are listed below. Depending on condition, gold, diamonds, etc., prices may be much more. NOTE: No longer buying women's or any type of quartz watches.

James Lindon
5267 W Cholla St.
Glendale, AZ 85304
602-878-2409

	We Pay
Audemars Piquet	350.00
Benrus	20.00
Breitling	100.00
Bucherer	20.00
Bulova	20.00
Cyma	20.00
Ebel	30.00
Gruen	30.00
Hamilton	30.00

Heuer	**40.00**
Hyde Park	**20.00**
Illinois	**30.00**
Le Coultre	**100.00**
Longines	**50.00**
Mido	**30.00**
Movado	**80.00**
Omega	**50.00**
Patek Philippe	**500.00+**
Rolex	**300.00**
Tiffany	**100.00**
Ulysse Nardin	**80.00**
Universal Geneva	**100.00**
Vacheron Constantin	**1,000.00**
Wittnauer	**30.00**
Any Character Watches	**Call or Write**
Any Advertising Watches	**Call or Write**
Any Watch-Related Advertising	**Call or Write**

We have been the advisor for *Schroeder's Antiques Price Guide* for watches for years and have over 33 years' experience in the field of **antique pocket watches and vintage wristwatches**. We are a leading authority for watches worldwide. **Watches currently needed include:**

Pocket watches and vintage better wristwatches, both American and European

Especially interested in: Patek Philippe, Howard, Illinois, Hamilton, Rolex, railroad (signed railroad dials and railroad movements), keywinds, watches that chime, up/down winding indicators, chronographs, enamels, calendars, and moon phases

Historical watches, sports-related watches, gold cases, novelty character watches, and unusual watches

Always buying any American pocket watch 21 jewels or higher.

We pay significant finder's fee for leads towards our purchase of large collections, estates, or accumulations. **Watches wanted dead or alive: need not run!** Prices highest for mint condition, original case, dial and movement, and vary according to watch. We are **not** interested in Timex, inexpensive watches made after 1965, nor any lady's wristwatches. We are **serious buyers** of any rare watch. Same day payment. All transactions strictly confidential. Buying prices vary according to condition and originality. Call Today!

Maundy International
P.O. Box 13028-BW
Shawnee Mission, KS 66282
Call Toll Free 1-800-235-2866 When You're Ready to Sell!

	We Pay
American Watch Co., 21 jewels & higher	**65.00+**
Ball Official RR Standard	**150.00+**
Hamilton, 21 jewels & higher	**75.00+**
Howard (Boston)	**75.00+**
Illinois, 21 jewels & higher	**100.00+**
Jules Jurgensen Copenhagen (pocket)	**500.00+**
Masonic Logo Dial & Movement	**550.00+**
Patek Philippe	**1,500.00+**
Railroad Watches, 21 jewels & higher	**150.00+**
Repeater (chimes on command)	**500.00+**
Up/Down Winding Indicators (pocket)	**325.00+**

We have been seeking and reselling antiques for over twenty years in Central New York. Our taste is for unusual items of good quality that are from the 1700s through 1800s when possible. We like to think we are as fair as possible and are willing to travel for substantial purchases.

Also, we are always looking for **military items — especially those of the Civil War.** These can be photographs, metals, weapons, etc. (No dead horses, please!) If you have something, I would like to hear from you.

We look for old banks — preferably mechanical. And will pay up to $2,000.00 for these.

Wilson's Antiques Service
1732 E Homer Rd.
Cortland, NY 13045
607-753-1076

	We Pay
Pocket Watches, Dudley Watch Co, Mason's model	**500.00-1,000.00**
Pocket Watches, Dudley Watch Co, other models	**Call or Write**
Watch, Fusee type, English, 1700-1800s	**up to 1,000.00**
Mechanical Banks	**up to 2,000.00**

I collect a variety of things, but special interests are **1970s LED watches and calculators.** I also want **old computers and related materials, old video game stuff from the 1970s and 1980s, and pre-1990s metal trash cans featur-**

ing advertising or comic characters.

I buy and sell **commercial art (prints, calendars, and magazines); advertising signs, calendars, characters, and products; toys (banks, action figures, Disney, Fisher-Price, etc.); and miscellaneous items such as Steiff stuffed animals, Kewpies, character-related items, etc.**

Robb Sequin
P.O. Box 1126
Dennisport, MA 02639
508-760-2599
rsesquin@capecod.net

Wedding Cake Toppers

I would like to hear from anyone having **older wedding cake toppers (bride and grooms) for sale that were made prior to the 1950s. Bisque, porcelain, chalkware, and celluloid ones will be considered.** Please, no plastic types. Of particular interest would be grooms in military uniforms. A topper might be in poor condition and still be considered. The true wedding topper is fragile and not meant as a play item. Please, **no** doll sets. A photo or rough sketch is very helpful. Prices reflect toppers in excellent condition.

Jeannie Greenfield
310 Parker Rd.
Stoneboro, PA 16153-2810

	We Pay
WWII Military Couple, plaster w/paper base	**25.00**
Art Deco, single molded set, shiny plaster, 1930s	**25.00**
Wood Figures on Plaster Base, 1900s	**40.00**
All Bisque Couple in 1920s Dress	**35.00**

Western Collectibles

We are buyers of old pre-1930 cowboy material — items used on a farm or ranch. We do **not** buy modern mass-market pieces but prefer the one-of-a-kind item with character. Feel free to send photos (will return).

Sam Kennedy
212 N 4th St.
Coeur d'Alene, ID 83814
208-769-7575

	We Pay
Chaps, leather	**100.00-800.00**
Chaps, wooly	**200.00-1,000.00**
Spurs	**50.00-500.00**
Cowboy Cuffs	**50.00-500.00+**
Six-Guns (need not be working)	**50.00-1,000.00+**
Leaver-Action Saddle Guns	**100.00-1,000.00+**
Handcuffs	**50.00+**
Badges	**100.00+**
Saddles	**100.00-1,000.00**
Old Photos	**Varies**
Original Paintings	**100.00-5,000.00**
Quirts	**50.00-150.00**

We are interested in purchasing **cowboy and rodeo memorabilia from the '40s and '50s as well as memorabilia relating to Gene Autry, Roy Rogers, Hoppy, etc. Also wanted are records, autographed photos, banks, plates, and lamps; cowboy vases, planters and cookie jars are desired.**

Cityslickers Cowboy Collectibles
Richard and Anni Frey
61 Marine St.
Bronx, NY 10464
718-885-0898

	We Pay
Hamilton Classic TV Western Plates	20.00
Cowboy Guitars	50.00+
Rodeo Programs	5.00+
Til Goodan Items	25.00+

Whimsical Children's Cups

Whimsical children's cups had whistles or figures on their handles and writing or saying about juice or milk. I will pay $20.00 to $40.00 for these cups, depending on condition.

Deborah Gillham
47 Midline Ct.
Gaithersburg, MD 20878
301-977-5727
dgillham@erols.com

Winchester

We are buyers and collectors of Winchester. We are mostly looking for pre-1950 pieces but unusual pieces are also of interest. We also want old ammunition boxes that are bright and undamaged. All pieces must be clearly marked Winchester. Feel free to send photos (will return).

Sam Kennedy
212 N 4th St.
Coeur d'Alene, ID 83814
208-769-7575

Winchester	We Pay
Advertising Pieces, cardboard	20.00-50.00
Ball Bats & Gloves	75.00+

Chisels	**10.00+**
Golf Clubs	**50.00+**
Planes	**20.00-200.00**
Posters	**100.00-1,000.00**
Screwdrivers	**10.00-30.00**
Shotgun Shell Boxes, 2-pc	**20.00-50.00+**

Windmill-Related Items

Only items related to US-made water-pumping windmills are wanted. Such things would include literature, salesman samples, calendars, dealers signs, and promotional items. Sorry, I am **not** interested in any Dutch windmill items.

Dennis L. Schulte
708 Allamakee St.
Waukon, IA 52172-1240

World's Fair Memorabilia

I'm primarily interested in the **New York World's Fair of 1939, although I do buy other fairs if you have something unusual.** I'm **not** looking for postcards or pamphlets from the exhibits, but almost anything that pictures the Trylon and Perisphere or the Unisphere (1964 NY World's Fair) is of interest to me. As I have many collecting interests, please let me hear about other items you have for sale. See my listing in this book under Toys.

Judith Katz-Schwartz
P.O. Box 6572
New York, NY 10128-0006
212-876-3512
http://antiques.miningco.com

World's Fair Memorabilia

	We Pay
Porcelier Teapots, Creamers, Pitchers	75.00-250.00
Original Posters	75.00-600.00
Souvenir Jewelry or Watches	20.00-600.00
Dolls or Stuffed Animals	100.00-400.00
Inkwells or Paperweights	75.00-250.00

OTHER INTERESTED BUYERS OF MISCELLANEOUS ITEMS

In this section of the book we have listed buyers of miscellaneous items and related material. When corresponding with these collectors, be sure to enclose a self-addressed stamped envelope if you want a reply. Do not send lists of items for appraisal. If you wish to sell your material, quote the price that you want or send a list of items you think they might be interested in and ask them to make you an offer. Be sure to throughly describe your items and mention any marks. You can sometimes do a pencil rubbing to duplicate the mark exactly. Photocopies and photographs are most helpful. If you want the list or photograph back, be sure to send an SASE large enough for them to be returned.

It's a good idea to include your phone number if you write, since many people would rather respond with a call than a letter. And suggesting that they call back collect might very well be the courtesy that results in a successful transaction. If you're trying to reach someone by phone, always stop to consider the local time on the other end of your call. Even the most cordial person when dragged out of bed in the middle of the night will very likely *not* be receptive to you.

Abingdon
Louise Dumont
579 Old Main St.
Coventry, RI 02816
Alternative address:
318 Palo Verde Dr.
Leesburg, FL 34749
LOUISED452@aol.com

Action Figures
Super Hero,
Planet of the Apes
Barbara Brecker
76 Sicard St.
New Brunswick, NJ
08901
732-246-1589
SalandRei@aol.com

Advertising
Aunt Jemima
Fee charged for appraisal
Judy Posner
R.R. 1, Box 273
Effort, PA 18330
http://www.tias.com/
stores/jpc
judyandjef@aol.com

Big Boy
Steve Soelberg
29126 Laro Dr.
Agoura Hills, CA 91301
818-889-9909

Campbell's Soup
Authors of book
Dave and Micki Young
414 Country Ln. Ct.
Wauconda, IL 60084
phone, fax 847-487-4917

Cereal boxes, premiums
Author of books; editor of
magazine: Flake
Scott Bruce;
Mr. Cereal Box
P.O. Box 481
Cambridge, MS 02140
617-492-5004
Buys, sells, trades,
appraises; books available
from author

Elsie the Cow, Mr.
Peanut, Reddy Kilowatt,
Pepsi, Freedomland, tins,
all advertising
Marty Blank
P.O. Box 405
Fresh Meadows, NY
11554
516-485-8071
MartyAdver@aol.com

Gasoline/Petroliana
Peter Capell
1838 W Grace St.
Chicago, IL 60613-2724
773-871-8735

Gasoline globes, pumps,
signs and promotional
items
Author of book
Scott Benjamin
411 Forest St.
LaGrange, OH 44050
216-355-6608

General line
Patrice McFarland
P.O. Box 400
Averell Park, NY 12018-0400
greatgames@webtv.net

Gerber Baby dolls
Author of book
($44 postpaid)
Joan S. Grubaugh
2342 Hoaglin Rd.
Van Wert, OH 45891
419-622-4411
fax 419-622-3026

Green Giant
Edits newsletter
Lil West
2343 10000 Rd.
Oswego, KS 67356
316-795-2842
Also other related Pillsbury memorabilia

Jewel Tea products and tins
Bill and Judy Vroman
739 Eastern Ave.
Fostoria, OH 44830
419-435-5443

Mr. Peanut
Judith and Robert Walthall
P.O. Box 4465
Huntsville, AL 35815
205-881-9198

Poppin' Fresh (Pillsbury Doughboy)
Editor of newsletter: The Lovin' Connection
Lil West
2343 10000 Road
Oswego, KS 67356
316-795-2842, 7am - 7pm
Also other related Pillsbury memorabilia

Reddy Kilowatt and Bordon's Elsie
Lee Garmon
1529 Whittier St.
Springfield, IL 62704

Smokey Bear
Glen Brady
P.O. Box 3933
Central Point, OR 97502
541-664-7674

Tins
Author of book
Linda McPherson
P.O. Box 381532
Germantown, TN 38183
KPCY12A@prodigy.com

Watches
Editor of newsletter: The Premium Watch Watch
Sharon Iranpour
24 San Rafel Dr.
Rochester, NY 14618-3702
716-381-9467
fax 716-383-9248
SIranpour@aol.com

Airline Memorabilia
Richard Wallin
P.O. Box 1784
Springfield, IL 62705
217-498-9279

Akro Agate
Rena Hubbard
640 W. Main St.
Campbellsville, KY 42718
Scottie and Colonial Girl powder tops; some bottoms, any color; also children's dishes

Aluminum
Author of book
Everett Grist
P.O. Box 91375
Chattanooga, TN 37412-3955

Richard Haigh
P.O. Box 29562
Richmond, VA 23242
804-741-5770 (until 9pm EST)

Author of book
Dannie Woodard
P.O. Box 1346
Weatherford, TX 76086
817-594-4680

American Bisque
Author of book
Mary Jane Giacomini
P.O. Box 404
Ferndale, CA 95536-0404
707-786-9464

Americana
Patrice McFarland
P.O. Box 400
Averell Park, NY 12018-0400
greatgames@webtv.net

Angels
Specializing in birthday and Zodiac
Jim and Denise Atkinson
555 East School St.
Owatonna, MN 55060
507-455-3340

Sonja K. Rothstein
1308 Medical Dr.
Fayetteville, NC 28304

Animal Dishes
Author of book
Everett Grist
P.O. Box 91375
Chattanooga, TN 37412-3955
417-451-1910
Has authored books on aluminum, advertising playing cards, letter openers, and marbles

Appliances
Jim Barker
Toaster Master General
P.O. Box 41
Bethlehem, PA 18106

Art
Oils, lithos, watercolors, old framed pictures
Steve and Susie Arnhold
3085 F 1/2 Rd.
Grand Junction, CO 81504
970-434-8064

Ashtrays
Author of book
Nancy Wanvig
Nancy's Collectibles
P.O. Box 12
Thiensville, WI 53092

Autograph Albums
Sherry and Mike Miller
303 Holiday Dr.
Tuscola, IL 61953
217-253-4991
miller@tuscola.net

Autographs
Don and Anne Kier
2022 Marengo St.
Toledo, OH 43614
419-385-8211
ozrktrmn@clandjop.com

Automobilia
Tire ashtrays
Author of book ($12.95 postpaid)
Jeff McVey
1810 W State St., #427
Boise, ID 83702

Autumn Leaf
Gwynneth Harrison
P.O. Box 1
Mira Loma, CA 91752-0001
909-685-5434

Avon Collectibles
Author of book
Bud Hastin
P.O. Box 11530
Ft. Lauderdale, FL 33339

Badges
Game warden, fire, and forest warden
Bob Bowering
P.O. Box 420
E Wilton, ME 04234
207-778-6724

Banks
Modern mechanical banks
Dan Iannotti
212 W Hickory Grove Rd.
Bloomfield Hills, MI
48302-1127

Barware
Especially cocktail shakers
Arlene Lederman
Antiques
150 Main St.
Nyack, NY 10960

Specializing in vintage cocktail shakers
Author of book
Stephen Visakay
P.O. Box 1517
W Caldwell, NJ 07707-1517
cocktailshakers@webtv.net

Bathing Beauties
Gwen Daniel
18 Belleau Lake Ct.
O'Fallon, MO 63366
314-978-3190
GWENDANIEL@aol.com

Beanie Babies
Jerry and Ellen L.
Harnish
110 Main St.
Bellville, OH 44813
419-886-4782

Beatnik and Hippie Collectibles
Richard M. Synchef
22 Jefferson Ave.
San Rafael, CA 94903-4104
415-507-9933
fax 415-507-9944

Beatrix Potter
Nicki Budin
679 High St.
Worthington, OH 43085
614-885-1986
Also Royal Doulton

Beer Cans
Dan Andrews
27105 Shorewood Rd.
Rancho Palos Verdes, CA
90275
310-541-5149
brewpub@earthlink.net

Bells
Unusual; no cow or school
Author of books
Dorothy J. Anthony
2401 S Horton St.
Ft. Scott, KS 66701-2790

Bicycles and Tricycles
Consultant, collector, dealer
Lorne Shields
Box 211
Chagrin Falls, OH 44022-0211
905-886-6911 or
fax 905-886-7748
vintage@globalserve.net

Black Americana
Ed Natale
P.O. Box 222
Wyckoff, NJ 07481
201-848-8485

Buy, sell, and trade; lists available; fee charged for appraisal
Judy Posner
R.R. 1, Box 273
Effort, PA 18330
http://www.tias.com/stores/jpc
judyandjef@aol.com

Black Glass
Author of book
Marlena Toohey
703 S Pratt Pky.
Longmont, CO 80501
303-678-9726

Blue Ridge
Oscar Hubbert
P.O. Box 1415
Fletcher, NC 28732
828-687-0350

Author of several books; columnist for The Depression Glass Daze
Bill and Betty Newbound
2206 Nob Hill Dr.
Sanford, NC 27330
Also milk glass, wall pockets, figural planters, collectible china, and glass

Blue Willow
Author of several books
Mary Frank Gaston
900 Bob White
Bryan, TX 77802
Also china and metals

Bobbin' Heads by Hartland
Author of guide; newsletter
Tim Hunter
1668 Golddust
Sparks, NV 89436
702-626-5029

Bookends
Author of book
Louis Kuritzky
4510 NW 17th Pl.
Gainesville, FL 32605
352-376-3884

Art Deco, cowboy and Indian
T.J. Ahlberg
1000 Irvine Blvd.
Tustin, CA 92780
714-730-1000 or
fax 714-730-1752

Books
Big Little Books
Ron and Donna Donnelly
6302 Championship Dr.
Tuscaloosa, AL 35406
205-507-0789 or
fax 205-507-0544

Big Little Books, Disney, pop-up and comic-related books
Ken Mitchell
710 Conacher Rd.
Willowdale, Ontario
Canada M2M 3N6

Children's
Marvelous Books
Dorothy (Dede) Kern
P.O. Box 1510
Ballwin, MO 63022
314-458-3301 or
fax 314-273-5452

Children's
My Bookhouse
27 S Sandusky St.
Tiffin, OH 44883
419-447-9842

Children's illustrated, Little Golden, etc.
Ilene Kayne
1308 S Charles St.
Baltimore, MD 21230
410-685-3923
Ilenegold@aol.com

Children's
Bob and Gail Spicer
Ashgrove Treasure Trove
1250 Ashgrove Rd.
Cambridge, NY 12816-9801

Fine books and antique toys
Bromer Booksellers, Inc.
607 Boylston St., on
Copley Sq.
Boston, MA 02116

Little Golden Books, Wonder and Elf
Author of book on Little Golden Books
Steve Santi
19626 Ricardo Ave.
Hayward, CA 94541

Paperback originals, TV and movie tie-ins, etc.
Tom Rolls
230 S Oakland Ave.
Indianapolis, IN 46201

Bottle Openers
Charlie Reynolds
2836 Monroe St.
Falls Church, VA 22042
703-533-1322

Bottles
Carmel Dairy
T.J. Ahlberg
1000 Irvine Blvd.
Tustin, CA 92780
714-730-1000 or
fax 714-730-1752

Bitters, figurals, inks, barber, etc.
Steve Ketcham
P.O. Box 24114
Minneapolis, MN 55424
612-920-4205
Also advertising signs, trays, calendars, etc.

Dairy and milk
Author of books
John Tutton
R.R. 4, Box 929
Front Royal, VA 22630
703-635-7058

Painted-label soda
Author of books
Thomas Marsh
914 Franklin Ave.
Youngstown, OH 44502
216-743-8600 or 800-845-7930 (book orders)

Painted-label soda; Bergen/Passaic Co. NJ Dairy
Ed Natale
P.O. Box 222
Wyckoff, NJ 07481
201-848-8485

Boyd
Joyce M. Pringle
Chip and Dale Collectibles
3708 W Pioneer Pky.
Arlington, TX 76013
Also Summit and Mosser

Boyd's Bears
Editor of secondary market price guide
Rosie Wells Enterprises, Inc.
R.R. #1
Canton, IL 61520
Also Hallmark, Precious Moments, Cherished Teddies

Breweriana
Dan Andrews
The Brewmaster
27105 Shorewood Rd.
Rancho Palos Verdes, CA 90275
310-541-5149
brewpub@earthlink.net

Tip and change trays; New Jersey items
Ed Natale
P.O. Box 222
Wyckoff, NJ 07481
201-848-8485

Breyer
Carol Karbowiak Gilbert
2193 14 Mile Rd. 206
Sterling Hts., MI 48310

British Royal Commemoratives
Author of book
Audrey Zeder
6755 Coralite St., S
Long Beach, CA 90808
Catalog available

Brownies by Palmer Cox
Don and Anne Kier
2022 Marengo St.
Toledo, OH 43614
419-385-8211

Brush-McCoy Pottery
Authors of book
Steve and Martha Sanford
230 Harrison Ave.
Campbell, CA 95008
408-978-8408

Bubble Bath Containers
Matt and Lisa Adams
1234 Harbor Cove
Woodstock, GA 30189
770-516-6874

Buckles
E. Bohlin, Hollywood Saddlery, etc.
T.J. Ahlberg
1000 Irvine Blvd.
Tustin, CA 92780
714-730-1000
fax 714-730-1752

Buffalo Pottery
Fred and Lila Shrader
2025 Hwy. 199 (Hiouchi)
Crescent City, CA 95531
707-458-3525

Butter Pats
Fred and Lila Shrader
2025 Hwy. 199 (Hiouchi)
Crescent City, CA 95531
707-458-3525

Cake Toppers
Jeannie Greenfield
310 Parker Rd.
Stoneboro, PA 16153-2810
724-376-2584

Calculators
Author of book
Guy Ball
14561 Livingston St.
Tustin, CA 92780

California Perfume Company
Not common; especially items marked Goetting Co.
Dick Pardini
3107 N El Dorado St., Dept. G
Stockton, CA 95204-3412
Also Savoi Et Cie, Hinze Ambrosia, Gertrude Recordon, Marvel Electric Silver Cleaner, and Easy Day Automatic Clothes Washer

California Pottery
Susan N. Cox
Main Street Antique Mall
237 East Main Street
El Cajon, CA 92020
619-447-0800
Want to buy: California pottery, especially Brayton, Catalina, Metlox, Kay Finch, etc.; Also examples of relatively unknown companies. Must be mint. (Susan Cox has devoted much of the past 15 years to California pottery research which caught her interest when she was the editor and publisher of the *American Clay Exchange.* She would appreciate any information collectors might have about California pottery companies and artists.)

Especially Hedi Shoop, Brad Keeler, Howard Pierce, Kay Finch, Matthew Adams, Marc Bellaire, Twin Winton, Sascha Brastoff; many others
Pat and Kris Secor
P.O. Box 158
Clarksville, AR 72830
Editor of newsletter: The California Pottery Trader
Michael John Verlangieri Gallery
P.O. Box 844
W Cambria, CA 93428-0844
Holds cataloged auctions

Cleminsons
Robin Stine
P.O. Box 6202
Toledo, OH 43614
419-385-7387

Camark
Tony Freyaldenhover
P.O. Box 1295
Conway, AR 72033
501-329-0628
camarket@cyberback.com

Cameras
Classic, collectible and usable
Gene's Cameras
2614 Artie St., SW Ste. 37-327
Huntsville, AL 35805
205-536-6893

Candy Containers
Glass
Jeff Bradfield
90 Main St.
Dayton, VA 22821
703-879-9961
Also advertising, cast-iron and tin toys, postcards and Coca-Cola

Glass
Author of book
Doug Dezso
864 Paterson Ave.
Maywood, NJ 07607
Other interests: Tonka Toys, Shafford black cats, German bisque comic character nodders, Royal Bayreuth creamers, and Pep pins

Cape Cod by Avon
Debbie and Randy Coe
Coes Mercantile
Lafayette School House
Mall #2
748 3rd (Hwy. 99W)
Lafayette, OR 97137
Also Elegant and Depression glass, art pottery, Golden Foliage by Libbey Glass Company, and Liberty Blue dinnerware

Carnival Chalkware
Author of book
Thomas G. Morris
P.O. Box 8307
Medford, OR 97504-0307
541-779-3164
chalkman@cdsnet.net
Also Ginger Rogers memorabilia

Cast Iron
Door knockers, sprinklers, figural paperweights and marked cookware
Craig Dinner
P.O. Box 4399
Sunnyside, NY 11104
718-729-3850

Cat Collectibles
Editor of newsletter: Cat Talk
Marilyn Dipboye
33161 Wendy Dr.
Sterling Hts., MI 48310
810-264-0285

Goebel, Josef, Hagen-Renaker, others
Renae Giles
P.O. Box 6
Carver, MN 55315-0006

Ceramic Arts Studio
BA Wellman
P.O. Box 673
Westminster, MA 01473

Character and Personality Collectibles
Author of books
Dealers, publishers, and appraisers of collectible memorabilia from the '50s through today
Bill Bruegman
Toy Scouts, Inc.
137 Casterton Ave.
Akron, OH 44303
330-836-0668
fax 330-869-8668
toyscout@akron.infi.net

Any and all
Terri Ivers
Terri's Toys
206 E Grand
Ponca City, OK 74601
580-762-8697 or
580-762-5174
fax 580-765-2657
toylady@poncacity.net

Any and all
John Thurmond
Collector Holics
15006 Fuller
Grandview, MO 64030
816-322-0906

Any and all
Norm Vigue
3 Timberwood Dr., #306
Goffstown, MA 03045
603-647-9951

Batman, Gumby, and Marilyn Monroe
Colleen Garmon Barnes
114 E Locust
Chatham, IL 62629

Beatles
Bojo
Bob Gottuso
P.O. Box 1403
Cranberry Twp., PA
16066-0403
phone or fax 724-776-0621

Betty Boop
Leo A. Mallette
2309 Santa Anita Ave.
Arcadia, CA 91006-5154

California Raisins
Ken Clee
Box 11412
Philadelphia, PA 1911
215-722-1979

California Raisins
Larry De Angelo
516 King Arthur Dr.
Virginia Beach, VA 23464

Dick Tracy
Larry Doucet
2351 Sultana Dr.
Yorktown Hts., NY 10598

Disney, Western heroes, Gone With the Wind, character watches ca 1930s to mid-1950s, premiums and games
Ron and Donna Donnelly
6302 Championship Dr.
Tuscaloosa, AL 35405
205-507-0789 or
fax 507-0544

Disney, radio, TV or cereal
Ken Mitchell
710 Conacher Rd.
Willowdale, Ontario
Canada M2M 3N6

Disney
Buy, sell, and trade; lists available; fee charged for appraisal
Judy Posner
R.R. 1, Box 273
Effort, PA 18330
http://www.tias.com/stores/jpc
judyandjef@aol.com

Elvis Presley
Author of book
Rosalind Cranor
P.O. Box 859
Blacksburg, VA 24063

Elvis Presley
Lee Garmon
1529 Whittier St.
Springfield, IL 62704

Garfield
Adrienne Warren
1032 Feather Bed Ln.
Edison, NJ 08820
908-381-7083 (EST)
Also Smurfs and other characters, dolls, monsters, premiums; Lists available

I Dream of Jeannie, Barbara Eden
Richard D. Barnes
1520 W 800 N
Salt Lake City, UT 84116
801-521-4400

Lil' Abner
Kenn Norris
P.O. Box 4830
Sanderson, TX 79848-4830

The Lone Ranger
Terry and Kay Klepey
c/o *The Silver Bullet* newsletter
P.O. Box 553
Forks, WA 98331

Lucille Ball
Author of book
Ric Wyman
408 S Highland Ave.
Elderon, WI 54429

Moxie 'doll house' bottle carton; mesh purse promotional items
Sherry and Mike Miller
303 Holiday Dr.
Tuscola, IL 61953
217-253-4991
miller@tuscola.net

Peanuts and Schulz Collectibles; also Wizard of Oz
Gwen Daniel
18 Belleau Lake Ct.
O'Fallon, MO 63366
314-978-3190
GWENDANIEL@aol.com

Peanuts and Schulz Collectibles
Freddi Margolin
P.O. Box 5124P
Bay Shore, NY 11706
516-666-6861 or
fax 516-665-7986
snupius@li.net

Roy Rogers and Dale Evans author; biographer for Golden Boots Awards
Robert W. Phillips
1703 N Aster Pl.
Broken Arrow, OK 74012-1308
918-254-8205 or
918-252-9362
rawhidebob@aol.com
One of the most widely-published writers in the field of cowboy memorabila and author of *Roy Rogers, Singing Cowboy Stars, Silver Screen Cowboys, Hollywood Cowboy Heroes*, and *Western Comics: A Comprehensive Reference*; research consultant for TV documentary *Roy Rogers, King of the Cowboys* (AMC-TV/ Republic Pictures/Galen Films)

Shirley Temple
Gen Jones
294 Park St.
Medford, MA 02155

Smokey Bear
Glen Brady
P.O. Box 3933
Central Point, OR 97502
541-664-6764

Three Stooges
Harry S. Ross
Soitenly Stooges Inc.
P.O. Box 72
Skokie, IL 60076

Tom Mix
Author of book
Merle 'Bud' Norris
1324 N Hague Ave.
Columbus, OH 43204-2108

TV and movie collectibles
TVC Enterprises
P.O. Box 1088
Easton, MA 02334
508-238-1179

Video game characters and related items
David Gross
76 Sicard St.
New Brunswick, NJ 08901
732-246-1589
SalandRei@aol.com

Wizard of Oz
Bill Stillman
Scarfone & Stillman Vintage Oz
P.O. Box 167
Hummelstown, PA 17036
717-566-5538

Character and Promotional Drinking Glasses

Authors of book; editors of Collector Glass News
Mark Chase and Michael Kelly
P.O. Box 308
Slippery Rock, PA 16057
724-946-2838 or
724-794-2540
fax 724-946-9012
cgn@glassnews.com
www.glassnews.com

Character Clocks and Watches

Author of book
Howard S. Brenner
106 Woodgate Terrace
Rochester, NY 14625

Bill Campbell
1221 Littlebrook Ln.
Birmingham, AL 35235
205-853-8227
fax 405-658-6986
Also character collectibles, advertising premiums

Character Nodders
Matt and Lisa Adams
1234 Harbor Cove
Woodstock, GA 30189
770-516-6874

Chicago Items
Donald Friedman
660 W Grand Ave.
Chicago, IL 60610
312-226-4741
DFRIED4141@aol.com

Children's Things
Vintage clothing (especially shoes), old books, dolls and accessories, china and tea sets
Joyce Andresen
7330 Hudson Hts.
Hudson, IA 50643

China and Porcelain
Marlow by Minton Co.; buy and sell
Mary Faria
P.O. Box 32321
San Jose, CA 95152-2321
408-258-0413

Chintz
Loretta DeLozier
1101 Polk St.
Bedford, IA 50833
712-523-2289 (M-F, 9 am to 4 pm)
fax 712-523-2624
LeftonLady@aol.com
http://members.aol.com/leftonlady/

Marge Geddes
P.O. Box 5875
Aloha, OR 97007
503-649-1041

Mary Jane Hastings
310 West 1st South
Mt. Olive, IL 62069
phone, fax 217-999-7519

Author of book
Joan Welsh
7015 Partridge Pl.
Hyattsville, MD 20782
301-779-6181

Christmas Collectibles
Especially from before 1920 and decorations made in Germany
J.W. 'Bill' and Treva Courter
3935 Kelley Rd.
Kevil, KY 42053
phone, fax 502-488-2116

Plastic or celluloid Santa and sleigh led by reindeer, mounted on a green base; small tree in sleigh
Jo Carol Gentry
481 Tanner Road
Searcy, AR 72143
Will pay $50.00

Winston Churchill Items
Donald Friedman
660 W Grand Ave.
Chicago, IL 60610
312-226-4741
DFRIED4141@aol.com

Clocks
All types
Bruce A. Austin
40 Selborne Chase
Fairport, NY 14450
716-223-0711

1940s–50s cowboys
T.J. Ahlberg
1000 Irvine Blvd.
Tustin, CA 92780
714-730-1000
fax 714-730-1752

Clothes Sprinkler Bottles
Ellen Bercovici
5118 Hampden Ln.
Bethesda, MD 20814
301-652-1140

Clothing and Accessories
Author of book
Sue Langley
101 Ramsey Ave.
Syracuse, NY 13224-1719
315-445-0133
langhats@aol.com

Teresa Clawson, Customer Service
Flying Deuce
1224 Yellowstone
Pocatello, ID 83201
208-237-2002 or
fax 208-237-4544
flying2@nicoh.com

Pat Campensa
'The Hat Lady'
414 E Heman St.
E Syracuse, NY 13057
315-431-4441

Coca-Cola
Also Pepsi-Cola and other brands of soda
Craig and Donna Stifter
P.O. Box 6514
Naperville, IL 60540
630-789-5780

Coin-Operated Vending Machines
Ken and Jackie Durham
909 26th St., NW
Washington, D.C. 20037

Coins
David W. Mayer
33 Mt. Vernon Pl.
Jamestown, NY 14701
716-487-0556

Collections
California picker buys/sells all
Hellinger
11791 Steele Dr.
Garden Grove, CA 92840-2124

Colorado Pottery (Broadmoor)
Carol and Jim Carlton
8115 S Syracuse St.
Englewood, CO 80112
303-773-8616
Also Coors, Lonhuda, and Denver White

Comic Books
Avalon Comics
Larry Curcio
P.O. Box 821
Medford, MA 02155
617-391-5614

Also Sunday newspaper comic sections and comic-strip art
Ken Mitchell
710 Conacher Rd.
Willowdale, Ontario
Canada M2M 3N6

Compacts
Souvenir styles
Kayla Conway
4500 Napal Ct.
Bakersfield, CA 93307
805-833-0291

Unusual shapes, also vanities and accessories
Author of book
Roselyn Gerson
P.O. Box 40
Lynbrook, NY 11563

Coney Island Memorabilia
Judith Katz-Schwartz
P.O. Box 6572
New York, NY 10128-0006
212-876-3512

Cookbooks
Author of book
Bob Allen
P.O. Box 56
St. James, MO 65559
Also advertising leaflets

Cookie Cutters
Author of book and newsletter
Rosemary Henry
9610 Greenview Ln.
Manassas, VA 20109-3320

Cookie Jars
Joe Devine
1411 3rd St.
Council Bluffs, IA 51503
712-232-5233 or
712-328-7305
Also Russel Wright

Buy, sell, and trade; lists available; fee charged for appraisal
Judy Posner
R.R. 1, Box 273
Effort, PA 18330
http://www.tias.com/stores/jpc
judyandjef@aol.com

Phil and Nyla Thurston
82 Hamlin St.
Cortland, NY 13045
607-753-6770
Other interests listed under Figural Ceramics

Cookware
Vintage only
Judith Katz-Schwartz
P.O. Box 6572
New York, NY 10128-0006
212-876-3512

Corkscrews
Antique and unusual
Paul P. Luchsinger
1126 Wishart Pl.
Hermitage, PA 16148

Cowan
Author of book
Mark Bassett
P.O. Box 771233
Lakewood, OH 44107

Cracker Jack Items
Phil Helley
Old Kilbourn Antiques
629 Indiana Ave.
Wisconsin Dells, WI 53965
Also banks, radio premiums and wind-up toys

Wes Johnson, Sr.
106 Bauer Ave.
Louisville, KY 40207

Author of books; editor of newsletter
Larry White
108 Central St.
Rowley, MA 01969-1317

Crackle Glass
Authors of book
Stan and Arlene Weitman
101 Cypress St.
Massapequa Park, NY 11758
516-799-2619 or
fax 516-797-3039

Credit Cards and Related Items
Walt Thompson
Box 2541
Yakima, WA 98907-2541

Cruise Ship Items
Richard Haigh
P.O. Box 29562
Richmond, VA 23242
804-741-5770 (until 9pm EST)

Cuff Links
National Cuff Link Society
Eugene R. Klompus
P.O. Box 346
Prospect Hts., IL 60070
phone, fax 847-816-0035

Also tie tacks
Harriet Myers
1132 Woodview Rd.
Burr Ridge, IL 60521
Also related items

Dakins
Jim Rash
135 Alder Ave.
Pleasantville, NJ 08232
609-646-4125

Decanters
Homestead Collectibles
Art and Judy Turner
R.D. 2, Rte. 150
P.O. Box 173
Mill Hall, PA 17751
717-726-3597
fax 717-726-4488

Degenhart
Linda K. Marsh
1229 Gould Rd.
Lansing, MI 48917

deLee
Authors of book
Joanne and Ralph Schaefer
3182 Williams Rd.
Oroville, CA 95965-8300
916-893-2902 or
800-897-6263

Depression Glass
Also Elegant glassware
John and Shirley Baker
673 W Township Rd. #118
Tiffin, OH 44883
Also Tiffin glassware

Green Parrot Sylvan
Clara Louthan
HC 64 Box 58
Coldwater, KS 67029
316-582-2850

Devils
No paper items wanted
Donald Friedman
660 W Grand Ave.
Chicago, IL 60610
312-226-4741
DFRIED4141@aol.com

Dinnerware
Cat-Tail
Ken and Barbara Brooks
4121 Gladstone Ln.
Charlotte, NC 28205

Fiesta, Franciscan, Russel Wright, Lu Ray, Metlox, and Homer Laughlin
Fiesta Plus
Mick and Lorna Chase
380 Hawkins Crawford Rd.
Cookeville, TN 38501
615-372-8333

Author of books
Mary Frank Gaston
900 Bob White
Bryan, TX 77802

Homer Laughlin China
Author of book
Darlene Nossaman
5419 Lake Charles
Waco, TX 76710

Johnson Brothers
Author of book
Mary Finegan, Marfine Antiques
P.O. Box 3618
Boone, NC 28607
828-262-3441

Liberty Blue
Gary Beegle
92 River St.
Montgomery, NY 12549
914-457-3623
Also most lines of collectible modern American dinnerware as well as character glasses

Restaurant China
Author of book
Barbara J. Conroy
Santa Clara, CA 95055-2369
408-248-4840
restaurantchina@earthlink.net

Royal China
BA Wellman
88 State Rd. W
P.O. Box 673
Homestead Farms #2
Westminster, MA 01473-1435
Also Ceramic Art Studios

Russel Wright, Eva Zeisel, Homer Laughlin
Charles Alexander
221 E 34th St.
Indianapolis, IN 46205
317-924-9665

Dolls
Annalee Mobilitee Dolls
Extensive lists sometimes available
Jane's Collectibles
Jane Holt
P.O. Box 115
Derry, NH 03038

Baby dolls
Marcia's Fantasy
Marcia Fanta
R.R. #1, Box 107
Tappen, ND 58487-9635
701-372-4441

Barbie
Gwen Daniel
18 Belleau Lake Ct.
O'Fallon, MO 63366
314-978-3190
GWENDANIEL@aol.com

Betsy McCall and friends
Marci Van Ausdall, Editor
P.O. Box 946
Quincy, CA 95971-0946
916-283-2770

Boudoir dolls
Bonnie M. Groves
402 N Ave. A
Elgin, TX 78621
512-281-9551

Celebrity and character dolls
Henri Yunes
971 Main St., Apt. 2
Hackensack, NJ 07601
201-488-2236

Dolls from the 1960s-70s, including Liddle Kiddles, Dolly Darlings, Petal People, Tiny Teens, etc.
Author of book on Liddle Kiddles; must send SASE for info
Paris Langford
415 Dodge Ave.
Jefferson, LA 70121
504-733-0667

Chatty Cathy and Mattel talkers
Authors of books
Don and Kathy Lewis
Whirlwind Unlimited
187 N Marcello Ave.
Thousand Oaks, CA 91360
805-499-8101
chatty@ix.netcom.com

Dolls from the 1960s-70s, including Liddle Kiddles, Barbie, Tammy, Tressy, etc. Co-author of book on Tammy
Cindy Sabulis
P.O. Box 642
Shelton, CT 06484
203-926-0176

Holly Hobbie
Helen McCale
1006 Ruby Ave.
Butler, MO 64730-2500

Holly Hobbie
Editor of newsletter: The Holly Hobbie Collectors Gazette
Donna Stultz
1455 Otterdale Mill Rd.
Taneytown, MD 21787-3032
410-775-2570

Ideal
Author of book; available from author or Collector Books
Judith Izen
P.O. Box 623
Lexington, MA 02173-5914
781-862-2994
jizenrez@aol.com

Liddle Kiddles and other small dolls from the late '60s and early '70s
Dawn Parrish
20460 Samual Drive
Saugus, CA 91530-3812
805-263-TOYS

Strawberry Shortcake
Geneva D. Addy
P.O. Box 124
Winterset, IA 50273

Vogue Dolls, Inc.
Co-author of book; available from author or Collector Books
Judith Izen
P.O. Box 623
Lexington, MA 02173-5914
781-862-2994
jizenres@aol.com
Vogue Dolls, Inc.
Co-author of Book; available from author or Collector Books
Carol J. Stover
81 E Van Buren St.
Chicago, IL 60605

Dollhouse Furniture and Accessories
Renwal, Ideal, Marx, etc.
Judith A. Mosholder
R.D. #2, Box 147
Boswell, PA 15531
814-629-9277

Door Knockers
Craig Dinner
Box 4399
Sunnyside, NY 11104
718-729-3850

Dorothy Kindell Ceramics
Bob Huxford
1202 7th St.
Covington, IN 47932
Want items with nude as handle or stem

Egg Beaters
Author of Beat This: The Egg Beater Chronicles
Don Thornton
Off Beat Books
1345 Poplar Ave.
Sunnyvale, CA 94087

Egg Cups
Author of book
Brenda Blake
Box 555
York Harbor, ME 03911
207-363-6566

Egg Timers
Ellen Bercovici
5118 Hampden Ln.
Bethesda, MD 20814
301-652-1140

Jeannie Greenfield
310 Parker Rd.
Stoneboro, PA 16153-2810
724-376-2584

Elegant Glass
Cambridge, Fostoria, Heisey
Deborah Maggard
Antiques
P.O. Box 211
Chagrin Falls, OH 44022
440-247-5632
debmaggard@worldnet.att.net

Also china and Victorian art glass
Roselle Schleifman
16 Vincent Rd.
Spring Valley, NY 10977

Erich Stauffer Figurines
Joan Oates
685 S Washington
Constantine, MI 49042
616-435-8353
Also Phoenix Bird china

Ertl Banks
Homestead Collectibles
P.O. Box 173
Mill Hall, PA 17751
Also decanters

Eyewinker
Sophia Talbert
921 Union St.
Covington, IN 47932
317-793-3256

Farm Collectibles
Editor of newsletter: Farm Antique News
Gary Van Hoozer, Editor
812 N Third St.
Tarkio, MO 64491-0812
816-736-4528

Fast-Food Collectibles
Author of book
Ken Clee
Box 1142
Philadelphia, PA 19111
215-722-1979

Authors of several books
Joyce and Terry Losonsky
7506 Summer Leave Lane
Columbia, MD 21046-2455
Illustrated Collector's Guide to McDonald's ® Happy Meal ® Boxes, Premiums and Promotions ($9 plus $2 postage), McDonald's® Happy

Meal® Toys in the USA and *McDonald's® Happy Meal® Toys Around the World* (both full color, $24.95 each plus $3 postage), and *Illustrated Collector's Guide to McDonald's ® McCAPS®* ($4 plus $2) are available from the authors
Bill and Pat Poe
220 Dominica Cir. E
Niceville, FL 32578-4085
850-897-4163 or
850-897-2606
McPoes@aol.com
Also cartoon and character glasses, Pez, Smurfs and California Raisins; Send $3 (US delivery) for 70-page catalog

Fenton Glass
Ferill J. Rice
304 Pheasant Run
Kaukauna, WI 54130

Figural Ceramics
Especially cookie jars; California pottery; Kitchen Prayer Lady, Fitz & Floyd, Head Vases, and Kreiss as well as other imports; American pottery
Phil and Nyla Thurston
82 Hamlin St.
Cortland, NY 13045
607-753-6770

Especially Kitchen Prayer Lady, Enesco, and Holt Howard
April and Larry Tvorak
P.O. Box 94
Warren Center, PA 18851
570-395-3775
april@epix.net

Fire-King
Authors of price guide
April and Larry Tvorak
P.O. Box 94
Warren Center, PA 18851
570-395-3775
april@epix.net

Fisher-Price
Co-author of book
Brad Cassity
1350 Stanwix
Toledo, OH 43614
419-389-1100

Fishing Collectibles
Publishes fixed-price catalog
Dave Hoover
1023 Skyview Dr.
New Albany, IN 47150
Also miniature boats and motors

Flashlights
Editor of newsletter
Bill Utley
P.O. Box 4094
Tustin, CA 92681
714-730-1252
fax 714-505-4067

Flatware
Alexis by Oneida; buy and sell
Mary Faria
P.O. Box 32321
San Jose, CA 95152-2321
408-258-0413

Florence Ceramics
Author of book
Doug Foland
1811 NW Couch #303
Portland, OR 97209

John and Peggy Scott
4640 S Leroy
Springfield, MO 65810

Flower Frogs
Nada Sue Knauss
12111 Potter Rd.
Weston, OH 43569
419-669-4735

Fountain Pens
Very old mother-of-pearl, silver or gold filled; no wood
Kayla Conway
4500 Napal Ct.
Bakersfield, CA 93307
805-833-0291

M. Jane Crane
132 Dillion Dr.
Lemont Furnace, PA 15456
724-437-1209

Sonja K. Rothstein
1308 Medical Dr.
Fayetteville, NC 28304

Frankoma
Authors of book
Phyllis and Tom Bess
14535 E 13th St.
Tulsa, OK 74108

Author of books
Susan N. Cox
Main Street Antique Mall
237 East Main St.
El Cajon, CA 92020
619-447-0800
Also unsharpened advertising pencils, complete matchbooks, Horlick's advertising, women's magazines from 1900 to 1950. (Susan Cox has written 3 books and 5 price guides on Frankoma pottery and is currently working on an updated price guide and a Frankoma advertising book. She has devoted much of the past fifteen years to California pottery research and welcomes any information collectors might have about California companies and artists.)

Fruit Jars
Especially old, odd or colored jars
John Hathaway
Rte. 2, Box 220
Bryant Pond, ME 04219
Also old jar lids and closures

Fulper
Douglass White
P.O. Box 5400672
Orlando, FL 32854
407-839-0004

Gambling and Related Items
Robert Eisenstadt
P.O. Box 020767
Brooklyn, NY 11202-0017

Games
Paul Fink's Fun and Games
P.O. Box 488
59 S Kent Rd.
Kent, CT 06757
203-927-4001

Americana
Patrice McFarland
P.O. Box 400
Averell Park, NY 12018-0400
greatgames@webtv.net

Paul David Morrow
1045 Rolling Point Ct.
Virginia Beach, VA 23456-6371

Gay Fad Glassware
Donna S. McGrady
154 Peters Ave.
Lancaster, OH 43130
614-653-0376

Geisha Girl Porcelain
Author of book
Elyce Litts
P.O. Box 394
Morris Plains, NJ 07950
Also ladies' compacts

Glass Animals
Author of book
Lee Garmon
1529 Whittier St.
Springfield, IL 62704

Glass Knives
Michele A. Rosewitz
3165 McKinley
San Bernardino, CA 92404
909-862-8534
rosetree@sprintmail.com

Glass Shoes
Author of book
The Shoe Lady
Libby Yalom
P.O. Box 7146
Adelphi, MD 20783

Graniteware
Author of books
Helen Greguire
716-392-2704
Also carnival glass and toasters

Griswold
Grant Windsor
P.O. Box 3613
Richmond, VA 23235-7613

Hallmark
The Baggage Car
3100 Justin Dr., Ste. B
Des Moines, IA 50322
515-270-9080

Halloween
Author of books; autographed copies available from the author
Pamela Apakarian-Russell
Chris Russell & The Halloween Queen Antiques
P.O. Box 499
Winchester, NH 03470
halloweenqueen@top.monad.net
Also other holidays, postcards, and Joe Camel

Judith Katz-Schwartz
P.O. Box 6572
New York, NY 10128-0006
212-876-3512

Hartland Plastics, Inc.
Author of book
Gail Fitch
1733 N Cambridge, Ave. #109
Milwaukee, WI 53202

Specializing in Western Hartlands
Buy and sell; hold consignment auctions specializing in vintage toys
Kerry and Judy Irwin
Kerry and Judy's Toys
1414 S. Twelfth St.
Murray, KY 42071
502-759-3456
kjtoys@apex.com

Specializing in sports figures
James Watson
25 Gilmore St.
Whitehall, NY 12887

Holt Howard
Pat and Ann Duncan
Box 175
Cape Fair, MO 65624
417-538-2311

April and Larry Tvorak
P.O. Box 94
Warren Center, PA 18851
570-395-3775
april@epix.net

Homer Laughlin
Author of book
Darlene Nossaman
5419 Lake Charles
Waco, TX 76710

Horton Ceramics
Darlene Nossaman
5419 Lake Charles
Waco, TX 76710

Hotel Menus and Brochures
Hotel De Monte, Drake-Wiltshire, Canterbury, Maurice Hotels
T.J. Ahlberg
1000 Irvine Blvd.
Tustin, CA 92780
714-730-1000 or
fax 714-730-1752

Hull
Author of several books on Hull
Brenda Roberts
R.R. 2
Marshall, MO 65340

Mirror Brown, also Pfaltzgraff Gourmet Royale; rare items only
Bill and Connie Sloan
4965 Valley Park Rd.
Doylestown, PA 18901

Imperial Glass
Joan Cimini
63680 Centerville-Warnock Rd.
Belmont, OH 43718
Also has Candlewick matching service

Imperial Porcelain
Geneva D. Addy
P.O. Box 124
Winterset, IA 50273

Indy 500 Memorabilia
Eric Jungnickel
P.O. Box 4674
Naperville, IL 60567-4674
630-983-8339

Insulators
Mike Bruner
6980 Walnut Lake Rd.
W Bloomfield, MI 48323
313-661-8241
Also porcelain signs, light-up advertising clocks, exit globes, lightening rod balls and target balls

Jacqueline Linscott
3557 Nicklaus Dr.
Tutusville, FL 32780

Japan Ceramics
Author of books
Carole Bess White
PO Box 819
Portland, OR 97207

Jewel Tea
Products or boxes only; no dishes
Bill and Judy Vroman
739 Eastern Ave.
Fostoria, OH 44830
419-435-5443

Jewelry
Marcia Brown (Sparkles)
P.O. Box 2314
White City, OR 97503
514-826-3039
fax: 541-830-5385

Copper items
Richard Haigh
P.O. Box 29562
Richmond, VA 23242
804-741-5770 (until 9pm EST)

Vintage costume
Judith Katz-Schwartz
P.O. Box 6572
New York, NY 10128-0006
212-876-3512

Men's accessories and cuff links only; edits newsletter
The National Cuff Link Society
Eugene R. Klompus
P.O. Box 346
Prospect Hts., IL 60070
phone or fax 847-816-0035

Old and new; gem stones
David W. Mayer
33 Mt. Vernon Pl.
Jamestown, NY 14701
716-487-0556

Bakelite, carved pins and hinged bracelets; 1920-1935 circa catalogs
Sherry and Mike Miller
303 Holiday Dr.
Tuscola, IL 61953
217-253-4991
miller@tuscola.net

Costume and plastic, 20 years or older
Harriet Myers
1132 Woodview Rd.
Burr Ridge, IL 60521

Josef Originals
Authors of books
Jim and Kaye Whitaker
Eclectic Antiques
P.O. Box 475
Lynnwood, WA 98046

Kay Finch
Animals and birds, especially in pink with pastel decoration
Mike Drollinger
1202 Seventh St.
Covington, IN 47932
765-793-2392

Co-authors of book, available from authors
Mike Nickel and Cynthia Horvath
P.O. Box 456
Portland, MI, 48875
517-647-7646

Kentucky Derby and Horse Racing
B.L. Hornback
707 Sunrise Ln.
Elizabethtown, KY 42701

Kewpie Items
Wilma Schiebel
HCR 63 Box 116C
Yellville, AR 72687
870-436-5874

Key Chains
Veterans of Foreign Wars License Plates
Kayla Conway
4500 Napal Ct.
Bakersfield, CA 93307
805-833-0291

Kitchen Prayer Ladies; issues price guide ($6.96 plus $1 postage and handling)

April and Larry Tvorak
P.O. Box 94
Warren Center, PA 18851
570-395-3775
april@epix.net

Lamps
Aladdin
Author of books
J.W. Courter
3935 Kelley Rd.
Kevil, KY 42053
502-488-2116

Figural Lamps
Dee Boston
2299 N Pr. Rd. 475 W
Sullivan, IN 47882
Also dresser, pincushion and half dolls

Motion lamps
Eclectic Antiques
Jim and Kaye Whitaker
P.O. Box 475
Lynwood, WA 98046

Authors of book
Sam and Anna Samuelian
P.O. Box 504
Edgmont, PA 19028-0504
610-566-7248
Also motion clocks, transistor and novelty radios

Perfume Lamps
Tom and Linda Millman
231 S Main St.
Bethel, OH 45106
513-734-6884 (after 9 pm)

Law Enforcement and Crime-Related Memorabilia
Tony Perrin
1401 N Pierce #6
Little Rock, AR 72207
501-868-5005 or
501-666-6493 (after 5 pm)

Lefton
Especially #4908 Napoleon, Colonial men and women
Author of books
Loretta DeLozier
1101 Polk St.
Bedford, IA 50833
712-523-2289 (M-F, 9 am to 4 pm)
fax 712-523-2624
LeftonLady@aol.com
http://members.aol.com/leftonlady

Letter Openers
Author of book
Everett Grist
P.O. Box 91375
Chattanooga, TN 37412-3955
423-510-8052

License Plates
Richard Diehl
5965 W Colgate Pl.
Denver, CO 80227

Clara Louthan
HC 64 Box 58
Coldwater, KS 67029
316-582-2850

Licenses
Hunting, fishing, trapping; guide licenses and pin-back buttons from any state and Canada issued before 1950
Bob Bowering
P.O. Box 420
E Wilton, ME 04234
207-778-6724

Lunch Boxes
Norman's Ole and New Store
Philip Norman
126 W Main St.
Washington, NC 27889-4944
919-946-3448

Terri's Toys and Nostalgia
Terri Ivers
206 E. Grand
Ponca City, OK 74601
580-762-8697 or
580-762-5174
fax 405-765-2657
toylady@poncacity.net

MAD Collectibles
Michael Lerner
32862 Springside Ln.
Solon, OH 44139
phone, fax 216-349-3776

Magazines
Issues price guides to illustrators, pinups, and old magazines of all kinds
Denis C. Jackson
Illustrator Collector's News
P.O. Box 1958
Sequim, WA 98382
360-683-2559
ticn@olypen.com

Pre-1950 movie magazines, especially with Ginger Rogers covers
Tom Morris
P.O. Box 8307
Medford, OR 97504
541-779-3164
chalkman@cdsnet.net

National Geographic
Author of guide
Don Smith's National Geographic Magazines
3930 Rankin St.
Louisville, KY 40214
502-366-7504

Pulps circa 1930s-50s
Ken Mitchell
710 Conacher Rd.
Willowdale, Ontario
Canada M2M 3N6

Pulps Issues catalogs on various genre of hardcover books, paperbacks, and magazines of all types
J. Grant Thiessen
Pandora's Books Ltd.
Box 54
Neche, ND 58265-0054
fax 204-324-1628
jgthiess@mts.net
http://www.pandora.ca/pandora

Maps
Charles R. Neuschafer
New World Maps, Inc.

Apple Hill Rd.
Bennington, VT 05201-9544
802-442-2846
maps@sover.net
http://pages.prodigy.com
/maproom

Marbles
Author of books
Everett Grist
P.O. Box 91375
Chattanooga, TN 37412-3955
423-510-8052

Match Safes
George Sparacio
P.O. Box 791
Malaga, NJ 08328
609-694-4167

Kayla Conway
4500 Napal Ct.
Bakersfield, CA 93307
805-833-0291

Matchcovers
Author of books
Bill Retskin
P.O. Box 18481
Asheville, NC 22814
704-254-4487 or
704-254-1066
bill@matchcovers.com
http://www.matchcovers.com

McCoy Pottery
Authors of book
Robert and Margaret Hanson
16517 121 Ave. NE
Bothell, WA 98011

Melmac Dinnerware
Co-author of book
Gregg Zimmer
4017 16th Ave. S
Minneapolis, MN 55407

Co-author of book
Alvin Daigle, Jr.
Boomerang Antiques
Gray, TN 37615
423-915-0666

Metlox
Author of book; available from author
Carl Gibbs, Jr.
P.O. Box 131584
Houston, TX 77219-1584
713-521-9661

Miller Studios
Paul and Heather August
7510 West Wells St.
Wauwatosa, WI 53213
414-475-0753
packrats@execpc.com

Morton Pottery
Authors of books
Doris and Burdell Hall
B&B Antiques
210 W Sassafras Dr.
Morton, IL 61550-1245

Motion Clocks
Electric; buy, sell, trade, and restore
Sam and Anna Samuelian
P.O. Box 504
Edgmont, PA 19028-0504
610-566-7248
Also motion lamps, transistor and novelty radios

Motorcycles
Bruce Kiper
Ancient Age Motors
2205 Sunset Ln.
Lutz, FL 33549
813-949-9660
Also related items and clothing

Movie Memorabilia
Lobby card, Moulin Rouge, 1934
Sherry and Mike Miller
303 Holiday Dr.
Tuscola, IL 61953
217-253-4991
miller@tuscola.net

Pre-1970 posters
Ken Mitchell
710 Conacher Rd.
Willowdale, Ontario
Canada M2M 3N6

Movie Poster Service
Cleophas and Lou Ann Wooley
Box 517
Canton, OK 73724-0517
580-886-2248 or
fax 580-886-2249
mpsposters@pldi.net
In business full time since 1972; own/operate mail-order firm with world's largest movie poster inventory

Music and Entertainment Related Items
Old radios, toys, rock and roll autographs, movie star autographs, Beatles, Elvis, Dylan punk rock stuff, books, magazines, posters, Marilyn Monroe, western memorabilia, tin robots, sci-fi stuff, tv stuff, JFK, Patti Page, Mickey Mouse, Disney, old concert ticket stubs, lunch boxes, Barbie dolls, 8-track and reel-to-reels, 78s, amusement park stuff, Las Vegas, Andy Warhol, games, buttons, and more. Call:
Bill
617-364-1854

Sherry and Mike Miller
303 Holiday Dr.
Tuscola, IL 61953
217-253-4991
miller@tuscola.net

Napkin Dolls
Co-Author of book
Bobbie Zucker Bryson
1 St. Eleanoras Ln.
Tuckahoe, NY 10707
914-779-1405
napkindoll@aol.com
http:/www/his.com/~judy
/reamers.html

Newspaper Collector Society
Rick Brown
P.O. Box 19134
Lansing, MI 19134

Niloak Pottery
Fred and Lila Shrader
2025 Hwy. 199 (Hiouchi)
Crescent City, CA 95531
707-458-3525

Novelty Radios
Authors of several books
Sue and Marty Bunis
R.R. 1, Box 36
Bradford, NH 03221-9102

Nutcrackers
Earl MacSorley
823 Indian Hill Rd.
Orange, CT 06477

Ocean liners
Books/collectibles/ephemera on ocean liners, merchant ships, and the Titanic. All queries promptly answered.
Maiden Voyage Booksellers
P.O. Box 4669
Portsmouth, NH 03802-4669
603-436-9759
fax: 603-443-0942
mdnvybks@nh.ultranet.com

Orientalia and Dragonware
Susie Hibbard
2570 Walnut Blvd. #20
Walnut Creek, CA 94596

Paden City Glassware
George and Mary Hurney
Glass Connection (mail-order only)
312 Babcock Dr.
Palatine, IL 50067
847-359-3839

Paper and Ephemera
Patrice McFarland
P.O. Box 400
Averell Park, NY 12018-0400
greatgames@webtv.net

Paper Dolls
Author of books
Mary Young
P.O. Box 9244
Wright Bros. Branch
Dayton, OH 45409

Pencil Sharpeners
Phil Helley
629 Indiana Ave.
Wisconsin Dells, WI 53965
608-254-8659

Advertising and figural
Martha Hughes
4128 Ingalls St.
San Diego, CA 92103
619-296-1866

Pennsbury
Author of price guide; video book available
BA Wellman
88 State Rd. W
P.O. Box 673
Homestead Farms #2
Westminster, MA 01473-1435

Joe Devine
1411 3rd St.
Council Bluffs, IA 51503
712-232-5322 or
712-328-7305

Shirley Graff
4515 Graff Rd.
Brunswick, OH 44212

Pepsi-Cola
Gwen Daniel
18 Belleau Lake Ct.
O'Fallon, MO 63366
314-978-3190
GWENDANIEL@aol.com

Craig and Donna Stifter
P.O. Box 6514
Naperville, IL 60540
630-789-5780
Other soda-pop memorablia

Perfume Bottles
Especially commercial, Czechoslovakian, Lalique, Baccarat, Victorian, crown top, factices, miniatures
Buy, sell, and accept consignments for auctions
Monsen and Baer
Box 529
Vienna, VA 22183
703-242-1357

Pez
Richard Belyski
P.O. Box 124
Sea Cliff, NY 11579
516-676-1183

Pfaltzgraff
Gourmet Royale
Bill and Connie Sloan
4965 Valley Park Rd.
Doylestown, PA 18901

Photo Albums and Stands
Mary Faria
P.O. Box 32321
San Jose, CA 95152-2321
408-258-0413

Photographica
Photo albums, photos circa 1925 of women with purses, Art Deco picture frames with reverse-painted designs
Sherry and Mike Miller
303 Holiday Dr.
Tuscola, IL 61953
217-253-4991
miller@tuscola.net

Tom Molecea
Box 100
North Lima, OH 44452-0100
330-549-3245
himages@cisnet.com

Pin-Back Buttons
Michael and Polly McQuillen
McQuillen's Collectibles
P.O. Box 50022
Indianapolis, IN 46250
317-845-1721

Playing Cards
Buy and sell Petty, Vargas, Elvgrin
Mary Faria
P.O. Box 32321
San Jose, CA 95152-2321
408-258-0413

Pocket Calculators
Author of book
International Assn. of Calculator Collectors
Guy D. Ball
P.O. Box 345
Tustin, CA 92781-0345
phone, fax 714-730-6140
mrcalc@usa.net

Political
Michael and Polly McQuillen
McQuillen's Collectibles
P.O. Box 50022
Indianapolis, IN 46250
317-845-1721

Before 1960
Michael Engel
29 Groveland St.
Easthampton, MA 01027

Pins, banners, ribbons, etc.
Paul Longo Americana
Box 490
Chatham Rd., South Orleans
Cape Cod, MA 02662
508-255-5482

Poodle Collectibles
Author of book
Elaine Butler
233 S Kingston Ave.
Rockwood, TN 37854

Porcelier
Jim Barker
Toaster Master General
P.O. Box 41
Bethlehem, PA 10106

Author of book
Susan Grindberg
1412 Pathfinder Rd.
Henderson, NV 89014
702-898-7535
porcelier@anv.net
http://www.coyote.accessnv.com/porcelier/

Post Office Lock Box Door Fronts
Oscar Hubbert
P.O. Box 1415
Fletcher, NC 28732
828-687-0350

Postcards
C.J. Russell and Pamela Apakarian-Russell
Halloween Queen Antiques
P.O. Box 499
Winchester, NH 03470
Also Halloween and other holidays

Judith Katz-Schwartz
P.O. Box 6572
New York, NY 10128-0006
212-876-3512

Anthony, Kansas only
Clara Louthan
HC 64 Box 58
Coldwater, KS 67029
316-582-2850

Powder Jars
John and Peggy Scott
4640 S Leroy
Springfield, MO 65810

Sharon Thoerner
15549 Ryon Ave.
Bellflower, CA 90706
562-866-1555
Also slag glass

Purinton Pottery
Author of book
Susan Morris
P.O. Box 656
Panora, IA 50216
515-755-3161

Purses
Glass beaded
Kayla Conway
4500 Napal Ct.
Bakersfield, CA 93307
805-833-0291

Glass beaded, 20-22 beads per inch
Sherry and Mike Miller
303 Holiday Dr.
Tuscola, IL 61953
217-253-4991
miller@tuscola.net

Veronica Trainer
P.O. Box 40443
Cleveland, OH 44140

Puzzles
Wooden jigsaw type from before 1950
Bob Armstrong
15 Monadnock Rd.
Worcester, MA 01609

Especially character related
Norm Vigue
62 Bailey St.
Stoughton, MA 02072
617-344-5441

Radio Premiums
Bill Campbell
1221 Littlebrook Ln.
Birmingham, AL 35235
205-853-8227
fax 405-658-6986

Radios
Buy, sell, and trade; Repairs radio equipment using vaccuum tubes
Antique Radio Labs
James Fred
Rte. 1, Box 41
Cutler, IN 46920

Authors of several books on antique, novelty, and transistor radios
Sue and Marty Bunis
R.R. 1, Box 36
Bradford, NH 03221-9102

Author of book
Harry Poster
P.O. Box 1883
S Hackensack, NJ 07606
201-410-7525
Also televisions, related advertising items, old

tubes, cameras, 3-D viewers and projectors, View-Master and Tru-View reels and accessories

Railroadiana
Any item; especially china and silver
Catalogs available
John White, 'Grandpa'
Grandpa's Depot
1616 17th St., Ste. 267
Denver, CO 80202
303-628-5590 or
fax 303-628-5547
Also related items

Also steamship and other transportation memorabilia
Fred and Lila Shrader
Shrader Antiques
2025 Hwy. 199
Crescent City, CA 95531
707-458-3525
Also Buffalo, Shelley, Niloak and Hummels

Razor Blade Banks
David Geise
1410 Aquia Dr.
Stafford, VA 22554
703-569-5984

Debbie Gillham
47 Midline Ct.
Gaithersburg, MD 20878
301-977-5727

Reamers
Co-author of book, ordering info under Napkin Dolls
Bobbie Zucker Bryson
1 St. Eleanoras Ln.
Tuckahoe, NY 10707
914-779-1405
napkindoll@aol.com
http://www.his.com//~judy/reamer.html

Records
45 rpm and LP's
Mason's Bookstore, Rare Books, and Record Albums
Dave Torzillo
115 S Main St.
Chambersburg, PA 17201
717-261-0541

Picture and 78 rpm kiddie records
Peter Muldavin
173 W 78th St.
New York, NY 10024
212-362-9606

Especially 78 rpms
L.R. 'Les' Docks
Box 691035
San Antonio, TX 78269-1035
Write for want list

Red Wing Artware
Hold cataloged auctions
Wendy and Leo Frese
Three Rivers Collectibles
P.O. Box 551542
Dallas, TX 75355
214-341-515
rumrill@ix.netcom.com

Regal China
Van Telligen, Bendel, Old MacDonald's Farm
Rick Spencer
Salt Lake City, UT
801-973-0805
Also Coors, Shawnee, Watt, Silverplate (especially grape patterns)

Rooster and Roses
Jacki Elliott
9790 Twin Cities Rd.
Galt, CA 95632
209-745-3860

Rosemeade
NDSU research specialist
Bryce Farnsworth
1334 14 1/2 St. S
Fargo, ND 58103
701-237-3597

Roseville
Andrew E. Thomas
4681 N 84th Way
Scottsdale, AZ 85251
602-947-5693 or fax 602-994-4382

Royal Bayreuth
Don and Anne Kier
2022 Marengo St.
Toledo, OH 43614
419-385-8211

Royal Copley
Author of books
Joe Devine
1411 3rd St.
Council Bluffs, IA 51503
712-323-5233 or
712-328-7305

Buy, sell, or trade; Also pie birds
Willard and Dianne Purcell
P.O. Box 166
Wimbledon, ND 58492-0166

Royal Haeger
Author of book
David D. Dilley
L-W Book Sales
5243 S Adams St.
Marion, IN 46953
765-284-7443
dink@comteck.com

Co-author of book
Doris Frizzell
Doris' Dishes
5687 Oakdale Dr.
Springfield, IL 62707
217-529-3873

Royal Windsor
Willard and Dianne Purcell
P.O. Box 166
Wimbledon, ND 58492-0166

Ruby Glass
Author of book
Naomi L. Over
8909 Sharon Ln.
Arvada, CO 80002
303-424-5922

RumRill
Hold cataloged auctions
Wendy and Leo Frese
Three Rivers Collectibles
P.O. Box 551542
Dallas, TX 75355
214-341-5165
rumrill@ix.netcom.com

Russel Wright
Author of book
Ann Kerr
P.O. Box 437
Sidney, OH 45365

Salt and Pepper Shakers
'30s-50s square Jade-ite; white with black letters: Shawnee animals, chickens, birds; and Lefton roosters
Clara Louthan
HC 64 Box 58
Coldwater, KS 67029
316-582-2850

Figural or novelty
Buy, sell, and trade; lists available; fee charged for appraisal
Judy Posner
R.R. 1, Box 273
Effort, PA 18330
717-629-6583 or
http://www.tias.com/stores/jpc
judyandjef@aol.com

Scottie Dog Collectibles
Donna Palmer
2446 215th Ave. SE
Issaquah, WA 98027

Scouting Collectibles
Author of book
R.J. Sayers
P.O. Box 629
Brevard, NC 28712

Sebastians
Jim Waite
112 N Main St.
Farmer City, IL 61842
800-842-2593

Sewing Machines
Toy only; Authors of book
Darryl and Roxana Matter
P.O. Box 65
Portis, KS 67474-0065

Sewing Needle Kits
Ed Natale
P.O. Box 222
Wyckoff, NJ 07481
201-848-8485

Shawnee
Rick Spencer
Salt Lake City, UT
801-973-0805

Corn King and Queen
Andrew E. Thomas
4681 N 84th Way
Scottsdale, AZ 85251
602-947-5693 or
fax 602-994-4382

Sheet Music
Maid of Mesh by Irving Berlin (1932)
Sherry and Mike Miller
303 Holiday Dr.
Tuscola, IL 61953
217-253-4991
miller@tuscola.net

Shot Glasses
Author of book
Mark Pickvet
Shot Glass Club of America
5071 Watson Dr.
Flint, MI 48506

Silhouette Pictures (20th Century)
Author of book
Shirley Mace
Shadow Enterprises
P.O. Box 1602
Mesilla Park, NM 88047
505-524-6717
fax 505-523-0940
shadow-ent@zianet.com

Silverplated Flatware
Rick Spencer
Salt Lake City, UT
801-973-0805

David W. Mayer
33 Mt. Vernon Pl.
Jamestown, NY 14701
716-487-0556

Skookum Indian Dolls
Jo Ann Palmieri
27 Pepper Rd.
Towaco, NJ 07082-1357

Snow Domes
Author of book and newsletter editor
Nancy McMichael
P.O. Box 53310
Washington, DC 20009

Soda Fountain Collectibles
Harold and Joyce Screen
2804 Munster Rd.
Baltimore, MD 21234
410-661-6765

Soda-Pop Memorabilia
Craig and Donna Stifter
P.O. Box 6514
Naperville, IL 60540
630-789-5780

Painted-label soda bottles
Author of books
Thomas Marsh
914 Franklin Ave.
Youngstown, OH 44502
216-743-8600 or 800-845-7930 (order line)

Spaulding Co. Pottery
Willard and Dianne Purcell
P.O. Box 166
Wimbledon, ND 58492-0166

Sports Collectibles
Sporting goods
Kevin R. Bowman
P.O. Box 471
Neosho, MO 64850-0471
417-781-6418 (6–9 pm CST)

Equipment and player-used items
Don and Anne Kier
2022 Marengo St.
Toledo, OH 43614
419-385-8211

Bobbin' head sports figures
Tim Hunter
4301 W Hidden Valley Dr.
Reno, NV 89502
702-856-4357
fax 702-856-4354
thunter885@aol.com

Paul Longo Americana
Box 490
Chatham Rd., South Orleans
Cape Cod, MA 02662
508-255-5482
Also stocks and bonds

Golf collectibles
Pat Romano
32 Sterling Dr.
Lake Grove, NY 11202-0017

Sports Pins
Tony George
22431-B160 Antonio Pky. #252
Rancho Santa Margarita, CA 92688
714-589-6075

St. Clair Glass
Ted Pruitt
3382 W 700 N
Anderson, IN 46011
Book available ($15)

Stangl
Birds, dinnerware, artware
Popkorn Antiques
Bob and Nancy Perzel
P.O. Box 1057
4 Mine St.
Flemington, NJ 08822
908-782-9631

Statue of Liberty
Mike Brooks
7335 Skyline
Oakland, CA 94611

Steamship China
Fred and Lila Shrader
2025 Hwy. 199 (Hiouchi)
Crescent City, CA 95531
707-458-3525

String Holders
Ellen Bercovici
5118 Hampden Ln.
Bethesda, MD 20814
301-652-1140

Swanky Swigs
Joyce Jackson
900 Jenkins Rd.
Aledo, TX 76008
817-441-8864
jjpick@fastlane.net

Syroco and Similar Products
Doris J. Gibbs
3837 Cuming #1
Omaha, NE 68131
402-556-4300
DDGIBBS@TOP.NET

Teapots and Tea-Related Items
Author of book
Tina Carter
882 S Mollison
El Cajon, CA 92020

Tire Ashtrays
Author of book ($12.95 postpaid)
Jeff McVey
1810 W State St., #427
Boise, ID 83702-3955

Toothbrush Holders
Author of book
Marilyn Cooper
8408 Lofland Dr.
Houston, TX 77055
713-465-7773

Toys
Any and all
June Moon
245 N Northwest Hwy.
Park Ridge, IL 60068
847-825-1441 or fax 847-825-6090

Aurora model kits, and especially toys from 1948–1972
Author of books
Dealers, publishers, and appraisers of collectible memorabilia from the '50s through today
Bill Bruegman
137 Casterton Dr.
Akron, OH 44303
330-836-0668 or fax 330-869-8668
toyscout@salamander.net

Building blocks and construction toys
Arlan Coffman
1223 Wilshire Blvd., Ste. 275
Santa Monica, CA 90403
310-453-2507

Campus Cuties by Marx
Bettye Puckett
177 Pottershop Rd.
Bardstown, KY 40004
fax 502-348-8210
PBuckett@BMS.Btown.K12.KY.US

Daffy and Taz, Looney Tunes with these characters
Bob Stinson
P.O. Box 21341
Louisville, KY 40221
Also M&M collectibles, old cb's, air magazines, 1/24 slot cars and mags, O scale trains (old steam)

Diecast vehicles
Mark Giles
P.O. Box 821
Ogallala, NE 69153-0821

Diecast vehicles
Mary Faria
P.O. Box 32321
San Jose, CA 95152-2321
408-258-0413

Fisher-Price pull toys and playsets up to 1986
Co-author of book; available from the author
Brad Cassity
1350 Stanyx
Toledo, OH 43614
419-389-1100

Games and general line
Phil McEntee
Where the Toys Are
45 W Pike St.
Canonsburg, PA 15317

Hot Wheels
D.W. (Steve) Stephenson
11117 NE 164th Pl.
Bothell, WA 98011-4003

Mechanical tin toys
La Gail Daniel
P.O. Box 494
Roland, OK 74954
918-427-1828

Model kits other than Aurora; edits publications
Gordy Dutt
Box 201
Sharon Center, OH 42274-0201

Model plane kits
Richard Haigh
P.O. Box 29562
Richmond, VA 23242
804-741-5770 (until 9pm EST)

Monsters as Frankenstein, Dracula, etc.
Barbara Brecker
76 Sicard St.
New Brunswick, NJ 08901
732-246-1589
SalandRei@aol.com

Plastic figures and Playsets
David Gross
76 Sicard St.
New Brunswick, NJ 08901
732-246-1589
SalandRei@aol.com

Puppets and marionettes
Steven Meltzer
670 San Juan Ave. #B
Venice, CA 90291
310-396-6007

Rings, character, celebrity, and souvenir
Bruce and Jan Thalberg
23 Mountain View Dr.
Weston, CT 06883-1317
203-227-8175

Sand toys
Authors of book
Carole and Richard Smyth
Carole Smyth Antiques
P.O. Box 2068
Huntington, NY 11743

Slot race cars from 1960s–70s
Gary T. Pollastro
4156 Beach Dr. SW
Seattle, WA 98116
206-935-0245

Tin litho, paper on wood, comic character, penny toys and Schoenhut
Wes Johnson, Sr.
106 Bauer Ave.
Louisville, KY 40207

Tootsietoys
Author of books
David E. Richter
6817 Sutherland
Mentor, OH 44060
216-255-6537

Tops and Spinning Toys
Bruce Middleton
5 Lloyd Rd.
Newburgh, NY 12550
914-564-2556

Toy soldiers, figures, and playsets
The Phoenix Toy Soldier Co.
Bob Wilson
P.O. Box 26365
Phoenix, AZ 85068
602-863-2891

Transformers and robots
David Kolodny-Nagy
3701 Connecticut Ave. NW #500
Washington, DC 20008
202-364-8753

Walkers, ramp-walkers, and wind-ups
Randy Welch
Raven'tiques
27965 Peach Orchard Rd.
Easton, MD 21601-8203
410-822-5441

Trolls
Author of book
Pat Peterson
1105 6th Ave. SE
Hampton, IA 50441-2657
SASE for information

TV Guides
Price guide available
TV Guide Specialists
Jeff Kadet
P.O. Box 20
Macomb, IL 61455

Twin Winton
Author of book; available from the author or through Collector Books
Mike Ellis
266 Rose Ln.
Costa Mesa, CA 92627
714-645-4697
fax 714-645-4697

Typewriter Ribbon Tins
Kayla Conway
4500 Napal Ct.
Bakersfield, CA 93307
805-833-0291

Valentines
Judith Katz-Schwartz
P.O. Box 6572
New York, NY 10128-0006
212-876-3512

Author of book; fee charged for appraisal
Katherine Kreider
Kingsbury Productions
P.O. Box 7957
Lancaster, PA 17604-7957
717-892-3001

Vallona Starr
Author of book
Bernice Stamper
7516 Eloy Ave.
Bakersfield, CA 93308-7701
805-393-2900

Van Briggle
Dated examples, author of book
Scott H. Nelson
Box 6081
Santa Fe, NM 87502
505-986-1176
Also UND (University of North Dakota), other American potteries

Vandor
Lois Wildman
175 Chick Rd.
Camano Island, WA 98282

Vernon Kilns
Maxine Nelson
873 Marigold Ct.
Carlsbad, CA 92009

View-Master and Tru-View
Roger Nazeley
4921 Castor Ave.
Philadelphia, PA 19124

Harry Poster
P.O. Box 1883
S Hackensack, NJ 07606
201-410-7525

Walter Sigg
3-D Entertainment
P.O Box 208
Swartswood, NJ 07877

Wade
Author of book
Ian Warner
P.O. Box 93022
Brampton, Ontario
Canada L6Y 4V8

Wallace China
All patterns
T.J. Ahlberg
1000 Irvine Blvd.
Tustin, CA 92780
714-730-1000 or fax 714-730-1752

Watt Pottery
Author of book
Susan Morris
P.O. Box 656
Panora, IA 50216
515-755-3161

Western Collectibles
Author of book
Warren R. Anderson
American West Archives
P.O. Box 100
Cedar City, UT 84720
801-586-9497
Also documents, autographs, stocks and bonds, and other ephemera

William Manns
P.O. Box 6459
Santa Fe, NM 87502
505-995-0102

Western Heroes
Author of books, ardent researcher, and guest columnist
Robert W. Phillips
Phillips Archives of Western Memorabilia
1703 N Aster Pl.
Broken Arrow, OK 74012
918-254-8205
fax 918-252-9363

World's Fairs and Expositions
D.D. Woollard, Jr.
11614 Old St. Charles Rd.
Bridgeton, MO 63044
314-739-4662

1893 Columbian Exposition and 1932 Century of Progress
Donald Friedman
660 W Grand Ave.
Chicago, IL 60610
312-226-4741
DFRIED4141@aol.com

1904 St. Louis
Gwen Daniel
18 Belleau Lake Ct.
O'Fallon, MO 63366
314-978-3190
GWENDANIEL@aol.com

1939-40 International Exposition, Treasure Island, San Francisco
T.J. Ahlberg
1000 Irvine Blvd.
Tustin, CA 92780
714-730-1000
fax 714-730-1752

Zell
Fred and Lila Shrader
2025 Hwy. 199 (Hiouchi)
Crescent City, CA 95531
707-458-3525